CHILD

❦ OF THE ❧

FIGHTING
TENTH

Dec. 24, 18

Lieut. G. L. Cooper.   and Family.

Jo. B. Baynnacke
Photographer

CHILD

✺ OF THE ✺

FIGHTING

TENTH

ON THE FRONTIER WITH
THE BUFFALO SOLDIERS

FORRESTINE C. HOOKER

EDITED BY
STEVE WILSON

OXFORD
UNIVERSITY PRESS

OXFORD
UNIVERSITY PRESS

Oxford   New York

Auckland   Bangkok   Buenos Aires   Cape Town   Chennai
Dar es Salaam   Delhi   Hong Kong   Istanbul   Karachi   Kolkata
Kuala Lumpur   Madrid   Melbourne   Mexico City   Mumbai   Nairobi
São Paulo   Shanghai   Singapore   Taipei   Tokyo   Toronto

and an associated company in Berlin

Copyright © 2003 by Jacqueline Hughes and Steve Wilson

Published by Oxford University Press, Inc.
198 Madison Avenue, New York, New York 10016
www.oup.com

Oxford is a registered trademark of Oxford University Press

Library of Congress Cataloging-in-Publication Data

Hooker, Forrestine C. (Forrestine Cooper), 1867-1932.
Child of the Fighting Tenth : on the frontier with the Buffalo Soldiers / Forrestine C.
Hooker; edited by Steve Wilson.
p. cm.
Summary: A memoir detailing the frontier childhood and young adulthood of the daughter
of Charles Cooper, one of the officers in the Tenth U.S. Cavalry.
Includes bibliographical references and index.
ISBN 0-19-516158-0 (alk. paper)
1. Hooker, Forrestine C. (Forrestine Cooper), 1867-1932—Childhood and youth—Juvenile
literature. 2. Children of military personnel—West (U.S.)—Biography—Juvenile literature.
3. Frontier and pioneer life—West (U.S.)—Juvenile literature. 4. United States. Army. Cavalry,
10th—Juvenile literature. 5. United States. Army—Military life—History—19th century—
Juvenile literature. 6. African American soldiers—West (U.S.)—History—19th century—
Juvenile literature. 7. Indians of North America—Wars—1866-1895 —Juvenile literature.
8. West (U.S.)—History—1860-1890—Juvenile literature. 9. West (U.S.)—Biography—Juvenile
literature. [1. Hooker, Forrestine C. (Forrestine Cooper), 1867-1932. 2. Frontier and pioneer
life—West (U.S.) 3. United States. Army.—African American troops. 4. United States. Army.
Cavalry, 10th. 5. West (U.S.)—History—1860-1890. 6. African Americans—Biography.
7. Women—Biography.] I. Wilson, Steve. II. Title.
F594 .H76 2003
973.8—dc21   2003007872

On the cover: Tenth Cavalry officers and Apache scouts seek renegades in the Arizona desert
during the Geronimo campaign of 1886. *Cover inset:* Forrestine "Birdie" Cooper about 1873.

Frontispiece: The Cooper family at Fort Concho, Texas, December 1875: First Lieutenant
Charles L. Cooper and his wife, Flora; Forrestine (eight years old);
son Harry (six years old); and daughter Florence (three years old).

Book design by Nora Wertz

1   3   5   7   9   8   6   4   2

Printed in the United States of America on acid-free paper

To the memory of the Buffalo Soldiers and their officers,
who led the way, opening the American West
for future generations

CONTENTS

~ૹ~

INTRODUCTION

Forrestine Cooper Hooker was a curious and obser-vant child, filing away in her mind countless adven-tures—and misadventures—of a lifetime before committing a word to print. She grew up in the frontier army when the U.S. Cavalry was helping open up the vast American West to settlement. As the daughter of a cavalry officer, she was in a unique position to witness the end of the nineteenth-century frontier. As the adopted daughter of the Tenth U.S. Cavalry, she witnessed history in the making.

Hooker's father, Charles Lawrence Cooper, was a nat-ural choice to serve in the Tenth Cavalry. In 1862, at the age of seventeen, he enlisted as a private in the Seventy-first New York State Militia. Two years later, he entered the Philadelphia Military Academy as an applicant for an offi-cer's commission in the newly formed African-American regiments. Charles passed his examination and was appointed a second lieutenant in Company A of the 127th U.S. Colored Infantry Regiment.

During the Civil War, the 127th joined other Union forces operating against Richmond, Virginia, capital of the Confederacy. In early 1865 Cooper's division joined the Twenty-fifth Corps and fought in the Second Battle of Hatcher's Run. On April 9 at seven o'clock, the Union troops overtook the enemy at Appomattox Court House. When the Confederate forces broke through General Phil Sheridan's cavalry, they encountered General William Birney's Second Colored Division of eight to ten thousand men. At ten o'clock that same morning, General Robert E. Lee surrendered his army to U.S. General Ulysses S. Grant.

On New Year's Day of 1863, President Abraham Lincoln signed the Emancipation Proclamation, freeing the slaves in Confederate-held territory. That act also opened the armed services to African Americans. No fewer than 179,000 black soldiers served their country in the Civil War, and about 33,000 gave their lives to secure the freedom of all Americans. After the war there was no longer a need for the 1.5 million volunteers to defend the Union, and the regular army soon reverted to its prewar size of 18,000.

The nation's interest soon turned to the opening of the American West and its vast unsettled regions. The need to protect the masses of settlers who were now displacing Native Americans forced Congress to again enlarge the regular army. To provide a place for the black soldier, Congress decreed in July 1866 the formation of six black regiments for the regular army—four of infantry and two of cavalry. The new black infantry regiments were designated as the Thirty-eighth, Thirty-ninth, Fortieth, and Forty-first Infantries. The new black cavalry regiments were the Ninth and Tenth Cavalries.

Charles Cooper's training had served him well, and in 1866 he was appointed to the Thirty-ninth U.S. Infantry. At a time when the army needed to be enlarged, Congress instead reduced it again. Further reorganization in 1869 eliminated twenty infantry regiments, primarily through consolidation, and merged the four black infantry regiments into the Twenty-fourth and Twenty-fifth Infantries. Funds were appropriated to recruit no more than 25,000 enlisted men and about 2,000 officers.

After the reorganization of the army, Cooper was assigned as first lieutenant of Company A in the Tenth U.S. Cavalry, then serving in Indian Territory (now Oklahoma).

The Tenth was organized at Fort Leavenworth, Kansas, and Company A was the first of twelve companies (later called troops) formed in early 1867. Each company was designated by a letter of the alphabet, consisting of A through M, with the exception of J. Infantry regiments were composed of ten companies each.

The Tenth Cavalry was authorized 1,092 recruits. Recruitment took place in such cities as Philadelphia, Boston, New York, Pittsburgh, Memphis, and St. Louis. The Tenth's commander, Colonel Benjamin H. Grierson, sent Captain Louis H. Carpenter to Philadelphia on recruiting duty, and reminded him: "I requested you to be sent there to recruit colored men sufficiently educated to fill the positions of non-commissioned officers, clerks and mechanics in the regiment. You will use the greatest care in your selection of recruits. Although sent to recruit men for the positions specified above, you will also enlist all superior men you can who will do credit to the regiment."

Enlistment in the cavalry was for five years, whereas the infantry required only three, the thinking being that it required longer to train a cavalryman. Pay for a private was thirteen dollars a month, and payday came every other month. But a soldier's life offered African Americans the opportunities of a career and camaraderie that were often nonexistent in civilian occupations, where prejudice often ruled.

The regiment had a colonel, lieutenant colonel, and three majors, and a regimental band composed of enlisted men. Each company had three officers: a captain, first lieutenant, and second lieutenant. Most officers were Civil War veterans, and its commander, Colonel Grierson, was famous for his 1863 cavalry raid through Mississippi. The regimental band was the special pride and joy of Colonel Grierson, who was a musician from an early age and played a variety of instruments, often entertaining his visitors with a violin or guitar.

The band always remained at headquarters, where it entertained the soldiers, officers and their families, or visitors on special occasions, breaking the monotony of a lonely, isolated post. Unique with the black regiments was the addition of a regimental chaplain, who, because many of the enlisted men were former slaves and unable to read or write, would also serve to teach the soldiers their three R's: reading, 'riting, and 'rithmetic.

Captain Nicholas Nolan organized the Tenth's first troop, Company A, in February 1867. Born in Ireland, he joined the army as a private in 1852, when only seventeen, and rose through the ranks until appointed a second lieutenant in the Sixth Cavalry in 1862 and captain four years later. Twice wounded in action, Nolan was cited "for gallant and meritorious service" at the Battles of Brandy Station and Dinwiddie Courthouse, Virginia. Captain Nolan's company of black cavalrymen were all mounted on bay-colored horses: three officers and sixty-plus enlisted men consisting of the first sergeant, four sergeants, three corporals, one trumpeter, two farriers (horseshoers) and blacksmiths, one saddler, and fifty-four privates. Some of the senior enlisted men had served with black volunteer regiments in the Civil War.

As soon as the Tenth was readied for service, they moved onto the western plains of Kansas to protect Kansas Pacific Railroad workers and almost immediately encountered resistance from the Plains Indians. The Comanches soon called their adversaries the "Buffalo Soldiers," believing the black soldiers' hair resembled that of the buffalo. The Tenth was proud of its nickname and placed the likeness of the buffalo atop its own regimental crest. Soon all the black regiments—which formed about 20 percent of the cavalry and 8 percent of the infantry in the West—came to be known as the Buffalo Soldiers.

Fighting Indians was only a small part of the duties of the Buffalo Soldiers. Building forts, roads, bridges, telegraph lines between garrisons; mapping remote regions; guarding and escorting wagon trains, stagecoaches, and railroad construction workers; chasing and capturing horse thieves, cattle rustlers, whiskey peddlers and bootleggers, and bandits and desperados of all types; ejecting white interlopers from the Indian reservations; and protecting the Indians from whites and occasional Texas Rangers while hunting off the reservation were among the many duties of the Buffalo Soldiers and their officers.

During those hard years on the frontier, the black regiments consistently enjoyed higher reenlistments, and fewer desertions, than any of the white regiments. By the end of the Indian wars and the winning of the West, eighteen African-American soldiers, and four of their officers, had received the Medal of Honor for bravery under fire.

Forrestine Cooper, or Birdie, as she was nicknamed early in life, grew up in the frontier army, admiring the officers and black troops alike. Fortunately for us all, she was a keen observer and later chronicler of her life and times. In this memoir, she captures much of the behind-the-scenes activity at the frontier army posts before all twelve troops of the Tenth Cavalry came together at Camp Rice, Texas, and rode to Arizona to participate in the Apache campaign in 1885. Hooker entertains us along the way with stories of family events, tales about her playmates, and details about her father's and fellow officers' official duties. She chronicles events and makes observations not recorded elsewhere.

Hooker does not tell us just when she learned to play the piano, but it became an important part of her life. Army records do tell us, however, when Lieutenant Cooper bought his daughter her own piano. Between November 12 and 29, 1878, a six-mule team wagon and driver made the 306-mile, 18-day round trip from Fort Sill to the railhead at Caddo, Indian Territory, to transport Lieutenant Cooper's piano. Forrestine was not yet twelve years old. It might not have been the first piano at Fort Sill, but it certainly must have been among the very few at the frontier garrison. The piano would long follow the Coopers on their journeys to other western posts.

Hooker's writing career began rather late in life. The first of her nine novels was not published until she was fifty-two. Her daughter, also named Forrestine, must take credit for launching her mother's writing career in 1904. Home from school for Christmas, the younger Forrestine found a story that she, her brother, and mother had all contributed to while Hooker wove it together at the typewriter at their home in Willcox, Arizona. Upon its rediscovery, Hooker instructed her daughter to just put it in the stove "with the rest of the trash." Instead, she read it, thought it better than many others she had read, and mailed it to a publisher without return postage, hoping the editor would not return it if it were rejected.

A month later while opening her mail, Hooker noticed an envelope with the return address of F. M. Lupton, Publisher, 25-27 City Hall Place, New York City, N.Y. Thinking it was merely an advertisement, and about to tear it in two, Hooker got curious and opened it. When she did, a check for twenty-five dollars fell into her lap. It was payment for her story. Lupton asked for more stories, and soon Hooker was writing regularly. More than a hundred published stories followed in the years ahead.

Hooker loved hearing from the old soldiers of the Tenth. When Sergeant Michael Finnegan visited her father in

Philadelphia, his first question was, "Where is Miss Birdie now?" Hooker wrote to a friend: "If I live to be a hundred, the only name officers or enlisted men of the Tenth Cavalry would know for me would be Birdie Cooper of the Tenth. I am more proud of that name than any title royalty could confer."

As early as 1921, New York publisher Russell Doubleday asked Hooker to write her own story, seeing the potential of a wonderful pioneer memoir. But other books took precedence and her ninth novel was published in 1929. Because of failing health, Hooker left Washington, D.C., where she had lived for almost a decade, and in early 1931 returned to Los Angeles, her former home where her children now lived.

Los Angeles Times columnist Lee Shippey interviewed the now famous author and observed: "No child ever had a more romantic girlhood than did Forrestine Cooper. She was a mischievous, impudent, unrestrained little girl. Today her home in West Fifty-third place is a place of mementos in which nearly every object on the walls or tables or mantel is historic. Many a historical novelist of the future will study Mrs. Hooker's books to get true pictures of the West that was."

Unfortunately, Hooker did not live to see her memoirs published. She had amassed a rough manuscript of several hundred pages when she died on March 20, 1932, just twelve days past her sixty-fifth birthday. Her manuscript remained with her family and many years later passed to her granddaughter, who was only nine when Hooker died. My research into the Tenth Cavalry, and its first black officer, Henry O. Flipper—who joined Company A upon graduation from the United States Military Academy at West Point in 1877, and served with Lieutenant Charles Cooper—eventually led me to Hooker's forgotten memoirs. Her memoir was found only a few miles from Fort Grant, where much of her story takes place.

The manuscript was a hidden gem of frontier adventures begging to be told. I have tried to be judicious in editing her memoirs. She often omitted first names, and I added them when possible, often finding them in company muster rolls. Occasional dates were added when discovered in the records, whereas events unrelated to her story or the Tenth Cavalry were deleted. Occasional portions were rearranged into chronological order. The reader should remember, too, that Hooker recalled much of her story from memory, without the use of records. She may have occasionally erred, or forgotten, but after all, it is her story, based on the knowledge she had at hand.

Hooker grew up in a different time, far removed from the racial sensitivity of our modern era. She understood the plight of Native Americans scattered over the Great Plains and Southwest, and personally observed that the officers would not stand by and allow them to starve when game was scarce, or when Indian agents cheated on their rations. Hooker's references to the black soldiers and Indians, using such descriptions as colored, Negro, squaws, or greaser, were never intended to slight or demean, but were simply common usage of the day. They should be so interpreted in her memoirs as a chronicle from another time.

The story she left us is a tribute to her life of adventure—and those she knew and loved—and a lifelong desire to share a part of the now-forgotten frontier she rode with her parents over the great Southwest.

——Steve Wilson

⊰ 1 ⊱

FATHER IN THE CIVIL WAR, MARRIAGE, AND OFF TO SHIP ISLAND

It was the Fourth of July 1863. All day the people of Philadelphia had breathlessly waited while anxious-faced men and women whispered to one another that the Confederates had reached Chambersburg and were marching on to Philadelphia. The city had been practically depleted of organized forces by the call of the President on June 15. Philadelphia, Baltimore, and Washington seemed doomed.

That night thunder crashed incessantly, like the firing of heavy artillery on a battlefield. Few people in Philadelphia slept, and those who did, dreamed of soldiers, marching, fighting, dying. The sound of thunder mingled with the roar of cannons and rattle of musketry in their dreams. Those lying awake whispered prayers for loved ones who might be lying wounded or dead on the battlefield of Gettysburg.

Then came the news that George Gordon Meade, commander of the Army of the Potomac, by a terrific forced march had swung into line before the Confederate forces at Gettysburg. During July first, second, third, and part of the Fourth, the struggle continued desperately. Then at sunset of July Fourth came the glorious news that the Army of the Potomac had been victorious. Philadelphia was safe. Worn from the strain, the men and women of Philadelphia went to bed, thankful and yet dreading the coming of dawn when they would learn the price of victory.

A SPECIAL CANNON

The story that night was one of the worst ever known to Philadelphians. It was midnight when, above the thunder, a cannon shot roused them all. My mother, then a girl of seventeen, was up and on her feet before Auntie Green called to her: "Get up, Flora! Fort Brown is calling us."

"Fort Brown" was not a garrison. It was the name of a little cannon that was fired to call the assemble of the men and women who made up the committee of the Volunteer Refreshment Saloon of Philadelphia. This work began when Brown, importer of tea and coffee, distributed food brought to his store by neighborhood people for soldiers passing through Philadelphia to the front.

The famous little cannon stood at the foot of a flagstaff, ready for service that was far different from its former records. It had been cast years before at the armory of Springfield and had gone to Mexico with the American Army under Zachary Taylor. Captured by the Mexicans, it had been mounted at an old Mexican fortress named San Juan de Ulloa. While being transferred from there on a Mexican gunboat, the Americans recaptured it, and sent it to Philadelphia. It was upon the receiving ship, *Union*, when that boat was sunk in the Delaware River.

Then the cannon was raised and sent to the Navy Yard at Philadelphia where it remained until the Civil War began. First it was used to defend the railroad bridge at Perryville, and at last loaned to the committee of the Union Volunteer Refreshment Saloon to call the members together, day or night, when their services were needed to feed the soldiers going to the front, or nurse the wounded who were being brought back from fields of battle.

My mother tramped beside Auntie Green through the deluge of rain, the lantern Auntie carried making a mere point of light between the glaring flashes of the storm. Reaching Washington Avenue where the railroad ran, the long train of box cars blockaded their passage. Auntie did not hesitate. Climbing between the cars, she reached the opposite side of the street. My mother followed her.

As she turned to join the older woman, a flash of lightning showed rows and rows of men, wounded, dying, or dead, lying on the sidewalk, while still others were being carried from the box cars. The rain was beating down on them. Houses had been filled with the wounded until the sidewalk had to be used. When my mother hesitated, Auntie Green commanded her to hurry. Between flashes of lightning they stepped over and around the men who had done their share on the field of Gettysburg.

At the Union Volunteer Refreshment Saloon, the committee was ready when the wounded were brought in. Armed with sponges and basins, Auntie thrust a basin into my mother's hands and bade her to hold it. A young soldier whose entire breast was one gaping wound, looked up as Auntie began washing the blood away. My mother closed her eyes. She felt faint, but Auntie's curt voice roused her. "It's no time for squeamishness. You have two brothers at the front. Someone may have to do this for them."

Through that night and the following days, the work went on and Auntie contributed to the cause with dauntless devotion. But there was one incident my mother never forgot or forgave the old lady, whose patriotism bordered on fanaticism. Among those who arrived one day was a mere boy. He was mortally wounded. Auntie leaned down to care for him, but when she saw the gray uniform of a Confederate, she straightened up, and refused to touch a "rebel." The anguish and pathetic appeal in his eyes as he heard her words have always haunted my mother. Others cared for him.

FATHER RECEIVES HIS COMMISSION

It was during September 1864 that my mother and a party of girl friends were invited to go to Camp William Penn for the afternoon and dinner. Major Arthur Greene was engaged to be married to my mother's most intimate friend, Ellie Lowry. Leaving his guests to watch dress parade, he hastened up country to purchase a horse. Field officers were mounted.

Camp William Penn held the unique distinction of having been the first place in the United States where black men were enlisted and trained to serve as soldiers of the regular army. Congress had authorized such action and Taggart's "Free Military School for Applicants for Command of Colored Troops" was established in Philadelphia. There men who had served as privates in the white regiments were sifted and selected, then trained for appointments as commissioned officers to serve in regiments of colored men. Among the men who graduated was Second Lieutenant Charles Lawrence Cooper.

That September afternoon just before parade was formed, Colonel John Gibbon was standing a short distance from Major Greene's guests. None of the girls was acquainted with him, but he walked over to them. He held a long narrow box in his hand and a dark red silk sash such as officers wear.

"Will one of you young ladies take care of this for me?" the colonel asked. "It is a sword to be presented to a young officer by his former comrades with whom he served as an enlisted man. I have some duties to attend to, but will soon return." Although each of the girls was eager to hold the sword, the officer laid the box containing the sword, then the silk sash, and finally a smaller one which held the shoulder straps for the newly appointed officer, in my mother's lap.

Parade formed and at its close, Colonel Gibbon presented the shoulder straps, sash, and sword to a very much embarrassed, but tall and handsome young officer as a token of esteem and affection from the comrades with whom he had served from the beginning of the war, when he had enlisted at the age of seventeen. Those comrades were proud of the nineteen-year-old soldier who had carried a bullet from the field of Gettysburg, but their gift was a complete surprise to Lieutenant Charles Cooper.

After parade and the sword presentation, an officer told the girls that an order had just been received and Major Greene would have to leave for the front early the next morning. Ellie Lowry, to whom Major Greene was engaged, had made all preparations for their wedding early in October. So the news was a shock to her and her girl friends, who were to have been bridesmaids.

At that moment, Mr. Elijah Cattell, brother of Senator Alexander Cattell, and Mr. Sam Moore, all relatives of Ellie Lowry, approached and were told the news. Instantly Elijah Cattell, Ellie's cousin, announced, "Ellie, you're going to be married tonight!"

"Oh, my! It can't be," she exclaimed, aghast.

"Yes, it can be!"

Then Mr. Cattell outlined the plans. The men would attend to getting the minister and take care of all the details of refreshments, while the girls were to hurry around to as many friends as possible and invite the guests. They were waiting on the platform to hasten to the city when Major Greene stepped from an incoming train and was utterly dumbfounded as the girls rushed at him crying out, "You're going to be married tonight! Your regiment leaves in the morning!"

So the wedding took place. Though the bridesmaids were hurried from the camp at seven that evening, donned silk gowns, and were as pretty as any bridesmaids could be, not one of them had found time to change the dusty, heavy shoes and stockings they had worn at Camp William Penn that afternoon. The wedding was always recalled as a beautiful one, and Major Greene came home safe and sound after the war was over.

The night of the wedding my mother and another girl, Annie Field, planned to get up before daybreak and go to a florist to buy flowers for the officers who were leaving that day for the front. Just before the regiment was ready to start, my mother said rather carelessly, "I think I will give my flowers to that Mr. Cooper."

So she watched him march past with his company, shoulder straps on his new blue uniform, red sash about his waist, and the shining sword held at the proper military angle. In his left hand he carried a little bunch of flowers. Those flowers went to Harpers Ferry. The petals fell and were trampled on ground that was soaked with blood. But memory flowers never lose their fragrance and never die. So the romance began, another first sword went through the war until the day when my father watched General Lee surrender.

While other men obtained leaves, or were mustered out, my father's regiment, the 127th Colored Infantry, was ordered at once from the battlefield to the Mexican border. There, with the American Army of Occupation, he served during the Maximilian trouble in Mexico, and not until after the tragic execution of Maximilian did he have an opportunity to again see the girl who had held his sword, and whose flowers he had carried down into the bloody fighting at Harpers Ferry.

But letters from battlefields, often written on scraps of paper with stumps of borrowed pencils on a canteen for a desk, and sewn together with black and white thread, were slipped by a sympathetic postman through half-closed slats when a girl's hand reached out. Auntie Green had forbidden the letters, saying, "I don't know who he is or anything about his family." Then Ellie Lowry Greene took up the cudgels for young Lieutenant Cooper, telling Auntie that his father was one of the staff on the *New York Tribune* with Horace Greeley, and the family went back to the founding of Southampton. "So it is as good as any family in Philadelphia." Auntie was mollified.

FATHER RETURNS HOME

In November 1865 Lieutenant Cooper was able to return to Philadelphia for the first time since he had marched away carrying the new sword and flowers. Auntie capitulated royally and the old friends gathered again. The girls who had been bridesmaids for Ellie Lowry acted as maids on December 20, 1865, for the wedding of Flora Green and young Lieutenant Charles Cooper, though he was not twenty-one years old until three months after his wedding day, and the bride was only nineteen.

Then came an unexpected climax to the evening. The caterer had confused the date. The elaborately planned refreshments had been delivered to another far-distant residence. It was late. Philadelphia had limited transit service in 1865 and no telephone to meet such emergencies. But the carriages of the guests were in front of the house. Making a rapid survey of necessities, the gentlemen of the wedding party commandeered carriages and drove hastily from place to place, rousing proprietors of shops where the articles on the list might be purchased. While the other guests, unaware of the catastrophe, were making merry in the big parlor, the scouts returned from their successful foray, and the supper that night did not betray how nearly the feast had been a "poor and hungry" affair.

OFF FOR NEW ORLEANS

Following their marriage, father was commissioned a regular second lieutenant in the Thirty-ninth U.S. Infantry (colored) and ordered to Ship Island, twelve miles south of Biloxi, Mississippi. My mother remained in Philadelphia with her family. Then shortly after my birth on March 8, 1867, my father was ordered to Philadelphia on recruiting duty. With the summer months the yellow fever became epidemic through the South, but was especially severe in Louisiana and Tennessee, and all officers absent from regiments in those sections received peremptory orders to remain north until further orders. It was not until the following year that he was able to return to duty.

On January 8, 1868, at five o'clock in the afternoon, New Orleans was celebrating the anniversary of the Battle of New Orleans that had been fought in 1814 by General Andrew Jackson, whose victory over the British ended the War of 1812. Though the Treaty of Peace had been signed between the British Commissioners and America, the commanders of the opposing forces at New Orleans were not aware of the fact owing to the lack of communication. So the Battle of New Orleans was fought and won by General Jackson. That achievement, and a pig that was caught in a fence, practically elected General Jackson as President of the United States.

Pigs were valuable. A Rhode Island farmer on his way to vote saw one of his pigs caught in a broken fence, and stopped to release it. When he reached the polls he was too late to cast his vote. That one vote lost the precinct for the Federalists at a time when the question of declaring war with England was a big issue. So a representative who favored war was elected and as a consequence of that lost vote, Congress declared war in 1812. A pig in a fence decided the issue. The Battle of New Orleans was fought and General Andrew Jackson was elected President of the United States. Louisiana never failed to celebrate that battle on the eighth day of January.

On January 8, 1868, at precisely five o'clock, my parents carried me, an infant nine months old, up the gangplank of a beautiful river packet named the *Selma*. It was to make its maiden voyage and the dock was thronged with people in holiday attire who cheered as the boat started on her first trip. Captain Thomas Rogers was in command.

The *Selma*, like all river packets, was built high above the water line, making her appear top-heavy. Usually such boats kept near the shore as they voyaged, but the *Selma* on her maiden trip was to take a course farther out in the Gulf of Mexico and deliver a cargo of commissary stores to the garrison on Ship Island. The trip ordinarily would have required less than twenty-four hours from New Orleans.

During the night of January 8, a terrific storm began. The *Selma* pitched to such an extent that Captain Rogers ordered everyone except the sailors on duty to remain in the cabins. Waves swept away the smokestacks of the boat and the engine broke down. Throughout the night the boat rolled helplessly. Dawn brought no relief.

The route of the *Selma* was out of the usual course of vessels. Efforts to mend the machinery seemed useless. The packet was at the mercy of the wind and the waves. My parents heaped pillows about me in the berth to protect me from being bruised by the pitching of the boat, while they sat on the floor of the cabin, clinging to the side of the berth and bracing themselves, though their bodies were stiff, and flesh black and blue from the violent motion. The storm continued to rage. It was during this time that the cabin door opened and a delicate little woman clothed in deepest mourning spoke as she clung to the doorway.

"Let me have the baby to take care of. I am next to you. My people have all been killed in the war. I have nothing to live for now, and I would give my own life gladly to save hers."

So the unknown Southern woman lifted me in her arms and took me into her own cabin next to the one my parents occupied. Probably I was the only human being on the *Selma* who was not worried over the situation. The rocking of the crippled boat might have seemed like the rocking of a huge cradle moved by an unseen hand.

That same evening a new problem faced the captain, crew, and passengers. There was no more food on the *Selma*. She had been provisioned for two days only. Captain Adams, also en route to Ship Island where his wife awaited him, was in charge of the government supplies on board the *Selma*. No officer of the army had any authority to open those boxes of foodstuffs, except for use by officers and soldiers at Ship Island. But my father and Captain Adams decided to speak to Captain Rogers. As a result of that conference, the boxes of government supplies were broken open and food was thus furnished for all hands on the *Selma*.

While the storm continued to rage, the engineers kept tinkering at the machinery, and so the boat limped on her way between long hours when she rolled at the mercy of the Gulf. Three weeks passed before the *Selma* managed to reach Ship Island. It had been reported that the ship had gone to the bottom of the Gulf of Mexico with all its passengers and crew. As the only boats that ever stopped at Ship Island were scheduled twice each month, the officers and soldiers there were amazed to see a strange boat built like a river packet limp slowly to the little wharf.

Then word passed that it was the lost *Selma*. Cheering and shouting and waving their caps, the soldiers and officers rushed down to welcome those who seemed like the dead arising from the sea. The wife of Captain Adams, believing her husband dead, had been making preparations to leave Ship Island and return to the home of her girlhood.

2

FRIENDS
AND MEMORIES OF
SHIP ISLAND

That day when the *Selma* reached Ship Island, there were tears as well as smiles, for practically the entire Regimental Band of the Thirty-ninth Infantry had been wiped out by yellow fever, a heavy percent of the enlisted men had died, and fully fifty percent of the officers. My father would ask, "Where is so-and-so stationed now?" Frequently the reply would be, "Died of the fever."

Lieutenant Colonel Frank Wheaton had been at Sedgewick Barracks just outside New Orleans. Only the devoted nursing of his wonderful wife had kept him from his grave, though so virulent had been the disease that his face remained terribly scarred until his death years after. A new band was being recruited. In the soldiers' barracks strange faces were seen where familiar comrades had vanished. Along officers' row stood empty houses that brother officers saluted as they passed by. A roll call of the Thirty-ninth Infantry when we arrived that day would have sounded like the roll call of a regiment at the close of a big battle.

Captain Rogers remained only long enough to get his machinery patched up to make the return voyage to New Orleans, then he said good-bye, and started homeward. It was later that the people on Ship Island learned that the *Selma*, after lying in the shipyards for over three weeks, once more sailed the Gulf, but within two months she burned to the water's edge, a total loss to her owners.

There is nothing left at the present day except one or two old newspapers that tell of her first voyage, then notice of her second trip. After that date no record can be found of the *Selma*. Marine insurance companies of Louisiana that thrived in those days exist no longer. Men who might have told the story are dead. And so the *Selma* is a lost bit of history today, except for what my mother remembers so vividly of my first adventure in life.

Ship Island was a little strip of dazzling white sand about eight miles long and only half a mile wide at low tide in the Gulf of Mexico. All houses were built on pilings. At high tide the water swept under them. My first attempt at fishing was by means of a stout string with a small hook. My father dropped this through a knothole in the floor, assuring me that if I caught a whale, I could not be pulled through the knothole. So I fished hopefully, but like Simple Simon, never caught a whale.

Ship Island had been made a military prison just after the Civil War. The only solid building was termed the "bombproof," and when I landed on the island, several hundred prisoners were in close confinement there. These were criminals and deserters, who were held in a stockade made of poles ten feet high, guarded day and night by sentinels. But at times a prisoner would take desperate chances, climb over the top of the stockade, risk a shot from the sentinels, and insanely hope to swim to the mainland. Any vessel that might pick up a man would be sure to turn him over to the authorities at the nearest port.

Colonel Joseph A. Mower commanded the Thirty-ninth Infantry at Ship Island. The officers who served under him were all first and second lieutenants, except Captain Delos Alphonzo Ward. Though there were five companies of soldiers on the island owing to the absence of captains, four companies were commanded by first lieutenants: R. Baxter Quimby, George Edward Ford, Michael Lewis Courtney, and my father, Charles L. Cooper, all of whom, though barely of age, had served during the four years of the Civil War and attained commissions as officers by meritorious service.

MY GUARD OF HONOR

The second lieutenants were George S. Grimes, Jonathan B. Hanson, Emmet Crawford, and Samuel K. Thompson, nick-named "Bleeding Kansas" Thompson because of his fiery red hair and his enlistment from Kansas when he entered the army as a private. Quimby, Ford, and Crawford were intimate friends of my parents, and these three young officers at once became my "Guard of Honor." Whenever they were not on official duty, they carried me about in their arms, and as soon as I was able to stand alone, they guided my first steps.

The bombproof was a round fortress. The only green herbage on the island was the grass that grew on the flat top of this building. Old cannons surmounted it, but they had not been fired for many years. The garrison proper was at the upper end of the island. There was also an ancient lighthouse that had been condemned as unsafe.

Two lines of buildings formed the garrison, like a street. At the extreme end stood Colonel Joseph Mower's quarters, facing down the street. The buildings nearest the Commanding Officer's quarters were occupied by the officers and their families. Below them the street continued with barracks for the enlisted men on either side. So Colonel Mower's house commanded a full view along the officers' quarters as well as the soldiers' barracks. When he walked down this line, every enlisted man and every officer had to stand in front of these quarters in official rigidity and salute the garrison commander.

From Colonel Mower's quarters, a railroad track led to the bombproof and between the rails a lifeboat stood upright. When a storm threatened to destroy the garrison, the boat was pushed to the bombproof where straw and canned provisions were kept for any emergency. A tall white post, marked like a huge yardstick, was another very important feature at the end of the island. A sentinel stood beside it night and day, watching the height of the tide, and when the water neared a certain mark, a shot from his gun gave warning to the entire garrison that it was time to seek safety in the bombproof.

Before I was old enough to walk, even assisted by my Guard of Honor, when passing this sentinel I believed that the salute he gave the officer was intended for me, and I never failed to lift my own hand as I saw the officers do. The tall white post, in my childish mind, was there for the sole purpose of measuring my own height when I stood beside it, and waited to learn how much taller I had grown during the night.

My first steps alone were encouraged in a peculiar way by my Guard of Honor, who would seat themselves on the little railroad track a short distance apart from one another, and persuade me to walk on the soft white sand between them. If I succeeded without a fall, I was entitled to grab handfuls of the fine sand and heap it upon the uncovered heads of the young officers until it poured like a shower bath over their faces and down their collars as they leaned forward. Uncle Emmet, Uncle George, and Uncle "Kimby" they were to me then, and even today those names identify them in my memory.

Furniture and dishes were limited. So when my mother decided to give a dinner party, dishes and chairs were loaned by the other ladies. Peter Wickerwack, a former soldier with a wooden leg, operated a tiny catboat. He was the one link connecting the mainland and the island during the two weeks that elapsed between scheduled trips of any other craft. Peter was not only a friend, he was an institution. He brought needles, pins, thread, matched dress goods, and also carried fresh vegetables, meats, and unofficial letters between the island and Mississippi City or Biloxi. No matter how rough the weather, Peter never failed to arrive with the articles ordered.

Though a frightful storm raged the night before the dinner party and continued the next day, Peter brought his tiny catboat safely to the island without one parcel missing. So the dinner proceeded as though the waves of the Gulf were not lashing against the pilings that supported our home. To glance through the windows gave an impression that the houses on Ship Island were simply floating on top of the Gulf of Mexico.

During the merriment, warning shots of the sentinel at the Marking Post rang out. Instantly hostess and guests deserted the feast. Wraps were snatched, and "Uncle Emmet" Crawford picked me up in his arms and wrapped a shawl about me. We all reached the lifeboat that stood upright between the tracks, and instantly it was shoved by waiting soldiers until the bombproof was reached, the only place of safety, where everyone hastened. Through the night the waves pounded against the walls, but the place had been well built. The straw that Colonel Mower had the forethought to place in the bombproof afforded rough beds. I am quite sure I slept as serenely as I had done during the voyage of the *Selma*.

When morning dawned, no one expected to see any buildings where the garrison had stood, but they were intact. How furious the storm had been was proven by the fact that a three-mast schooner that put into port before the storm had broken, and anchored on the inland side of the island, had sailed completely across the island and was floating on the opposite side unharmed. Though no lives were lost at Ship Island, no damage except dampness of articles left in the buildings, the Gulf of Mexico was strewn with wreckage. Many boats were helplessly drifting and others had gone fathoms deep during that night of my mother's first dinner party.

"BIRDIE" AND "CHIPS"

An amusing bit of family history of Ship Island has been handed down. After I learned to walk, I considered each house my own home, especially the quarters occupied by the unmarried officers. There one day my chatter interfered with official duties. Making out Muster Rolls was an exacting bit of clerical work. Instead of marching me home, Uncle Emmet, Uncle George, and Uncle Quimby resorted to putting a big drop of New Orleans molasses on my fingers and thumbs, then handing me a feather from a pillow, they instructed me to pick off the feather.

It kept me busy and silent. But when they next inspected, they found that I had secured the can of molasses, poked a big hole into the pillow, and not only decorated myself from head to feet like a plucked chicken, but had plastered the sides of the room with a frieze of feathers and molasses. I am firmly convinced that this episode was responsible for my nickname of "Birdie," the only name by which I was ever identified during my entire life by those who knew us in army circles.

Another incident occurred at Ship Island in which I had no part, but my father and my own Guard of Honor were responsible. "Bleeding Kansas" Thompson had convivial habits. His trips to the mainland meant his return rather the worse for indulgences. A small hairless dog of the Chihuahua breed was his one intimate associate on Ship Island. "Chips" was almost as unpopular as his master. On one occasion when Bleeding Kansas returned to his quarters late at night, he groped vainly for matches. A dog greeted him. He patted the dog. Chips was hairless, but this dog was woolly like a poodle. Bleeding Kansas swore at the dog and called for Chips. The poodle responded.

At last the matches were found, and Bleeding Kansas stood looking at a fuzzy white poodle that danced yapping about his feet. Bleeding Kansas started a wild marathon to escape the unfamiliar apparition. It followed him until he was entrenched behind a chair. There was something a bit familiar about that poodle, as he stared at it from the barricade.

"Hic—hic—Chips."

Chips wagged a knobby white tail and bounced happily, forgiving the kicks received. "Sit up!" hiccuped Bleeding Kansas. Chips sat up and waved white cotton paws.

"Tention! Walk (hic) like a solsher, Chups."

The white poodle stood erect and marched across the room on its hind legs. Then Bleeding Kansas set down the chair, and gravely remarked:

"You don't look like Chips. You don't feel like Chips. But you act like Chips. Come here, Chips."

Chips obeyed. A bucket of hot water and the job of plucking wads of cotton from a hairless dog kept Bleeding Kansas busy the rest of the night so that he was sober enough to attend to his duties when reveille was sounded at daybreak. He swore that he would shoot whoever transformed Chips into a white poodle, but the secret remained buried until long after Bleeding Kansas had been dismissed from the army. Crawford, Quimby, and Cooper were the guilty parties, though Bleeding Kansas never knew it as long as he lived.

ORDERS TO LEAVE

I was almost two years old when a boat arrived at Ship Island bringing orders for my father to proceed immediately to New Orleans for duty on the staff of Major General Robert Christie Buchanan. Luckily there was not much to be packed, and as it was obligatory to leave on the same boat that brought the orders, or risk a court-martial for disobeying orders, things were in wild confusion in our home. However, others in the garrison came to my mother's rescue, and Lieutenant Crawford was most active darting about, grabbing anything he happened to see, and thrusting it into one of the trunks.

So the packing turned into a comedy and broke the army tragedy that is attendant on moving from familiar places and separating from dear friends. Thus I said goodbye to Ship Island and my loyal little Guard of Honor. Without adventure the trip to New Orleans was completed in regulation time, and we went at once to the old St. Charles Hotel. As my mother sat with me in the big "parlor," while my father registered to obtain accommodations, she noticed quite a large group of men and women at the rear of the room. They were evidently people of good social standing. She watched them press eagerly forward, and the movement afforded an opportunity for her to see the man facing them.

It was General Jefferson Davis. Then she understood that these were friends and admirers of the Southern leader. No one noticed her until my father, conspicuous not only by his height of six feet two inches, but doubly so because he was wearing the blue uniform of an officer of the United States Army, entered the room and joined my mother. Instantly the voices ceased. Faces were turned toward us. General Davis looked steadily at my father. Then the Southern leader, with a slight bow to the friends who stood about him, passed from the room and soon we were left alone.

My parents always regretted this incident, because they learned that General Davis had been accustomed to receiving his close friends informally at the old St. Charles Hotel whenever he came to New Orleans from his country home. But after we arrived at the hotel, he never again held a reception, nor did he register there during the time we lived in the hotel. Probably he was aware that my father had been appointed Provost Marshal of New Orleans.

The new duties gave him authority over all prisoners and also in charge of distributing food to the many Southern families who applied for it, owing to their complete impoverishment during the war. Frequently he would return to the hotel and relate some pathetic incident about the people who had stood in line that day, women of culture who had formerly lived luxuriously, but compelled by actual necessity, had abandoned their pride to ask assistance from the conquerors of the South. He had a very sympathetic nature, being hardly more than a boy himself, and realized the humiliation of these men and women who appealed for food from the United States government through his hands.

Socially my mother was ostracized, as were the wives of other United States officers in New Orleans. Even on the streets and in a store they were marked. This was a mystery until one of the ladies discovered that "all Northern women wore bonnets," while the Southerners wore "hats."

It was during this time that I started a small war of my own. The nursemaid who dressed me had daily trouble combing my hair, which was very thick and hung in dark curls far below my waist. Naturally it tangled at night, and when the combing began, she had to follow me all around the room to finish her task. So I resolved to "run away."

I did so, accompanied by a huge Newfoundland dog owned by someone in the hotel. The dog and I were inseparable friends. When I was missed, a search was begun, and after quite a while I was discovered a long distance from the hotel, the dog at my side. I rebelled against returning, but was led back, still accompanied by my friend, the dog that had guarded me across crowded streets and safely passed moving vehicles.

During the period of reorganization of the army in 1869 and 1870, my parents were in Philadelphia. Officers were being held on waiting orders until they were either assigned permanently to a regiment in the regular United States Army, or else mustered out of the service. My father and his bosom friend, Lieutenant Emmet Crawford, were among those waiting orders. They were both eager to continue in the service, and as the limited vacancies were being rapidly filled, they grew anxious as to what might be their fate.

FATHER GOES TO WASHINGTON

Christmas Day of 1870 Crawford shared our family dinner in the old home where my mother had grown up and in which she and father were married on December 20, 1865. Crawford and my father became so concerned as to whether they would be assigned to one of the few vacancies still remaining, or be mustered out of the service for good, that they finally decided to go that very night to

Washington and try to "save their bacon." So immediately after dinner they started.

The next morning, following the regular procedure, they went to pay their official respects to the Commanding General of the United States Army. General William Tecumseh Sherman had been appointed to that rank on my second birthday, March 8, 1869. After the usual formalities, the important subject was broached by my father, who acted as spokesman. Crawford was always rather diffident, and at that time, this trait was more marked than in later years. General Sherman, tall, slim, and every inch a soldier, regarded my father intently.

"General, I am unassigned, and I do not want to be mustered out," my father said, hoping his voice was steady, but he was not sure. "I should like to be assigned to a white regiment, and would prefer the Third Cavalry."

Sherman was always very deliberate in action as well as word, and during the silence, Crawford broke in hastily. "I do not care what regiment I go to, as long as I am not mustered out of the service." That was all. The two young officers saluted and left the room. What the consequence might be, neither of them could say. Back to Philadelphia they returned, no wiser than before.

That memorable interview had taken place the morning of December 26, 1870. On December 31, my father was assigned to the Tenth Cavalry, a colored regiment, while Crawford received his assignment to the Third Cavalry, the white regiment which my father had told the Commanding General he "would prefer." Crawford's assignment was exactly the same date as that of my father's, December 31.

Neither of them was ever able to decide whether General Sherman had sent my father to a colored regiment as a matter of discipline, when he had asked for a white regiment, and had made the rebuke more pointed by assigning Crawford to the Third, or whether an accident had confused the names of the two in Sherman's mind. No one could solve that problem except the Commanding General of the Army, and neither Crawford nor my father dared open the matter again. They were not to be mustered out! That was enough.

3

THE TENTH U.S. CAVALRY
AND ASSIGNMENT TO
INDIAN TERRITORY

A few days after New Year's, 1871, my father left for his new regiment. Headquarters of the Tenth Cavalry was stationed at Fort Sill, Indian Territory, now Oklahoma, but the troop to which he had been assigned was at Camp Supply, then in the very heart of the Indian troubles. Owing to the roughness of life at that date in the West, it was considered advisable for my mother to remain in Philadelphia with me until conditions were more comfortable.

No officer could tell at what moment his troop would be "on the jump after Indians," and often for months the soldiers would never camp in the same place. My baby brother, Harry, two and a half years younger than I, was just old enough to walk and talk when we three started to join my father at Camp Supply. At Hays City, Kansas, the railroad terminal, he met us with transportation from Fort Hays, and we were driven to the garrison where Captain Augustus Robinson of the Quartermaster's Department and his wife welcomed us as their guests.

Fort Hays was a large, important garrison where we remained several days awaiting transportation to take us on to Fort Dodge. Owing to the danger from Indians, no families, in fact, not even an officer was permitted to go from one post to another except with an escort of armed soldiers. So when we left Fort Hays, we were accompanied by armed men.

When we reached Fort Hays on our way to Camp Supply, our first frontier army home, it was in the late spring of 1871. Colonel Nelson A. Miles commanded the Fifth Infantry at Fort Hays, with his regimental headquarters at that garrison. Mrs. Miles was with him. Two interesting incidents occurred to my parents at Fort Hays. Among the old army customs, officers and their wives in any garrison made it a point to call upon other army people who might be passing from one station to another.

That night, to my mother's delight, Captain Samuel Ovenshine was among the callers. He was then an officer in the Fifth Infantry. My mother had not met "Sam" Ovenshine since as a little girl in Philadelphia, she had attended her very first party, and that event had been a birthday party at the home of the Ovenshines in honor of Sam. My mother, even at the age of six, had been taught to dance, and felt very proud when Sam Ovenshine, who was in her opinion quite a young man, invited her to dance with him, while Auntie Green and the Ovenshine family smiled at the difference in the size of the two dancers.

FATHER VISITS TOM CUSTER

While she and Captain Ovenshine were laughing over the memory of that birthday, my father was sitting in the tent of Captain Tom Custer, smoking and talking over memories of the Civil War, when the Army of the Potomac, commanded by Major General George G. Meade, formed a central point in front of Richmond, father then recently promoted to first lieutenant in the 127th Infantry under Meade. To the left of Meade's command was the cavalry under Phil Sheridan. George Armstrong Custer, at the age of twenty-five, was a major general in Sheridan's cavalry. Tom, his younger brother, was under General Ulysses S. Grant. Fronting them was the Army of Northern Virginia with General Robert E. Lee commanding the Confederate Army. The line reached for thirty miles from a point on the north, near Richmond, to Appomattox on the south. Every foot of that stretch was earned by hard fighting, until on April 9, 1865, General Lee surrendered.

My father saw that surrender, when Lee's flag, which was merely a piece of white toweling on a stick, was accepted. George Custer and his younger brother, Tom, were also witnesses of that hour. Later that flag was presented to General George A. Custer by General Sheridan, and the table at which General Grant sat to write the terms of Lee's surrender was a gift to General Custer's wife.

After General Lee surrendered that day, my father penciled a note to a girl named Flora Green in Philadelphia, describing the scene, and telling the glad news that the war was over. My father was twenty years old on March 6, 1865, a month previous to Lee's surrender, and his admiration for the brilliant work of young Major General Custer of Sheridan's Cavalry was enthusiastic, though it was not until the Tenth Cavalry and the Seventh "cut trails" in the Indian country that the personal friendship began between my father and Tom Custer, whose career had won high honors, including two Congressional Medals.

When we were at Fort Hays, the Seventh Cavalry was under the command of George Custer, who was actually the second in command of the regiment, being only the lieutenant colonel of the Seventh. Colonel Samuel Sturgis was the commanding officer of the regiment, but he was absent, so Custer had full command. The Seventh was not at Fort Hays, but not far from the garrison and in temporary quarters, practically under canvas, and expecting orders to move. After our arrival at Fort Hays, my father learned that his dear friend, Tom Custer, was encamped just outside the garrison. The regiment, under orders to move, was packed and ready to march on command. Mrs. Custer was also at Hays.

As soon as the evening dinner was over, my father excused himself and hurried down to Tom Custer's tent. When he returned that night, he carried a small box made of walnut which he exhibited with pride. It was crudely made without a cover. One of the sides was a trifle smaller than the other three. It was intended to have measured about six inches across and seven high, but was slightly irregular.

My father told of his chat and smoke with Tom, and that when he arose to say "good-bye," Tom had reached across to where the tobacco box was standing on his camp table. They had both been filling their pipes from the tobacco in the box. Tom held it out to my father.

"One of the soldiers in my troop made this for me," he said. "Take it with you. Many a good fellow has had his hand in that box, Cooper. When you smoke up, think of me."

Good-byes were said at the tent door. They never met again. A very vivid and personal incident is associated with that box by myself. It occurred just after we left Fort Hays several days later to journey on to Fort Dodge. In some way a wild pigeon was caught and my father brought it to me. He attached a light cord to one of its legs, allowing a string about six feet with a small loop. This he slipped over my finger as I sat in the ambulance.

"Shut your hand tightly," he said, "then you can watch the pigeon fly as we drive along."

I watched for a while, but the tugging at the string made me fear the pigeon would break the string and escape. My father argued, but I insisted. Finally he had the driver stop. My father's small camp locker was on the "boot" of the ambulance. From this he took Tom Custer's tobacco box, and bringing it to me, he put the pigeon in the box, spreading my small hands over the opening.

"Now it can't get away," he said. But I wanted to see the pigeon. I had slipped the loop from my finger, and as I spread my hands apart, there was a flap, a flash of wings, and my pigeon darted on its way, taking the string with it, while I sat crying. I always regretted losing that pigeon, because the string was still tied to its leg when it disappeared from our sight.

FORT DODGE

We reached Fort Dodge that night. Where Dodge City stands today was then a stretch of prairie, the only habitation being Fort Dodge. So rare was the advent of travelers that the approach of even an unexpected horseman brought everyone outside the buildings of the garrison. It was at Fort Dodge that my mother met the first of our new regiment, the Tenth Cavalry. Lieutenant and Mrs. Samuel Colladay, who were charming, cultured people, acted as our host and hostess during the time we were forced to remain at Fort Dodge.

The garrison was so depleted on account of scouting after the Indians that the necessary number of armed soldiers to escort us on our way could not be furnished. Colonel De Lancey Floyd-Jones, the post commander, would not permit any officer, even though not accompanied by a family, to leave Fort Dodge unless under protection of a proper escort.

In those frontier garrisons there was no hotel, no stopping place, except the homes of the officers to shelter chance guests. Yet, no matter how small an officer's pay, or how limited the space in his home, or how many the invading party might number, someway was always found to care for visitors who were given a cordial greeting at the front door. The Indians were out making medicine, which meant more trouble for the soldiers. Medicine making included excited harangues and plans for an outbreak. When rumor of a medicine camp reached any garrison, the soldiers were at once dispatched to break it up. As Fort Dodge was almost depleted of its usual quota of men because they were out on Indian duty, we waited there for ten days.

In the ambulance, which was merely a three-seated covered carriage, we two children were settled on the back seat with my mother. On the second inside seat, which faced us, my father sat with a loaded carbine in his hand, while he sharply watched for the first suspicious sign of Indians, for even a small puff of dust might give warning of danger. The driver of our ambulance held the reins of the four fast-trotting mules, while at the same time a loaded carbine was propped beside him ready for instant use. In a big canvas-topped army wagon rode our escort of armed soldiers ready for action.

Young though I was, that drive is fresh in my memory. Everything was so unusual that it made as sharp an impression as when a sensitive photographic film is exposed to sunlight. I am confident that this trip really formed my life habit of observing the smallest details. My father kept calling my attention to things that seemed insignificant, such as a peculiar twist of a mesquite bush, a horned toad, distant dust, hoofprints in the soft road, the position of the sun compared with time by his watch. I acquired the trick of drinking from the gray woolen-covered tin canteens, two of which banged on the inside of our vehicle, and were kept moistened to ensure a drink that was not like water from a simmering teakettle.

I felt quite initiated as a westerner when I was able to pull the plug of the canteen, tip it, and "drink like a soldier," instead of pouring the water outside my chin and down my neck. No easy accomplishment for a tenderfoot of any age or sex, when in a carriage bumping over a rough road at fairly good speed. It was necessary to plan the drive on such trips from "water to water." Mules and horses had to be considered before human beings, but extra canteens were always kept in reserve for a "dry camp." Because of the importance of camping where water could be found, each spring or waterhole, every tiny creek, was marked on the handmade map my father carried. I learned the value of maps as we traveled over unsettled country.

Our first night out from Fort Dodge brought us to a little river called the Cimarron. It was a new and interesting experience for me when the soldiers pitched the tent where our family was to pass that night. Camp was arranged. I watched our supper being cooked over a campfire. A small box was placed for my mother to sit upon, another for my father. Tin plates, cups, and common iron forks adorned the red cloth spread upon the ground over a canvas. Many times after I had become what my father called "a camp follower," I saw soldiers dig up mesquite roots for fuel. The short, thick knobs made a very hot, lasting fire, like oak.

DUGOUT ON THE PRAIRIE

After the meal, my father showed us a dugout built against the embankment of the river. It could not be seen from level ground above the invisible roof. Only the short stovepipe betrayed it. I went with him to see that stovepipe. Then we went into the queer store that had been established by a typical pioneer. The one entrance was a stout door, but there were no windows. When the door was shut and barred, it made the dugout into a fortress.

The storekeeper had a small supply of matches, tobacco, pipes, chewing tobacco, and such things as teamsters might require on the road. In the back of this tiny store the owner had taken the precaution to dig a second room. It was so small that it barely permitted a good-sized man to crawl inside. He explained that in case Indians should get into the front of his home, he could retreat into the hole in the back of the store and stand them off with no risk to himself, until his ammunition had been used to the last bullet.

That bullet he would use on himself. Any white man captured by the Indians in those days preferred death for his family at his own hands. Though I did not know it for many years later, all through the unsettled Indian countries, women in lonely places were instructed, "Save the last bullet for yourself."

My brother and I were soundly sleeping, but my mother sat on the box in front of the tent. It was growing dark. Miles of lonely prairie reached about us. Coyotes, scenting human beings, began their shrill howls. Someone had told mother that the call of a coyote might be a signal of Indians. She remembered stories she had read about Indian cruelties.

My father came up and advised her, "Turn in and get a good night's rest. Tomorrow will be a hard day for you."

"I'm afraid to sleep in a tent," her voice quivered. "I'm afraid of Indians."

"What will you do?" father asked.

"If that man would let me go in his dugout, I would feel safer."

"The tent is just as safe and much cleaner. However, if you insist, I will ask him."

"Sure," was the man's hearty reply. "It's not fit for a lady, but she can have it if she wants it."

Soldiers carried our bedding into the hole at the back of the dugout. Into it my mother crawled with my brother and myself, and there we three slept until daylight. After camp breakfast, we started our second day's march. It was not monotonous. In fact, I never knew a monotonous day during my long years of frontier experiences. Each day held its own interests.

AN OCEAN OF BUFFALO

The second day from Fort Dodge we ran into immense herds of buffalo. They were coming north from their winter ranges, and the whole country was black with them. They kept ahead of us, one herd following the other. Sick buffalo, driven from the herds, straggled singly, in pathetic effort to keep up with the main bunches. All day long we were not out of sight of the big creatures that looked like an ocean of small black waves as they moved at a rapid gait, their immense heads lowered, and the hairy lumps on their backs rising and falling as they traveled along.

It was my first glimpse of a buffalo herd. My father lifted my brother to the driver's seat, and held him so that he could watch. Some of the mounted soldiers galloped their horses ahead until they were within shooting range of the rear herd. We had no fresh beef. As one of the animals toppled clumsily to the ground, my brother grew highly excited. When excited he often stuttered.

"See! See!" he shrieked at the top of his voice, staring in horror. "No! No! B—b—boy shoot b—b—bounce!"

I understood and explained. Katie Dougherty, who had been my own nursemaid until my brother usurped my cradle, used to take us both to see her brother's family, and there a big Newfoundland dog had become our staunch friend. The dog was big, black, and its name was Bounce. So it required quite a little bit of explaining to persuade my brother that the soldiers had not shot our friend, Bounce.

A few years later when we traveled over this same country, the only signs of buffalo we saw were the dried carcasses or bleaching bones. Every buffalo had been skinned. Wanton slaughter by buffalo hunters for the sake of selling the hides not only nearly exterminated the herds, but created much of the Indian troubles, because the meat of the buffalo, dried, afforded food for months, while the hides provided tepees, bedding, and protection to Indians when exposed to cold or stormy weather. Deer, also necessary to sustain life and provide clothing for the Indians, soon became almost as scarce as the buffalo.

WE SLEEP IN A REDOUBT

The second night brought us to a camp where one company of the Sixth Infantry was stationed. This was called a "redoubt." A circle ten feet high had been built from bags of sand, with one narrow opening barely permitting a man to pass in and out. An armed sentinel always stood guard, day or night, at this entrance. Inside the redoubt, tents were pitched for the soldiers stationed there, who were under the command of noncommissioned officers—sergeants and corporals.

Though a whole company of soldiers was at hand in addition to our own armed escort, my mother was very nervous. The mere fact that it was considered necessary to keep such a large force of soldiers at this point made her feel more certain that there was grave danger around us, and that the hidden Indians might dash upon our tent before the men could assemble outside the redoubt to protect us.

Our tent had been pitched about fifty feet away from the redoubt, but my mother again sat outside the opening of the tent and insisted that she was too nervous to sleep, and would not stay in the tent. Despite the presence of the company of soldiers and the sentinel on guard, she could not conquer her fear. At last she begged, "If I could have the tent inside that redoubt, I know I could sleep soundly."

It was an unusual situation. Officers' families never were quartered amidst enlisted men, but precedent and official regulations were mere words to her at that time. Her plea had reached the ears of an old Irish sergeant on duty. He stepped up, saluting my father, and said, "Liftenant, shure if the lady wants to stay in the redoubt, we'll put her there."

That settled it. The tent was taken down and set up inside the fortress of sandbags, our bedding arranged on the ground, and there, surrounded by a troop of the Sixth Infantry, while the sentinel at the entrance called each hour as it passed, my mother rested peacefully. "All is well," the man on guard called after naming each hour. She was safe.

WE REACH CAMP SUPPLY

The next day's journey would bring us to Camp
Supply. Fort Hays, Fort Dodge, and Camp Supply.
Then for forty years afterward, a succession of frontier
army homes. Yet, never once did my mother or I see any
army garrison built inside a stockade, as is erroneously represented in fiction, motion pictures, and illustrations of
western frontier stories by people who have never seen the
West except from windows of Pullman cars.

A terrific thunderstorm was raging when our ambulance
reached Camp Supply late in the afternoon. We were driven past a long row of squatty log cabins which were all
connected by small porches at the sides, giving an effect of
one continuous building. There were no doors to be seen at
the backs. The connecting porches were about four feet
across from building to building.

The driver stopped the ambulance and father got out.
Turning to my mother, he said, "Well, don't you want to
get down?"

"Not at these stables, but at the officers' quarters."

There was nothing to do but get down, but if those miles
of Indian dangers had not been so vivid, one officer of the
Tenth Cavalry would have been minus his wife and two
children that day. Two men came to the ambulance just then.
My father introduced Captain Nicholas Nolan, commanding
officer of Troop A, and Second Lieutenant Levi P. Hunt of the
same troop, my father being the first lieutenant of the troop.

My mother looked at these officers who wore scouting clothes, as they had just returned from a long, hard chase after Indians. Their trousers were of the kind issued to enlisted men, coarse cloth, lighter color than the handsome dark blue broadcloth used by officers. In those days, the "army blue" with yellow trimmings for cavalry, white for infantry, and red for artillery made the United States Army a thing of beauty on parade, very different from the later appearance when inferior dye of so-called olive drab made a line of soldiers look like a spilled omelet concocted from addled eggs.

My mother had so far only seen officers on garrison duty. The ones who were standing in the rain had on blue flannel shirts, their Mexican sombreros, sported unshaven faces, and wore Indian moccasins in place of boots. Their appearance could not be offset by their cordial words. She was very frigid in her resentment at being introduced to such rough characters, much to the amusement of the captain of her husband's troop, and the second lieutenant, who was a West Point graduate and a polished gentleman. My father was practically "between the devil and the deep sea" at that moment.

"You are to be the guests of Mrs. Nolan and myself, until your quarters are fixed comfortably," said Captain Nolan to her.

So we were helped to the ground, and as we went under the little side porch, a door opened. Those side doors, one at either side of the house, were the only entrances to the officers' homes at Camp Supply. Mrs. Nolan stood with her two children, Katie, about my age, and her boy, Eddie, a bit younger than my brother, beside her to welcome us to Camp Supply.

She was a refined, cultured woman from Washington, D.C., but the home over which she presided gracefully was like all the others in the garrison. Rough logs ran vertically, not horizontally as most log cabins, and the cracks between the logs were chinked in with dry mud. We were ushered into her bedroom to wash for dinner.

Spikes driven into the logs held clothing, while a collapsible iron frame supported a tin bowl and pitcher, such as was used in camps. The bed was of rough boards with a government bed sack filled with straw. The floor in this room was merely packed dirt, well swept. In the other room were chairs of crude, unpainted wood.

The rough board table in the center of the room was covered, but Mrs. Nolan could brag of being the only woman at Camp Supply who had a carpet on her living room floor. It was an ingrain carpet, carefully laid. On the dirt floor, hay had been thickly strewn, and over this, many layers of newspapers, donated by those who had slowly accumulated them. Thus the sacred carpet had been protected from contact with the earth beneath it.

While chatting with Mrs. Nolan, "Old Aunt Eliza" entered. She was an old-fashioned Southern darkey. All the enlisted men of the Tenth Cavalry were colored soldiers of the best type. Their wives became cooks, laundresses, and nursemaids for the officers. The old women bragged about how many "chillun ob de Tenth Ca'vry I done nussed and raised," long after those boys and girls had fully grown children of their own.

"Miss Annie, how many potatoes shall I done cook fo' dinnah?"

My mother was insulted at having potatoes doled out by her stingy hostess.

"How many will there be?" Mrs. Nolan counted, then replied, "Cook one potato for each person, and two potatoes for the four children." Eliza vanished. Mrs. Nolan, reading my mother's thoughts, said quietly, "When you have been here awhile, you will understand why we count potatoes."

It was seven months before we ate another potato, and then we paid seven dollars to a courageous peddler for half a bushel. In the Indian country, peddlers did not risk trips from the railroad towns to Camp Supply or such garrisons. The chance of an attack, loss of horses, burning of wagons, and theft of merchandise were serious enough matters without the additional possibility of losing one's scalp as a climax of the trading trip.

Neither potatoes nor any other fresh vegetables were then included in government rations. The soldiers, few in proportion to the area of scouting necessary, had no time to cultivate either "company gardens" or a "post garden." Indians kept them all busy. Fresh beef furnished by contractors was only issued at intervals. This was varied by buffalo meat, venison, quail, dove, wild turkeys, and small game shot by the soldiers. Canned stuffs from the commissary completed our menu, but the canning industry was just starting, so we were limited to peaches, tomatoes, and cove oysters in cans.

A HOME OF OUR OWN

We moved down to our own quarters—two log rooms with dirt floors, and a "lean-to" for a kitchen. At the front of the cabin, a small window looked out onto the walk and beyond that was the parade ground. It was evidently the rainy season, for when we entered our own side door, the rain was pouring down.

My mother had learned the reason why no house had a front or back door, and why those funny little side porches had been built. In case of attack by Indians, the families at the extreme ends of the garrison could retreat from house to house by those side porches, while soldiers fought on the outside edge of the porches to cover the retreat until the women and children were concentrated at the safest point of the garrison.

Our trunks had been set down in the largest room, and a huge chunk of mud fell from the ceiling as we entered the room. It left a hole through which the rain fell merrily. My mother sat down on the trunk and cried, announcing that she was going back to Philadelphia at the first opportunity. I was satisfied. I had found a big spider. My father promptly killed it, warning me about tarantulas, centipedes, scorpions, and many other interesting insects which he promised to show to me later.

Our beds were like Mrs. Nolan's. Short posts were driven into the dirt floors and on these were nailed flat boards. The soldier bed sacks filled with clean straw formed the mattress. On this was laid buffalo robes, fur side up, beneath the sheets to keep the sharp straws from scratching the flesh. As the rain drove the mud onto the bed at times, a canopy was eventually constructed on four upright posts, much like an old-fashioned four-poster bed. On this was tacked a canvas tent sheet. I am quite sure that the beautifully draped silken canopies originated centuries ago in the mind of an exasperated woman whose roof was not weatherproof.

Tent sheets were scarce. The quartermaster was held responsible for each one used. They could not be bought. Before our canopy had been erected over the bed, I distinctly recollect my mother rescuing me from a nice little mud puddle I had discovered during a rainstorm. I was plopped on the bed. There she climbed with my brother, so we were safe from the muddy spots on the floor. My father suggested opening an umbrella over us, but "umbrellas opened in a house are a sign of death." She rejected the proposition.

After the tent sheet had been erected over the bed, whenever it rained we took refuge there and I considered it a playhouse. The climax occurred when my mother opened her eyes one morning and looked right out through a big hole and onto the front walk. It was too much. That morning she gathered her precious newspapers and rammed them into the open places between the logs that formed the front of our home.

John W. Davidson, lieutenant colonel of the Tenth, and in command of Camp Supply, was passing on his way to the adjutant's office. He saw the papers and knocked at the door. My mother explained the predicament. My father was out with Troop A scouting after Indians as usual, and we were alone. Colonel Davidson studied the cabin. When he reached his office, he sent the quartermaster an order to "line Mrs. Cooper's quarters, ceilings, and sides with good canvas."

One of the ladies who had not yet acquired a canopy, took refuge from falling chunks of mud beneath her dining room table (a big box), until such time as there was sufficient canvas and enough men who were not scouting so that a rainstorm held no terror for her inside her home.

OUR STRIKER

While the officers' wives employed the wives of the soldiers, the need of a manservant was a feature of each home. So the officers were permitted to use an enlisted man, who was willing to work for extra pay during hours when certain duties did not require his attention. These men were termed "strikers" in the days before that term had its present association. Maybe the present application was founded on the fact that a soldier striker was not required to give his attention exclusively to official duty.

The Tenth Cavalry soldiers vied for such jobs. They had comfortable kitchens to sit in and talk with the cooks, and never lacked good things to eat, as they were entitled to their regular meals in the barracks, and then were able to devour delicacies prepared for the officer's table. Soldiers who were not strikers, probably because such positions were limited, called the strikers "dog-robbers," intimating that the family dog was deprived of tidbits by the presence of the striker.

Our striker at that time was unique. His name was John Hopkins. He was an expert card player among the soldiers, and when he had been lucky, Hopkins took the largest currency bill in his possession and thrust it through the buttonhole of his collar so that it formed a necktie of two flaring ends. The effect of this bow-tie below his solemn black face when he passed the dishes at our table, or tended to other chores, was ludicrous beyond comparison.

FATHER BUYS A CHAIR

Our only chairs were empty soap boxes, the dining table being a very large box which had contained uniforms for the soldiers. My bathtub was provided by sawing a whiskey barrel in half. Ropes formed the handles. The half-barrel had been burnt to destroy the strong whiskey odor. I was very proud of that bathtub. Similar tubs were used by the laundresses.

One memorable afternoon my father appeared at the side entrance carrying a real chair. He had bought it at the trader's store where it had been left by an officer formerly at Camp Supply. It was a folding chair with a gaudy carpet seat, and another strip of the same design forming the back. It was tried in every corner of the room, and just as my mother had decided where it should remain, a knock at the door brought Captain and Mrs. James Powell of the Sixth Infantry to call. They were new arrivals.

The chair, as a seat of honor, was offered to Mrs. Powell. She insisted that my mother should use it. Then in turn it was declined by Captain Powell and my father. As there were only three boxes to sit upon, and no one would sit in the chair, my father remained standing until the others combined to compel him to sit down in that chair. Very much against his will, he complied. He was six feet two and built in proportion, a typical cavalry officer.

Very cautiously he sat down, but as the conversation progressed, he forgot the new chair and leaned back. Instantly, it crashed to the floor and he went with it. The chair made good kindling wood, however, and an extra soap box came to our home the next day. We were prepared for more callers.

Dust storms often made candles necessary in midday. Coal oil was too valuable for constant use, even when it could be obtained from a venturesome peddler, for it was not carried by the government then. The fine sand sifted in clouds through the houses and filled the pots where our food was cooking, so that we literally ate our "peck of dirt," but not on the installment plan as most human beings do it.

I recall another storm at Camp Supply. A grasshopper storm. They came in a dense cloud, like hailstones, and fell around our doors and all over the ground. Colonel Davidson had two daughters, who were about ten and twelve. They frequently took me to play at their home, and just after the grasshopper storm, they came for me. In the house they showed me a big can covered with mosquito netting. It was filled with live hoppers.

I do not know who originated the new game. A bit of thread was fastened to a grasshopper, then about a yard of string intervened between that insect and another hopper. These were tossed to the ceiling, where they clung. The swinging thread between them afforded a place for a third hopper to cling. By the time the room was thick with swinging grasshoppers, someone discovered us and put an end to our fun.   '

By this time my mother had forgotten her determination to desert the army and return to civilization. She had grown accustomed to seeing officers with rough clothes and beards unkept, for my father was one of those officers, and he looked exactly like the others when he came home after weeks of constant scouting in dust, rain, cold, or grilling heat.

Then came the order for Troop A—Nolan, Hunt, and my father—to proceed to Fort Sill, Indian Territory, the heart of the Kiowa and Comanche Reservation. Only those who have traveled overland with the cavalry can understand the thrill that stirs each one, even to the youngest child, when the march begins.

The stomping of the troop horses, the jokes of the old Negro soldiers, the last good-byes of fellow officers and women who have shared hardships and mutual laughter, even mishaps, then the march begins. The officers and soldiers on their horses, followed by the ambulances with their families. Back of them a long line of white topped prairie-schooners loaded with troop property, each wagon drawn by a six-mule team, while the driver sits on one of the "wheel team" with his blacksnake whip hanging about his neck. So we started for Fort Sill.

5

OFF TO FORT SILL, HEART OF THE INDIAN COUNTRY

Ordinarily, three weeks were required for a troop, with its wagons, to move from Camp Supply to Fort Sill. Though the distance was only a hundred ninety miles, the unbroken roads, rivers swollen from bank to bank, or the regular crossing completely washed away, made travel slow. The cavalry, unimpeded and with every favorable condition, was supposed to make twenty-five miles a day over good roads.

On that trip I recall several episodes. One was when we reached a river where the usual ford had been cut away by floods. The soldiers unhitched the wagons, also our own ambulance, and tied picket ropes to the back wheels. One soldier had already ridden his horse through the muddy water, and after reaching the best possible landing place on the other bank, signaled. Then our vehicle bumped down the steep declivity toward the stream.

We practically dangled from the picket ropes held by a troop of cavalry soldiers, but touched bottom safely. Then the men scrambled down, untied the ropes from the back wheels, and hitched the four mules to the ambulance. Across the rushing water, with soldiers riding at either side of the leaders to keep them from turning downstream with the current, we finally reached the opposite bank where the other soldier sitting on his horse had indicated a safe landing place.

Once again the picket ropes were employed. This time they were fastened to the front wheels and the pole of our ambulance, then the soldiers seized the ropes and we were dragged to the top. No horses or mules could have hauled any of our wagons up that grade. At times we literally "hung 'twixt heaven and earth" like Mahomet's coffin.

There was another menace in crossing streams. Quicksand. Often there was no indication of its presence until a team would begin to flounder and sink. Then the troopers would dash their horses through the water and begin whipping the team with the flat blades of their sabers, and thus keep the animals moving. If a team balked under such circumstances, the traces had to be cut, so that each mule might fight for its own life, but the heavily loaded wagon soon disappeared beneath the water and was never recovered.

Herd after herd of buffalo was passed. They were going north to their summer range. When the weather turned cold, these same herds would travel south to their winter range. Not hundreds, but thousands were in sight of our troop. There was one day I have never forgotten. A big herd of buffalo, for some unknown reason, stampeded. They were just ahead of us and formed a solid mass. It was characteristic of them that they never swung aside, but kept right on in a direct line when they stampeded. So from early dawn until we stopped that night and made camp, those buffalo formed a solid wall of brown bodies in front of us.

In the morning they had vanished, but as we traveled along that day, we came across what had been a light wagon. It was a total wreck. No horses or human beings were near it. Later in the day we met the owners of the wagon, a man and his wife, who were riding their team. Nothing of any value was in the abandoned wagon, but they gladly climbed into one of the white-topped troop wagons, while their horses were tied to the back of it. In this way they reached the next settlement and said "good-bye."

ROAD MAKING ON THE PRAIRIE

The trip to Fort Sill required twenty-one days, camping each night. At times it was necessary to make a road. The river had cut away any sign of a crossing, leaving only a high bank overhanging a steep bluff. In order to get our wagons across and continue our journey, the soldiers, armed with picks and shovels, cut a road down the embankment, though the ground was frozen hard. That accomplished, another problem had to be met. The riverbed was so narrow that it would not permit a team of four mules to stand on it level, and even four mules could not possibly drag our heavy wagons up the opposite grade.

So eight mules were "doubled-up," thus making four teams, one team ahead of the others. These were hitched to the first wagon as an experiment, and old Sergeant Thomas Allsup took the reins while he sat astride the "near wheeler." We watched anxiously from our own ambulance on the edge of the bluff, knowing that we, too, must cross in that same manner if we were to cross at all. The mules were driven slowly, brakes held against the wheels by a soldier who sat on the driver's seat.

Near the bottom of the narrow riverbed, the men released the brakes. Wild yells of the men mingled with cracks of the whip while mounted soldiers at either side, with the flat blades of sabers, urged the mules as they dashed down the last few feet of the incline across the narrow bottom and up the opposite grade. The leaders of the four teams were struggling up the steep road while the wagon was still careening downward on the other side. The idea was similar to the rebound of a rubber ball.

There were no settlements, not even solitary houses. It was all open Indian country, and when we reached Sheridan's Roost (where General Phil Sheridan had once camped), a terrific norther overtook us. Sheridan's Roost was merely a name. There was no building of any description. However, heavy timbers surrounded our camp, and that was of vital importance in the month of January on the Great Plains when a norther was raging, and the only shelter was a tent.

A detail of soldiers at once started chopping wood to make fires, not only to warm the half-frozen men, but also to provide hot food for us all. Other soldiers were taking care of the horses and mules, for all of them were suffering from the intense cold after plunging through the icy water of the stream. As the men chopped wood, every drop of rain that fell on their overcoats froze, and their top capes were rigid with ice that cracked as they moved their arms.

All three officers of Troop A—Captain Nolan, my father, and Lieutenant Hunt—were total abstainers. On New Year's Day, when my mother was awaiting our ambulance to start on the trip, the post surgeon had brought a bottle of French brandy to my mother in case of any emergency on the road. He told her not to let any of the three officers know she had it, as he was aware of their objection to stimulants.

An extra pair of long riding boots belonging to my father were in our ambulance, ready to be changed when the ones he was wearing became water soaked, a very necessary precaution in freezing weather. She put the bottle of brandy in the leg of one of these boots. That evening before we reached our camp at Sheridan's Roost, while the norther pelted us viciously, my father and Lieutenant Hunt rode to the side of our ambulance to see how we were standing the conditions.

Their faces were absolutely purple from the cold and their teeth chattering so they could hardly speak. My mother said she had something to warm them, and insisted they take a drink of the brandy. Reaching down for the boot to get the bottle, she found that the cork had come out. All the liquor was in the foot of the boot. However, enough was poured out into a tin cup so that the half-frozen officers could get a swallow and start their blood circulating once more. So we went into Sheridan's Roost.

The wood gathered for fires was rain soaked, making it hard to start a blaze so that hot food could be prepared for the soldiers or ourselves. That night my father sat up till dawn, putting little chunks of wood into the Sibley stove in our tent, and thus prevented our freezing, though we had quantities of blankets and warm buffalo robes over us.

The next morning before breaking camp, we saw small Indian boys running around killing wild turkeys with sticks. So plentiful were the wild turkeys, that an Indian, who came into our camp carrying a load of turkeys, offered to sell them all for two cups of brown sugar. Thus for two cups of brown sugar there were enough turkeys to give a real turkey dinner to the entire command.

In those days we always faced the danger of prairie fires. On our trip to Fort Sill we encountered this menace. Luckily the wind was in our favor, but the heat and smoke of the fire reached us. At any hour we knew that the wind might change, and it was not until we had crossed a good-sized stream that we felt we were out of the path of the flames. It is a sight that once seen, is never forgotten. The flames were like an army of immense red demons, leaping and tossing long arms to clutch and destroy every vestige of life. I was too young to realize the danger of flying sparks on the dry prairie grass, even across the river, if the wind should shift.

An amusing incident on this trip arose because army regulations allowed a captain only fifteen hundred pounds of baggage, and that filled the front half of a government wagon. The first lieutenant was entitled to one-half of the back part of the same wagon, while the second lieutenant took what was left by the first lieutenant. Lieutenant Hunt, a bachelor, had only a trunk so he donated his share of the back end of the wagon to accommodate our overflow.

Among our limited possessions was a five-gallon can of coal oil, half-used. Coal oil was not provided by the government and had been very hard to procure at Camp Supply. One dollar a gallon had been paid by my mother for that can, so it was packed into the wagon with our other things. Mrs. Nolan's precious ingrain carpet had been stowed in the front of the wagon. That first night in camp when the cook went to get out things for supper, it was discovered that our can of coal oil was empty.

Two gallons and a half of the valuable fluid had leaked onto Mrs. Nolan's prized ingrain carpet. Mrs. Nolan was aggrieved. So was my mother. Each one felt she was the injured party. So for several days on the trip, neither one spoke to the other, but my father and Captain Nolan saw the humor of the situation. Anyway, it was "all in the line of duty," and soon the incident became a laughable memory.

FORT SILL AT LAST

Fort Sill was located in Indian Territory in the heart of the Indian Reservation, about a hundred ninety miles southeast of Camp Supply, thirty south of the Washita River, and forty miles north of the Red River. It was established by General Sheridan in his campaign during the winter of

1868 and 1869. Colonel Benjamin F. Grierson, commanding officer of my father's regiment, had called the place Camp Wichita before it received the name of Camp Sheridan, but in 1869 it was officially named Fort Sill.

At Camp Supply, all mail had been brought by mounted couriers, but at Fort Sill, an open buckboard carried the mail from Caddo, one hundred sixty miles southeastward. The buildings at Fort Sill were not so primitive as at Camp Supply. Two rows of neat stone cottages formed the officers' line, making two sides to the square parade ground in the middle of which was the flag staff. The soldiers' barracks faced the captains' line of quarters, and the hospital stood back on the northwest corner, while the chapel occupied the northeast point. All were made of quarried limestone.

Southeast of the garrison was the big plain on which the cavalry drills were held. About a mile beyond this plain in the same direction the Indian agency and Indian commissary building stood. The Caddo Indian School was also there. Our quarters were near the center of the east row of officers' quarters, and directly next to the officers' mess (dining hall). That fact is indelibly impressed upon my memory.

Cache and Medicine Bluff creeks joined near the post, then uniting, flowed to the Red River forty miles distant. The Red River was truly named, for the water, when it had water in it, was thick and red. In drinking this fluid, it was necessary to hold the teeth tightly together in order to avoid swallowing the slimy red sediment. Before I was thirteen years old, our family made the trip across the Red River eight times by wagon, en route between Fort Sill, Indian Territory, and Fort Concho, Texas, so we had ample opportunity to get acquainted with the Red River under varied conditions. Winter, summer, flood or drought, it was equally bad.

The country surrounding Fort Sill was beautiful. From the garrison one could see the Wichita Mountains, which extended fifty miles or more. The Wichita Mountains hid many small streams that were tributaries to Cache and Medicine Bluff creeks. Cache Creek especially was noted for excellent fishing, and I spent many hours with my father, sitting with dangling fishing lines. His catch was perpetual, mine occasional. Trout, bass, small catfish, and perch made up his string.

At Fort Sill the winter of 1871–72, and until a few months before the birth of my sister in November 1872, troops of soldiers were crowded together in the barracks, while the condition of the officers and their families was almost parallel to former tenement dwellers in the slums of New York City. Our own set of quarters was classed as a two-family set. The front room on the first floor was both living room and bedroom for my father, mother, myself, and younger brother. A bandbox of a room allowed us to have a table where we ate our meals, and out in the backyard stood our kitchen. It was a tent.

Another officer and his family, consisting of his wife, a young baby, and two children about the ages of my brother and myself, had the back room downstairs as their combined sleeping and living room. Our room was separated from theirs by sliding doors, so every sound in either room was audible in the other.

What had been a tiny kitchen was allotted to them as a dining room and in the backyard stood their own kitchen, like ours. Upstairs were two attics, each about six feet square and so low were the ceilings that a person of average height could not stand upright. Yet, even such so-called rooms were occupied at times by members of an officer's family. General Ord once remarked that Grierson's regiment was quartered in a manner that he would not stable his horses.

Fort Sill in those years was scourged with malaria each summer, so that often there were not enough soldiers to carry out necessary duties. The officers crawled from sickbeds between "chill day" to do the work for other officers whose "chill day" made them unable to be on their feet. It was an epidemic. I, myself, was a victim, and by an unexpected turn recovered when the post surgeon had no hope. I lay ill in one bed in that front room, while my father was ill in another bed in the same room. Eventually the fever passed.

One of the most interesting features near Fort Sill, even to those who were accustomed to frontier trails, was Medicine Bluff. It towered sheer and smooth from the bed of the creek to a point three hundred ten feet that seemed to defy anything but a fly to cling to its face. From the back, however, three distinct knolls were visible, the center being the highest point. Medicine Bluff was held in superstitious awe by the Indians. Upon the highest peak, they said, a good Medicine Man, dead for many years, had built an altar. It was a sanctuary for the Great Spirit when he descended from the sky to communicate with his children.

Long years after the death of this Medicine Man, the Comanches and Wichitas carried their sick to the altar when their living Medicine Man, who was both priest and doctor, could give no further aid. There the sick Indian was left alone. If worthy, he would be cured by the Great Spirit; but the one who had been wicked, or did not deserve help, was doomed to die beside the altar, and later the vultures and wolves would destroy his body.

At times, it was said, the sick one miraculously disappeared. Then it was whispered with awe that the Great Spirit had carried him away. Many Comanches and Wichitas insisted that the Medicine Man who had built the altar still met the Great Spirit there, face to face, as he had done in life. Whenever this occurred, an immense light illumined the center knoll, while wind and rain circled about the spot. But if the sick Indian beside the altar found favor with the Great Spirit, neither rain nor wind would touch him there. Down the jagged pathway back of the bluff, the Indians believed the spirit of the Medicine Man walked as he had done in life, and so the path became known as "Medicine Man's Walk."

None of the people living at Fort Sill in those days ever tried to make the ascent of Medicine Bluff, not only because of its great difficulty, but principally because they knew that the Comanches and Wichitas regarded the place as sacred. Apart from respecting the religious belief of the Indians, it would have been inviting an attack on the garrison of Fort Sill to have desecrated the altar built by the dead Medicine Man as a sanctuary of the Great Spirit.

OUR TRIP TO MOUNT SCOTT

Eight miles from Fort Sill, Mount Scott could be seen, its towering peak frequently swathed in veil-like clouds. We had settled down comfortably in our new home when my mother was invited to join a picnic party bound for Mount Scott. Mr. George Smith and his wife lived at the Indian Agency while Lawrie Tatum, a fine old Quaker gentleman, was in charge of the Indians.

Mr. Smith's mother, over sixty years of age, had come to visit her son, and as her visit was for a limited time, she wanted to see everything she possibly could before she started back to her Philadelphia home and friends. The old lady, having heard how difficult it was to climb Mount Scott, determined she would reach the very top. Arguments were useless.

Mr. Smith, his mother, wife, and two boys older than myself, my mother, my brother, not quite three, and I, now past four, constituted the party, except for an educated Indian who drove the team of the Smith carriage. My father had been appointed the post commissary officer, so knew nothing of the picnic plans, as the Smiths had driven to the house after my father left for his daily duties at the commissary building. My mother spoke hastily to the colored maid, just saying we were with the Smiths on a picnic at Mount Scott.

As it happened, my father did not come home at noon, so it was not until five o'clock when he received the message. He did not become really alarmed until it was growing dark. Each moment he expected to hear the carriage approaching, but it did not come. Then he hurried to the quarters of the commanding officer, and was ordered to take a detachment of his troop and ride out along the road leading to Mount Scott.

The Indians had been surly and defiant for several weeks. In the village of White Horse, two Indian Commissioners sent from Washington to investigate complaints had been seized and held as prisoners until notified that the soldiers would act at once unless the commissioners were released. My mother had not known this when we started on our picnic.

We drove along the officers' line and out on the road toward Mount Scott, passing many small Indian villages on our way. Though the Indians stared curiously at us, no one had any thought of danger, for we were all accustomed to having them wander about our houses and even peer through our windows. As usual, our greeting, "How?" brought responsive nods, grunts, grins, or an echoing "How?"

At the foot of Mount Scott, after the picnic luncheon had been enjoyed, it was decided that the junior Mrs. Smith should remain with all of us children and the driver, while the older lady and her son, together with my mother, were to make the ascent of the mountain. So they disappeared while the younger Mrs. Smith enjoyed a book and we children played various games. The afternoon passed and when the sun reached the horizon, Mrs. Smith watched anxiously, realizing that irresponsible Indians, singly or in groups, might have encountered the explorers.

Unable to leave her charges, and with no way of signaling, she and the driver consulted. She dared not order the man to hitch the team and return with us to the garrison, for her husband, the old lady, and my mother might return and be alarmed at not finding us there. Further, they would have no way of reaching the garrison themselves. So she sat in the carriage with all of us huddled about her. We were hungry, tired, cross, and sleepy. We wanted to go home. None of us realized her fear that her husband and the two women might have been killed, or that at any moment she might face the same fate, unable to protect herself or us.

Footsteps startled her and the driver. A moment later my mother stumbled into sight. She had made the ascent halfway, but becoming tired, had arranged to remain at the same spot until Mr. Smith and his mother should rejoin her there. After they had disappeared from her sight, she had found a convenient boulder for a seat. While sitting there enjoying the view, she noticed an arrow lying at her feet.

It was not weather beaten. Startled, she picked it up, and a hasty glance around proved that she was sitting in plain sight of an Indian village. Moving behind a sheltering rock, she waited nervously for the Smiths to return, knowing they would be alarmed and start searching for her if she did not remain as agreed. Twilight was turning to darkness. Unable to stand the fear that Mr. Smith and his mother had been victims of violence at the hands of Indians, she stumbled down the side of the mountain. Her only landmark was the distant light of Fort Sill, but by a stroke of good luck she found our camp.

Then the driver made a campfire, hoping it might help the wanderers; and yet there was real danger that such a fire might lure mischievous Indians, who would understand the utter helplessness of women and children with only one man to protect them. But two hours later Mr. Smith and his mother found us. He was carrying his mother who was completely exhausted.

While the team was being hitched, he told that they had actually gained the top of Mount Scott, but heavy clouds had shut off their view. Starting to descend, they sought an easier trail, and in so doing lost their bearings and had come down the opposite side of the mountain. This made it necessary for them to work around the base over rough surfaces and through heavy brush, many times retracing their steps because of gullies cut by storms. The old lady frequently was too exhausted to continue, and much time was lost while she lay on the ground resting, or was lifted and carried by her son. All this time he was worrying about my mother alone on the trail waiting their return. So it was a great relief to find her in the camp with the rest of us.

Taking a short cut back, we passed through the camp of White Horse, who was a subchief of the Kiowas. From that camp was an excellent road into Fort Sill, and mules were more reliable than horses on a dark road or a bad trail. When we reached the Indian village, a campfire was blazing at one side of our road. "Drive quickly," ordered Mr. Smith. The man whipped up the team, but as he did so, figures darted from lodges on either side of the road, and dashed toward the carriage. Loud cries, excited voices, and the yelping of Indian dogs, half-wolf and half-mongrel, startled us all. Indian hands gripped the bridles of our team and the carriage stopped.

Around us in the light of the campfire we could see a group of threatened faces. The Indians were muttering in the Kiowa tongue. One of the leaders, whom we afterwards knew to be White Horse, began talking to Mr. Smith, who understood what he was saying. My mother and Mrs. Smith supposed it some unimportant grievance, or indignation that we had disturbed their camp at that hour. For over an hour the conversation went on, while the Kiowas became more emphatic and Mr. Smith's voice betrayed irritation. Squaws kept throwing fresh wood on the fire, so that the threatening countenances could be plainly seen. Then White Horse stepped back. With an angry sweep of his arm, he motioned for us to go on.

Our driver whipped the mules to a swift gallop, but even then half-grown boys yelled derisively and ran after us, throwing good-sized rocks and clumps of dirt that fell around our carriage. Hisses, jeers, screams of hate and defiance followed after us. We crouched on the floor as the mules' gallop changed to a swift run, and the carriage bumped over the road to Fort Sill and safety.

While still some distance from the garrison, we met my father riding at the head of a detachment of his troop. Not till then did we fully realize our past danger. White Horse was in an ugly mood over his failure to enforce his demands by holding the two commissioners as hostages. The next morning it was learned that White Horse had disappeared with all his followers and entire camp equipment, which meant he was on the warpath.

Mr. Smith's assertion to White Horse that if we were not safely back in Fort Sill at a certain hour, the troops would search White Horse's village the first thing because of the way he had taken the commissioners captive, had brought our release. White Horse, at that moment, had made all preparations to decamp, and he realized that any investigation by the officers would betray and thwart his plans. Thus ended a picnic that might have been a serious tragedy, but the name of Mount Scott always brings back the memory of that day.

A MOMENT TO RELAX

When we arrived at Fort Sill in 1871, there were Comanches, Kiowas, and Southern Cheyennes in many large Indian villages surrounding the garrison. With them in other villages were lesser tribes: Wichitas, Keechis, Wacos, and Caddos, all of whom were on friendly terms with the more powerful bands of Indians. The nearest railroad point was Caddo, one hundred sixty miles distant. There were three thousand Indians living on the reservation surrounding Fort Sill. The Kiowas, Cheyennes, Arapahos, and Comanches had separate villages and each tribe its own chief and subchiefs.

Satanta, Big Tree, Kicking Bird, and Lone Wolf were leaders of the Kiowas. Each tribe had its own language, yet they all spoke Comanche. Kicking Bird's village was located on the north side of Beaver Creek, not far from Fort Sill; other bands lived on Rainy Mountain Creek forty miles to the northwest. Rivers, villages, and even the warriors were named after animals or some incident of importance. No Indian boy had a permanent name until he had earned a name and place among the strongest and bravest of the warriors of his tribe.

With the return of Kicking Bird to the reservation, and Satanta and Big Tree prisoners in the Huntsville Penitentiary, the officers and men at Fort Sill relaxed for a short time, well knowing that their inactivity was merely a lull between storms. With their families they went on picnics or fishing parties to Cache Creek. Many rode horse-back, others went in carriages, but the soldiers who drove them and those who accompanied the women and children were always armed with pistols and carbines loaded for any emergency.

～⚛6⚛～

LIFE AT FORT SILL IN ITS
EARLIEST YEARS

———————

Ration day at the Kiowa and Comanche Agency was always an interesting sight. When the weather was pleasant, the garrison people were usually ready to make that an excuse for an outing. Nobody walked, though the agency was within walking distance of Fort Sill. Men, women, as well as the cavalry children were so accustomed to riding, that they never thought of walking any distance. Most of the children had their own ponies, bought from the Indians.

The commissary was the main building at the agency. In it all provisions were stored. Around the commissary small houses sheltered the employees who were civilians. Indians whose villages surrounded Fort Sill were supposed to be on friendly terms with the whites, but were not permitted to leave their reservation. This prohibited them from roving at will to kill buffalo, deer, and other game as in former years, so the government established agencies near the principal garrisons on reservations. From these commissaries, rations or foodstuffs were distributed in proportion to the size of each family.

Different tribes on the reservation were located in separate sections, each tribe having its own chief to command it. There was a strong undercurrent of resentment against the white settlers. In addition to this, the Indians who had never wantonly slaughtered buffalo, but had merely killed what was needed for food and warm hides, saw buffalo hunters slaughter thousands for the mere purpose of selling the hides, while the carcasses were left to rot.

The Indian agent was a civil appointee and in no way under the authority of the army officers, yet in the event of any trouble caused by the agent, it was the duty of the officers and men to apprehend the rebellious Indians. Many Indian agents were dishonest or unfair, and at times, shortage of rations or spoiled rations started trouble which ended in a band of Indians "jumping the reservation," and retaliating by raids on homes of white settlers.

Lawrie Tatum, who was agent at Fort Sill, was a kindly, honest old Quaker, whose influence over the Indians was excellent. On ration day the Indians gathered from all directions, walking or riding ponies. Men and women apparently wore the same kind of garments, but the buckskin moccasins of the women came up higher on their legs. They all wore brilliantly colored blankets. The squaws had wicker baskets or cradles of rawhide tied to their backs by thongs of rawhide. These cradles were covered with blankets with space enough to permit the child to breathe and peep out. No Indian baby ever cries.

In addition to being the baby carrier, the squaw on ration day as well as other times had plenty to do. No warrior ever worked. The women cooked, kept the tepee in order, cleaned game that the men brought home, cured hides of deer, bear, buffalo, wolves, and with the fine sinews, sewed all garments and mended their tepees. It was also the duty of a squaw to take care of her husband's ponies and to saddle them when he wished to ride; or to pack their household goods on the ponies' backs and follow without questioning whenever the head of the family elected to move elsewhere. If a fight took place, the squaw was ready to do her part.

The Indians were represented by their chiefs. As the agency clerk announced the number of each ration ticket or tag, a chief who represented many families, or lodges, as they were called, would produce his ration ticket, which was proof that he was entitled to a certain number of pounds of salt pork, bacon, sugar, flour, coffee, and meat. The clerk measured the rations, then the squaws carried out the articles and loaded them on the backs of the waiting ponies.

The fact that babies were strapped to the backs of these squaws seemed to make no difference to either the babies or their mothers. Some of the Indians at once swapped goods, others drove their pack ponies to the Post Trader's Store at Fort Sill, where the food just issued to them might be exchanged for something almost useless, possibly a yard or two of gaudy calico, or a little round looking glass with a metal back. These mirrors were highly prized by Indians.

During the time required for issuing rations, the Indians held pony races, or engaged in shooting matches with bow and arrows. So ration day to them was almost like a circus day in civilized sections. Not until sunset did the last laden pony turn its nose toward the trail leading to its owner's village. Apparently they were on the most friendly terms with the white people at the agency and in the garrison, but everyone understood that the least incident might be like a lighted match thrown into a keg of gunpowder. However, I can safely state that during times of peace, no one thought of war, and when the crisis arrived, everyone was too busy to be afraid. There was a certain exhilaration in the danger. I cannot remember a time in my life on the frontier when I actually felt cowardly. Probably proof that "fools rush in."

The Comanche ponies, one of which we owned for years, were wonderfully trained and could be guided entirely by the knees of the riders, making an arc without the use of reins, or stopping within its own length when running full speed. No bridle bits were used. A bridle of braided hair formed a loop about the pony's nose and formed a single rein. Their saddles of wood were shaped with a high pommel and cantle made in several sections. Each part was perfectly fitted, then punctured with red hot tools and sewn together with green sinews from deer. A deer hair made an excellent needle. After this, all joints were glued with a sticky substance obtained from buffalo hooves.

The herd mark of a Comanche pony was a slit from the top of one ear for about an inch and a half. Duke, our Comanche pony, had such a slit ear. My father bought him at Fort Sill and he went with us through Texas, Indian Territory, Arizona, and Montana, where he died at Fort Keogh in 1898. Duke was mourned by the soldiers of H Troop, who gave him a military funeral.

THE INDIANS ARE MISTREATED

The situation at Fort Sill was becoming serious. Lawrie Tatum, the Quaker Indian Agent, whose honesty, kindliness, and sense of fair play had won the respect of the Indians as well as the army people living at the garrison, was relieved as agent and went back East. With him left the Smith family. A later successor was a different story entirely. With him arrived various relatives, each of whom held some kind of a "job" officially. Trouble began at once.

Indians came to the officers and complained that they were not receiving full weight rations, or that rations were unfit to eat. Other times only one kind of food was disbursed to them, instead of the various articles guaranteed by the government. Army officers were powerless to protest, or even officially report conditions to Washington authorities, since the agents were under the jurisdiction of the Indian Bureau, and army officers were under the War Department. Each was a distinct organization, neither of which could interfere with the other.

Back of our quarters were barrels into which garbage was dumped until the wagons collected it and hauled it away. At this time we saw starving women and children reaching into the barrels and scraping out garbage which they devoured. Starving creatures with sunken faces and eyes that were dull. Babies, children, old women. The men were too proud to join them. With unbelievable patience they waited for help from the authorities in Washington. They did not know what red tape meant.

Stories told at this time were so grave that the officers and many of the ladies rode down to the agency one ration day where they saw for themselves the rations issued. Soap. Bars of soap! Not another article. My mother and father were among those who saw that one ration issued to the starving Indians. Indignant at the situation, the officers held a consultation.

They fully realized that sooner or later the Indians would rebel and probably massacre all those at the agency. Then upon the army officers would fall the duty of punishing the desperate Indians. Through various indirect means, the officers, who were prohibited from expressing any personal opinion on official matters, had tried to bring the situation to the proper authorities in Washington. Now, believing a crisis was imminent, they decided to carry out a plan of their own.

An officer was allowed to buy his foodstuffs from the commissary, but only a person in the employ of the government could use the commissary. So each officer, according to his rank and size of his family, made out a list of articles of food for which he would pay. My father was then the post commissary officer at Fort Sill. The Indians were invited to come on a certain day for a "big feast and dance." I stood beside my mother on our front porch that day.

Around the flagstaff in the center of the parade ground, boxes and barrels and bundles were heaped high. The Indians came: men, women, and children all afoot, dressed in their best finery. Babies too small to walk were strapped to the backs of their mothers. It was a strange procession. Even now I can see it plainly in my memory. The right hand of every Indian, men and women alike, as well as the smallest toddler, held a long, slender bough of green willow, which was waved automatically to and fro. Then from one corner of the parade ground, a gaily decked group of warriors advanced, wearing war bonnets of feathers that trailed to the ground.

Their faces were streaked with colored paints as when starting on the warpath, but high in the air they waved in rhythmic unison the green boughs, emblems of peace, as they danced to the beating tom-toms and chanted in wild, weird monotones their song of Thanksgiving to the Great Spirit who had heard the prayers of their hungry people.

They held the boughs pointed upward toward the flag that fluttered at the top of the flagstaff as they circled beneath it. Then uttering a loud, shrill cry, they bent and laid the willow branches on the ground beside the boxes and barrels. After that followed strange dances with tom-toms beating time to droning voices. Beyond the garrison the cloud-tipped peak of Mount Scott loomed indistinctly against the sunset painted sky.

The dances ended, and at signals, the Indian women and children were seated on the ground. The warriors remained standing and stolid, while the soldiers ripped the tops from boxes and barrels filled with canned goods:

tomatoes, peaches, pears, meats, corn, sacks of rice, sugar, dried beans, and boxes of hardtack.

Not rotten, mildewed stuff, but such food as was used on the tables of officers' families, all bought by the officers at Fort Sill from their scanty monthly pay. Yet they gave generously and gladly that day, and probably not one of those officers connected a line in the Holy Book: "I was hungry and ye fed me." Yet at any hour the officers might be ordered to follow and capture those identical Indians, "dead or alive."

A bugle call sounded "retreat," the cannon was fired, and the flag lowered. Then the Indians, happy as children, left the garrison and went toward their villages, carrying with them the supplies that had been distributed among them. For awhile longer the danger of an uprising had been averted. Colonel Grierson, commanding officer of the Tenth Cavalry, was absent from Fort Sill, and the responsibility of the garrison fell upon the next ranking officer, Major George Wheeler Schofield, also of the Tenth.

OUR FRIEND MOLLY CURTIS

My father was commissary officer at Fort Sill during the summer of 1872. Owing to the swamps surrounding the garrison, malarial fever had practically put all the officers and enlisted men on the sick list. When an officer had his "chill day," another officer whose "chill day" did not occur at the same time took up the duties.

With my usual aptitude for being in the midst of things, even at the age of five, I also had "chills and fever" and had a very serious attack. While I was ill, one day my father came from the commissary and said to my mother, "Molly Curtis is back again, and is over at the commissary waiting for Hauser's work to be finished so they can be married. Her mother is with her, and the enlisted men are staring as they pass. I wish you would let them come here until Hauser gets through with his work." So Molly Curtis, her mother, and a small Cheyenne brother were brought to our home.

Everyone at Fort Sill knew the story of Molly. Her father was Dick Curtis, a white scout, her mother a Cheyenne squaw, whom Curtis had married. This gave Curtis a right to remain on the reservation, even had he not been an employee of the government. No other white people were permitted on the reservation in those days. A white man, Hauser, of good education and apparently of good family, was clerk in the commissary department under my father.

Hauser was a civilian employed by the government and lived in the garrison. He and Dick Curtis became associates fifteen years before. During a game of gambling, Curtis, then broke, put up his six-year-old daughter as a stake in the game. Hauser stipulated, however, that if he won the child, he would agree to educate her as a white girl, and marry her legally, if she should then agree.

Hauser won the game. Molly, as she was called, was given into his custody. Molly was at once sent to a convent at Leavenworth, Kansas, which was the nearest educational institution at that time. She remained there until her education had been completed at the age of eighteen. Every advantage had been given her at the convent, including music lessons. Then she came back to Fort Sill.

She entered the front room. I was lying in bed in the adjoining room, and called to my mother that I wanted Molly to come into my room. So she came to me. With her was an old fat, blanketed squaw, and a small Indian boy dressed in "store clothes" like my brother's. Molly was dressed nicely in a conventional traveling dress, hat, and gloves, and was very attractive and had pretty manners. She spoke excellent English, while her mother sat blinking, understanding not one word of the conversation between Molly and my own mother. Molly came over to my bed and showed me her gold watch which "Mr. Hauser" had given her that day.

I remember how she opened the case to show the wheels to me. Meantime her small brother, who had crawled under my bed, began amusing himself by bumping it up and down, until I demanded that he should be stopped. He was dragged out by Molly and with his mother departed to the kitchen.

Then Molly discovered that the keys of her watch were lost. They were found beneath the bed. At that moment the servant brought a box to the door. It had been sent from the Trader's Store for Molly. When opened, we saw a handsome silk dress, beautifully made of expensive material. Hauser had provided it for Molly to wear at their wedding. Molly rather resented the fact that he had not allowed her the privilege of selecting her own wedding gown, and was worried for fear it would not fit, as there was no time to alter it then.

It did fit. I saw her try it on while my mother examined it to see if it needed any stitches here and there. It was a beautiful dress, and must have cost Hauser many dollars of his pay. It was made in the prevailing style, a skirt separate from the waist. Then Molly and my mother discovered that there was no belt for it, and a belt was absolutely necessary. In the dilemma, I piped up from the bed, "Let Molly wear one of my sashes."

I had a collection of which I was very vain, so the box was taken from a bureau drawer, and a sash that harmonized with the dress was soon found. This was adjusted by my mother around Molly's waist. But as I studied Molly critically, I decided that she ought to wear a lace collar, such as my mother wore when "dressed up for a party."

I announced this at once, and my mother's box of choice lace collars was hauled out. A point lace collar was selected and fastened in place, and then my mother dug into another treasure box and produced a new pair of white kid gloves, which fitted Molly's hand as though purchased for her wedding day.

Hauser called with a carriage, and Molly, after thanking my mother who wished her much happiness, leaned over and kissed me. It puzzled me when I saw tears in her eyes. The ceremony was performed at the Kiowa agency by old Lawrie Tatum, the Quaker Indian agent, and a number of the officers and their wives were present at the wedding, after which refreshments were served by Mrs. Tatum.

The wife of one of the army officers, speaking to Molly immediately after the ceremony, made the tactless remark, "Molly, you must make Mr. Hauser a good wife, for he has done a great deal for you and will be very kind to you. He is a good man."

Molly looked at her steadily, then answered, "I have fulfilled the agreement made between my father and Mr. Hauser, but I will never live with Mr. Hauser as his wife. I am going back to camp with my mother."

Molly returned immediately after the wedding to the Cheyenne agency with her mother. Hauser proved his force of character by accepting the situation quietly. He continued his work in the commissary under my father. It was told around in army circles later that Molly had become a regular blanket squaw, who finally married an Indian called Big Mouth.

Not one of those who had been at Fort Sill when she married Hauser ever saw Molly after her wedding day. We never forgot her, and I often think of dressing the Indian bride in our home. The lace collar, gloves, and my sash were returned in perfect condition by an Indian squaw after the wedding.

Many years later the wife of Dr. Samuel Weireck of the U.S. Medical Corps met my mother, and in conversation quoted an incident at Fort Yates, Dakota Territory, as proof that educating an Indian will not prevent returning to primitive ways. Mrs. Weireck needed the assistance of a woman to clean her quarters, and another lady suggested that she hire an Indian woman who worked at intervals in various garrison homes. So the woman agreed to come on a certain day.

Mrs. Weireck said the woman was a typical blanket squaw, but seemed intelligent, so after explaining the work to be done, Mrs. Weireck went upstairs. Shortly afterward she heard music. The parlor organ owned by Mrs. Weireck was being played. She knew there was no one in the house but herself and the squaw, but concluded that one of the ladies had dropped in for a chat, so hurried downstairs. There she discovered the Indian squaw seated at the organ, playing music that Mrs. Weireck herself could not master.

She waited until the squaw stopped playing, then asked, "Where did you learn to play such music?" The squaw looked at her steadily, and replied in perfect English, "I was educated in the convent at Leavenworth and was graduated there. They used to call me Molly Curtis."

After that episode, Molly was not seen in the garrison at Fort Yates. Once again, and this time permanently, she had dropped away from contact with the army people who would gladly have helped make life different for her.

ALMOST RANKED OUT

When we were in any particular garrison long enough to feel settled down, still we were on the move. We could be ranked out of our quarters because a newly arrived officer, who held higher rank than my father, decided our own quarters were more desirable than any other to which he was entitled. There were specially assigned quarters for the colonel, lieutenant colonel, majors, captains, first lieutenants, and second lieutenants, each one according to his official rank.

When at Fort Sill, where my sister Florence was born November 13, 1872, an officer of infantry arrived, and as he outranked my father by twenty-four hours, his wife wanted our set of quarters. Another set identical with our own was vacant, and Colonel John W. Davidson, then commanding Fort Sill, offered to put in shelves and paint the kitchen the same color as our own, as that was the only explanation the other lady gave for wishing to oust our family. Her husband tried to persuade her to take the other quarters, but she was obdurate until I solved the issue.

My mother had received Madeira bulbs from Philadelphia. These were planted at the end of our front piazza. They thrived and formed a green screen. No one else had Madeira vines. I heard my mother remark to my father, "She wants those Madeira vines. If we had not planted them, we would not be ranked out now."

I went out of the room and in a little while when my father came out on the front porch, only broken strings were left of the green screen. I had not only torn down the vines, but having been told that the bulbs could be taken up in winter and planted again next summer, I had pulled up the bulbs and smashed them to a pulp with a stone.

Then the wife of the ranking officer decided that if her kitchen could be painted the color of our own, and a shelf in the kitchen like our own made for her, the vacant set of quarters would be quite satisfactory. So we did not move. And we did not plant anymore Madeira vines after that.

CHRISTMAS 1872

Christmas morning, 1872, is vividly impressed upon my memory, though I was not six years old until the following March. My only brother, Harry, who was two and a half years my junior, stood beside me at the closed door which led from the hallway into the living room of our quarters. My father opened the door and we gazed at our first real Christmas tree, decorated with the things that had been sent from Philadelphia for this event.

I can see that tree distinctly today. Under the tree were two tiny chairs. They were folding chairs with wooden legs, and arms of black, white canvas seats and backs bound with red braid. In one chair was an immense wax doll in a red dress. That was my chair; the other was for my brother.

Then I saw two strange objects on the mantel above the open fireplace. They had not been there when we had hung up our stockings the previous night. One was a boy in French bisque, holding a pole and strings of fish, and at the other end of the mantel stood a girl with a net full of fish. The statuettes were about fifteen inches high and tinted in colors. I assumed that they were gifts to my brother and me, and I claimed the fisher girl, generously permitting my brother to own the boy.

My parents explained to me that Mr. John Evans, the post trader at Fort Sill, had sent them as a Christmas gift, but I could call the fisher girl my own if I wanted to, while the boy could be called my brother's. From that day to this, the two little French bisque figures have been a feature in my mother's home, and in various sections of the country, frontier or civilized, the fisher boy and girl have stood as they stood that Christmas morning of 1872, looking down on a crude little walnut tobacco box that Tom Custer had given my father the year before.

I sat in my new chair (which my father and mother had selected from the articles displayed in the Trader's Store of John Evans), and held my new doll in my arms. At that moment, my mother carried my baby sister into the room and told me that I could hold her for a little while. My new sister, Florence, now six weeks old, was not much larger than my new wax doll. These events made that Christmas day stand out very plainly in my memory.

7

OUR UNFORGETTABLE
JOURNEY TO JOIN FATHER

After my sister was born at Fort Sill in November 1872, the following March my mother went on a visit to her family in Philadelphia, accompanied by the three of us children. During that summer my father's troop was ordered from Fort Sill to Fort Concho, in Tom Green County, Texas, just across the Concho River from what is now the thriving town of San Angelo.

In 1873 the town consisted of Veck's store, which was merely a dugout in the ground where the usual articles most in demand by frontiersmen: guns, ammunition, tobacco, and wet goods, were kept. Mr. William Veck had formerly been an employee in the Quartermaster's Department at Fort Concho and had seen the opportunity of such a business near the garrison, where he had no competition.

THE LONG TRAIN RIDE TO TEXAS

So when October 1873 arrived, my mother started from Philadelphia for Fort Concho with the three of us, my sister being less than a year old. We boarded the train and soon found on the Pullman, Colonel Jeremiah Dashiel and his stepdaughter, Miss Mary Ringold. She had just been graduated from St. Mary's Hall in Burlington, New Jersey, and they were returning to their home in San Antonio. He had been a graduate of West Point, but when the Civil War began, resigned from the regular army and joined the Confederates.

Another passenger en route to Texas was Mrs. Maud Young, officially rated as State Botanist of Texas. She had found twenty-three varieties of cacti, and had made the study of cacti a specialty. Nothing of special importance occurred to our little group of traveling companions until we reached Denison, Texas, then complications started and grew. Denison was a railroad junction where we knew it would be necessary for us to change to a southbound train. During the interval between our arrival and time for departure, our entire party went to the St. Elmo Hotel to have dinner.

Passing through the hallway, which had rooms on either side, the doors being wide open, my mother noticed the rooms were all filled with cots, and every cot was occupied. "There must have been an accident on the railroad near here," she said, as we sat down at a table in the dining room. "There are people on cots in all the rooms."

The usual comments gave place to consulting the menu and dinner was ordered for the whole party. Colonel Dashiel, glancing about the dining room, saw a placard attached to a pillar, and believing it might give information about the accident, he stepped up and read it. When he returned to the table he was smiling. "My old friends, Governor Edmund Davis and Judge William Alexander, are to speak here tonight," he explained. "They are staying in this hotel. I will send up my card while we are at dinner. I would like you to meet them."

A waiter took the card. Before the dinner had been placed on the table, Governor Davis and Judge Alexander hurried into the dining room. Colonel Dashiel had not time to introduce the ladies, for the governor exclaimed earnestly, but in a low voice, "Colonel, get the ladies out of this hotel at once. We have not only yellow fever, but also cases of cholera here in the hotel. Every place is filled with yellow fever patients in this town."

Then we learned that the Quarantine Law had gone into effect in Denison just fifteen minutes before our own train arrived. It was one of the tragic years when the scourge of the South was at its worst, Shreveport bearing the heaviest toll of lives. A consultation between Governor Davis, Judge Alexander, and Colonel Dashiel resulted in our leaving the table without eating a mouthful of the food for which we paid, and hurrying across to the railroad station.

Governor Davis said that under the Quarantine Law, no trains could leave Denison for the south. "I have no authority whatever in that matter," he explained, "but I can and will assume personal authority and responsibility of sending a local train to Navasota, as that point is the least affected on this line."

We boarded the special local and at midnight (six hours later) reached Navasota in a terrific downpour of rain. When it rains in Texas, it means a deluge. The inky darkness was broken by two points of light from lanterns in the hands of a couple of railroad employees. Before we had reached Navasota, Colonel Dashiel inquired from the conductor as to which was considered the best hotel in the town. The reply had been, "Only one in the town." Now the railroad men informed him that there was no chance of getting a conveyance of any kind to take us from the depot to the hotel.

"A big ball is going on at the next town, and everything's been hired to carry folks there. The hotel is a quarter of a mile from the station." So splashing in mud above our ankles, everyone trudged along, except my baby sister and small brother, who were carried, while the rain continued to beat in torrents that drenched us from head to feet.

Luckily for us, the storm prevented many of the hotel roomers from returning that night from the dance, so we were conducted to rooms. Our own room was typical of the others. Rough board partitions reached up only a distance of eight feet. Above this was open space. Between the boards that formed the sides of the room were cracks wide enough to permit the "guest" in the adjoining room to have full view of ours. My mother hastily undressed us, then extinguished the solitary candle so that her own preparations for bed might not be observed from the next room. During the night she was startled by moans, groans, and stifled calls for help which came from the next room. Her impression of some horrible crime vanished when she heard a man say, "Wake up. You're raising h——."

The other man woke. "Thought the herd was stampeding on top of me." The rest of the night was peaceful. For one week we were forced to remain in Navasota, as no trains were allowed to pass through. It was imperative that my mother should reach Austin, Texas, on the date set by my father in his letter of instruction to her at Philadelphia.

Army officers were limited as to time away from their commands, and overstaying that limit was considered as being absent without leave. Furthermore, my mother was worried at the additional expense of the trip for fear she should run short of funds. In event of my father having to return to Fort Concho without us, it would mean still another hotel bill until some way had been arranged to get us to the garrison.

One morning at Navasota, Mrs. Young invited my mother to take a walk with her, and added that Miss Ringold would look out "for the children a little while." Away from possible eavesdroppers, Mrs. Young told my mother that she was going over to the railroad station to send a telegram to her father, explaining that her father was one of the officials of the Houston and Texas Central Railroad, which had a branch line from Hempstead (fifty miles north of Houston) to Austin, a distance of a hundred fifteen miles.

The question of allowing mail cars to pass through the affected districts had been a heated problem. The government had ordered the mail cars should go through, but the districts beyond the quarantine lines had objected vehemently, and threats had been made to tear up the tracks if trains attempted to pass from the yellow fever sections. Mrs. Young was writing a telegram to her father while my mother stood nearby. The two railroad men in the office were busy, when one of them said suddenly, "Have you answered the telegram about tracing that army officer's family?"

"Yes, I sent a dispatch saying information had been received here that Mrs. Cooper and a doctor had left the train and caught the stage at Dallas to go across the country on account of the quarantine." My mother was astounded. "I am Mrs. Cooper. That is not true!"

The operators explained to her that telegrams had been sent from Austin to the mayors of different towns through which the train carrying us had been scheduled to pass. Wires had been sent as far as Philadelphia trying to trace her and her children, and it had been supposed that we all had been removed from our train at some point and were ill with the fever.

My mother was about to write a message when Mrs. Young stopped her by saying, "Wait, don't telegraph until I get an answer from my father. I am sending him a telegram." Her message told that she and a party of friends were quarantined at Navasota, then she added, "Is the

Texas Central sending United States mail through Navasota? Answer immediately."

The two operators understood and promised to hold the message strictly confidential, as it was to a railroad official on business. Two days later the answer came. "Mail will pass through Navasota tonight. Pullman attached to engine. Be ready."

The President of the United States had ordered that the United States mail must go through, but the frenzy of fear that gripped all sections was so great that even a presidential order could not have prevented the destruction of tracks had it been suspected that people were hidden in the Pullman coach that was carrying the mail. The Pullman and engine constituted the entire train. We had only hand luggage at the hotel. All trunks had been left at the depot on our arrival. After supper that night, Colonel Dashiel settled all bills, saying we had found other accommodations since we would have to remain at Navasota for an indefinite time. We went to the depot, but not in a group.

The station was in absolute darkness, and a little distance away we waited by the tracks until at ten o'clock, an engine with one car—a Pullman—arrived. There were no lights on the Pullman car as we stumbled hastily into it. The berths had all been made up and curtains drawn down at each window. The mail pouches were pulled at the front end of the Pullman. So we sneaked out of Navasota, running the blockade of the quarantine and not knowing what might happen next.

The engineer, following instructions, put on full speed while our car switched and jerked like the tail of a kite in a high wind. As we dashed through some of the small towns in the night, we heard the yells of those who discovered the Pullman. None of us could tell at what moment there might be a crash—a torn up track and tragic death—if the news of our car should be wired ahead of us to other towns.

We reached Hempstead just before noon the next day, where we all left the Pullman to await a local train to Austin. Mrs. Young said "good-bye" to us here, as her train for San Antonio soon arrived. We had not eaten any food since six o'clock the previous evening, and we three children were very hungry. Hempstead had no waiting room or station. A platform was the only building. No one was in sight except a woman who was sweeping the porch of a little shack some distance from the tracks.

Colonel Dashiel hopefully hastened toward her, intending to buy food, or at least have her make a pot of coffee for us to drink. As he approached, she waved the broom and ordered him to "keep away." He took a few more steps, but she darted into the house and banged the door, while he called out, "For pity's sake, Madam, let me have a pitcher of water. The ladies and children are suffering from hunger and thirst." The door remained closed, but the woman appeared at a window. She raised it, poked out the barrel of a gun, ordering him to "Git or I'll shoot. You folks come from the quarantine! Git, quick!"

He came back empty handed, and so we waited until the local train arrived and our weary party boarded it. That train did not touch the quarantine district. We were now ravenously hungry, but no food could be procured on the train. Colonel Dashiel went from car to car, asking if anyone would sell part of a lunch, or even a piece of bread for little hungry children. They would have given it, but no one had any food.

WE ARRIVE AT AUSTIN

At four o'clock that afternoon, Colonel Dashiel conferred with the conductor and porter, and it was agreed to have the train stop a few minutes at any point where food might be bought for us. Texas was thinly settled, and finally near a group of a few rough shacks, the train slowed and stopped for Colonel Dashiel and the porter to rush to a one-room shack over which hung a weather-beaten sign, LAGER BEER. They ran back, each carrying tin trays on which were schooners of beer and a pile of huge pretzels.

Everyone, even my baby sister, sipped the warm beer and nibbled at the stale pretzels. We were famished. That evening at seven o'clock we reached Austin and found my father awaiting us at the steps of the train. With the exception of the pretzels and beer, we had been nineteen hours without food. "Thank goodness!" my mother exclaimed, "our troubles are over at last!" But she was sadly mistaken.

It had taken exactly one month from the time we had left Philadelphia until we met my father at Austin. There were reasons why Colonel Wesley Merritt, at that time in command of Fort Concho, did not wish to grant any leaves of absence to officers except in dire necessity. But as an officer had to go in command of a detachment of soldiers who were to act as guards for prisoners on their way to civil authorities at Austin, Colonel Merritt had selected my father as that officer.

The Tenth Infantry, white soldiers, was stationed at Fort McKavett, and a detail of these soldiers was sent as guards under my father. He arrived at Austin, turned over the prisoners to proper authorities, and anticipated our arrival. But we did not come, nor could he get any information as to our whereabouts, though he wired to Philadelphia. The reply from there stated we had started two weeks previously. Telegrams were sent to mayors of all the towns on our route, but nothing could be learned that gave any clue.

It was time for him to start back to Fort Concho when the telegram arrived from Navasota, and so our family was reunited at last at Austin. The following day we were to begin our drive to Fort Concho. It was customary, when opportunity offered, for the officers to make out a list of supplies that were not carried in the commissary. So when my father had started for the railroad with the prisoners, he had a list of articles that otherwise could not be obtained by the officers and families.

In addition to our ambulance, drawn by four government mules, there was a white-topped army wagon in which the soldiers were to ride. These men, being all infantrymen, were not mounted as in the case of the cavalrymen. Inside their wagon was their camp equipment, rations, and so forth for the trip. Early that morning my father instructed the sergeant in charge of the detail to load the goods onto the wagon, and then proceed to the place where camp was to be made that night.

My father had already gone to a general store, checked over the list of articles, and authorized the owner of the store to deliver the goods to the sergeant and men so that everything could be loaded carefully onto the wagon when it reached the store door. We waited until my father saw the wagon and soldiers stop at the store for the goods, and the soldiers went into the store.

Then, and not until then, did he feel it was safe to order the driver of our ambulance to drive on ahead so that we could make camp by sundown. The wagon with the men, he knew, could reach camp shortly after our own, as they were traveling with a light load and good team of four mules.

George Washington, a Negro soldier of our own regiment, had been detailed from the Quartermaster's Department to drive our ambulance, and George Clark, a private of Troop A who had been acting as striker for us for some time even before my sister's birth, was on the front seat beside Washington. Clark was an excellent cook.

Arriving in camp at sundown, we had not long to wait for the escort wagon, and Clark at once went over to it to get out our mess chest to prepare supper for us. "The mess chest is empty," he reported. It was true. There was not one article of food for our supper. The soldiers had rations for themselves. Not one article that had been carefully listed had been loaded onto that wagon. It was empty except for the white soldiers, evidently the worse for liquor. Among articles on that list were things for Colonel Merritt. There was nothing to be done except return to Austin and get the missing articles.

BACK TO AUSTIN

The mules had already traveled twenty-five miles that day, a regular cavalry day's travel, and as my father had to be back at Fort Concho on a specific date, there was only one way to do it. Leaving us in the care of old George Clark, whom we all knew would protect us even at the cost of his own life, my father took Washington with him and started back to Austin.

He planned to drive back those twenty-five miles, get the goods, then once more drive twenty-five miles covered by the mules in less than twenty hours. But, after a short rest, it would be necessary for those mules to start another twenty-five-mile drive to make our next camp according to schedule and orders. After he had gone, and we were safely in our camp beds, the Tenth Infantry soldiers began drinking again. Their loud voices awoke my mother, who then discovered that George Clark was sitting just in front of the tent door near a fire he had built, and his carbine was lying across his knees while he watched the white men. They were whispering together, looking toward him and the tent. Then they started toward him.

My mother, whom I saw creeping on hands and knees near the front of the tent, pushed me down when I sat up curiously. She bade me to lie down and keep quiet, but she spoke in a whisper that frightened me. My brother and baby sister were asleep. I saw my mother reach the tent flap and heard her whisper, "Clark, do you think there is any danger?"

"Not so long as I'se alive, Ma'am!" he answered. After that I heard him call out, "I'll shoot the first man that comes near this tent. Keep back! I'll shoot to kill!"

They knew he meant it. So they kept drinking and fighting among themselves, and two of them, fighting, even rolled against the back of our tent where they snored in drunken stupor. Old George Clark, just a colored private of "A" Troop, sat all night long with his loaded carbine, protecting the wife and children of a Tenth Cavalry officer.

Before dawn we heard the ambulance coming and Clark's vigil was over. The men who had been the worst offenders were put under arrest and in irons, and then Clark cooked our long-delayed meal, while the mules were carefully rubbed and allowed to rest after their seventy-five-mile record that day. Washington was a fine driver. Otherwise there might have been sick or dead mules, for which my father would have been held financially responsible by the government if his explanation had not been approved.

The next twenty-five miles were uneventful, but the following day we found ample excitement at Menardsville, a small hamlet where an election was taking place. When the soldiers made camp, groups of citizens gathered at a distance. Many people in Texas were averse to the presence of United States soldiers; especially averse to them were men who had been driven from other sections and who were practically outlaws. And Washington and Clark were Negro soldiers: a double aggravation in those days of Texas.

We had barely settled in camp when a number of such men, mounted on ponies, began dashing through our camp, then turning in their saddles, they fired back without regard to the danger not only to the soldiers, but also to a woman and three little children. I think it was done to irritate my father. Again and again it was repeated, but my father, wishing to avoid precipitating an open conflict between citizens of Texas and the regular soldiers, refrained from retaliating. The outlaws, apparently believing they had intimidated the soldiers and their officer in command, became more bold and increased their dashes through our camp, firing more rapidly and nearer the men.

Then my father commanded the soldiers not under arrest to draw up in line and "make ready." The outlaws (usually termed bushwhackers) saw the action and heard his clearly given order that if another dash were made through camp, the men were to shoot. Not another dash through camp was made. The bushwhackers circled about in bravado and finally dispersed.

The next day we reached Fort McKavett, where the Tenth Infantry detail was turned over to the officer of the day. The soldiers who had been placed under arrest were tried later by court-martial, found guilty, and sentenced to terms of imprisonment in the guardhouse at Fort McKavett. The garrison was crowded, so my mother and we children were housed by Captain and Mrs. Francis Lacey, but my father shared the quarters of the adjutant. The garrison was divided into an old and new garrison. We were in the new garrison, my father in the old part.

He did not appear the next morning, and finally my mother and Mrs. Lacey, wondering why he did not come, walked down to the adjutant's quarters and found my father very ill, threatened with typhoid fever, which was prevalent at McKavett. The post surgeon was with him, and confidentially advised my mother to urgently request transportation to take my father at once to Fort Concho, which was much higher and healthier than Fort McKavett.

Colonel Henry Clitz, commander of the Tenth Infantry, and Lieutenant Colonel Alexander McCook of the same regiment, were both reluctant to allow an officer so seriously ill as my father to leave their garrison and medical aid. But they finally consented, and we were on our way once again.

ARRIVAL AT
FORT CONCHO
AT LAST

———

Two days were usually required to drive from Fort McKavett to Fort Concho under the most favorable conditions of road and weather, but on account of my father's serious condition, Colonel Clitz sent a relay team ahead of us to Kickapoo Springs. When we reached that point, four fresh mules replaced our first team, and we dashed on as fast as possible toward Fort Concho. It was a race I have never forgotten.

My father's life was at stake. In one day's time we covered two days' travel and reached Fort Concho the same night we left McKavett. The change of altitude and other conditions averted a tragic climax for that never-forgotten trip from Philadelphia to Fort Concho in October 1873. My mother still asserts that she should have known better than to start from Philadelphia on Friday, and in that way invite disaster.

Fort Concho was located between the North and Middle Concho rivers. At the time we arrived, Lieutenant Colonel Wesley Merritt, second in command of the Ninth Cavalry, commanded the garrison. Both the Ninth and Tenth Cavalry were composed of colored enlisted men. Five miles away to the southwest on the other side of the Middle Concho was a thrifty little settlement called Benficklin, headquarters of a stage line owned by James Metcalfe, whose daughters, Fanny and Zemmie, later became my close friends.

The front porches of the officers' homes looked across the banks of the North Concho, where the only attempt at human habitation at that date consisted of a dugout store known as Veck's. Children of the garrison who were old enough to stick on the backs of Indian ponies, which they all owned, were told emphatically that they must never cross the river unless a grown-up was with them. No ladies of the garrison ever drove across, or rode that way unless accompanied by an officer or a soldier.

Shooting affrays were common occurrences at Veck's, where Mexicans, outlaws, and unruly characters came to buy tobacco, ammunition, arms, and principally to get whiskey and gamble where there was no law to restrain them. They frequently finished their business with a general gunfight. Soldiers were prohibited from crossing the river, and though the shooting across the shallow stream could be heard in the garrison, the military had no legal right to even investigate. Their jurisdiction was confined to the military reservation only.

Between the garrison and Benficklin was a group of shacks known as Lone Wolf, where the most desperate characters congregated nightly. Often these men would mount their horses and ride full tilt from Lone Wolf to Veck's, or from Veck's to Lone Wolf, firing shots into the garrison as they dashed past in groups, yelling derision and insults at the soldiers and officers. Such were the conditions at Fort Concho when we reached there in the fall of 1873, when I was "half-past six," as my father rated my age.

The murmurs among army people regarding the post trader and Indian trader situations all over the frontier

Indian reservations were also touching Fort Concho, though that garrison was not immediately on any Indian reservation. The post trader, James Trainer, had resigned his position previous to our arrival and a man named Frank Conrad, who was much liked by the officers and men, was filling the place as trader. Conrad owned the buildings, and then he decided to make a formal application for appointment as post trader to succeed Trainer.

Colonel Merritt and all the other officers stationed at Fort Concho gladly gave their official endorsements and recommendations for his appointment because of his honesty and excellent character, apart from his close cooperation with the officers to prevent any condition on the military reservation that would be detrimental to military or moral conditions of the soldiers.

To the amazement and chagrin of the officers at Fort Concho, Conrad's application was denied, and Veck received the appointment, although Colonel Merritt himself wrote to those who held the appointing power (then vested in the Secretary of War) stating emphatically that "Veck's character made him unfit to put foot on a military reservation." Veck, previously to establishing his dugout store across the Concho River, had been employed by the government as wagon master, and had been in charge of the quartermaster's corral.

After arriving at Fort Concho, we had not time to unpack our limited household belongings before my father was ordered to San Antonio to bring recruits and horses back. No one anticipated that it would require over a week or ten days to make the round trip, but on his arrival at San Antonio, General E. O. C. Ord, the Department of Texas commander, ordered him to remain there to receive other recruits and more horses. These arrived irregularly, so that my father was not able to return to us until the following spring in 1874.

However, army families were accustomed to adapting themselves to unexpected conditions, so my mother, with the three of us children, settled down to everyday life, minus the necessity of considering bugle calls from sunrise to taps, when lights in the barracks went out, or hearing the rattle of saber or spurs, when my father hurried to his duties.

The garrison was rather crowded for quarters at that time, and the house in which we lived contained a "long side" which was occupied by Captain William Kennedy, a bachelor, who commanded Troop F of the Tenth. A very wide hall separated his part of the house from our own, the "short side." Officers were entitled to quarters according to their rank, not according to the size of their families. Our side had a large front room downstairs with an open fireplace. Back of this was a small room used as a dining room. Our kitchen was a tent in the backyard, while another tent housed the colored cook.

Captain Kennedy had two large rooms downstairs, as well as a board lean-to for a kitchen. Upstairs were two very large rooms, each with two dormer windows at the side and another dormer window in each room looked out over the backyard. Our bedroom was upstairs, but Captain Kennedy did not use his upper room. At that time two interesting events occurred.

Captain Kennedy's troop was ordered out of the garrison on a scout after Indians, and though he could retain possession of his part of the house, there would be no one else but ourselves in the building, which, of course, meant much more freedom for three energetic children during the day. Then a surprise happened, not only to ourselves, but also to Captain Kennedy.

LIEUTENANT GASMAN'S BRIDE

A nervous tapping at the upper door aroused my mother, who opened it, and to her amazement saw Captain Kennedy standing there. He never had come upstairs since we had moved into the house, but he looked very much disturbed. After apologizing for knocking, he said in a nervous voice, "Mrs. Cooper! I am in an awful fix. Can't you help me out? My new second lieutenant, Gasman, has just reported for duty with the troop, and he has brought a bride with him, and the troop is under orders to leave the garrison on a scout tomorrow morning. What on earth can I do with her?"

That was the attitude in those days, when troop commanders or the higher officers felt the responsibility of the women and children during the enforced absence of the heads of those families. There was a hurried conference, which ended by Captain Kennedy saying that the bride could occupy the upstairs bedroom across the hall from our own, and my mother agreed to let Mrs. Gasman have her meals with us until the lost bridegroom should return. Of course, Lieutenant Gasman paid the share of our commissary bill while his wife was boarding with us. That was understood without discussion.

A load lifted from his shoulders, Captain Kennedy went down to tell the bride of the arrangement, and to have her go into our living room while my mother followed him in a few moments. As she entered the room, the bride arose to meet her, demanding, "Where is Hans? I want to see Hans at once." Hans was on official duty and could not come at once, my mother explained. The bride was very tall and rather pretty, with large blue eyes, clear skin, and black hair, but her costume was absolutely unique.

She wore a small round, white straw hat, trimmed with gay flowers. A long, close-fitting garment of black alpaca, called a redingote, reached her knees. From under it a skirt of gay calico fell in sweeping folds and train. Her hands were encased in brown cotton gloves, and a blanket shawl of several tones of brown with a bright red border and fringe was folded across her shoulders so that the point hung down in back.

In spite of the command for me to stay upstairs, I sneaked down softly to peep at the bride, fully expecting to see a long white veil, white gloves, and other accessories shown in pictures of brides in *Godey's* fashion magazine from which my mother allowed me to cut paper dolls. I took one look, then hurried upstairs undetected.

So the bride was established in our family, much to my delight and my mother's worry, for Mrs. Gasman always did the unexpected and unconventional thing. She called herself a "Texas Yahoo." Her mother had died after the Civil War, leaving three children and husband. He was quite elderly and evidently the oldest daughter had done as she pleased, until he felt she was in need of additional education and training, so had sent her to San Antonio to an Ursuline convent.

Lieutenant Gasman had just been graduated from West Point and assigned to Troop F of the Tenth Cavalry under Captain Kennedy. On his way to report for duty he had stopped at San Antonio to visit friends. They took him with them to visit the convent and meet the Texas girl. The result was that the convent missed one of its students, who had slipped away unnoticed and joined young Lieutenant Gasman. The wedding took place at once, and accompanied by his runaway bride, the second lieutenant of "F Troop" reported at Fort Concho, only to find that he must leave on the following morning.

She was only a girl in ideas as well as years, so my mother had her hands full, but I felt I had found a playmate across the hall, where I was always made welcome, in spite of my incessant chatter. I remember vividly that when my mother would tell me not to talk so much, I would ask, "May I go over and call on Mrs. Gasman?"

We used wood in small stoves to heat the upper rooms, and many times Mrs. Gasman made candy, which she showed me how to pull into white sticks. Sometimes there was molasses candy filled with pecan meats. Pecans grew thickly along the banks of the Concho rivers. They were in green hulls, like English walnuts, and in the late fall the families would drive to the river and a soldier would climb the great trees.

As he shook the branches, the children would gather the nuts and put them into flour sacks. So we were all provided with nuts for the entire winter. Mrs. Gasman never used sugar in her coffee. She used black molasses, but she had a happy disposition and tried to be helpful in every way possible, frequently reading or entertaining my brother and myself in her room.

MRS. CONLEY

Another interesting individual was a Mrs. Conley, though she was the exact opposite of Mrs. Gasman. Mrs. Conley "belonged" to the infantry. She dressed magnificently in silks made of the latest style. Her father was very wealthy, and owned a chain of hotels in the West to Chicago.

On pleasant days, Mrs. Conley, in her very latest attire, would walk slowly along the front of the officers' quarters, a silk sunshade above her fashionable hat, kid gloves on her hands, and from her wrist would dangle a beauti-ful little silver-mounted pistol. Why she carried it was always an unsolved mystery, but it provided an idea for Mrs. Gasman.

One day after Mrs. Conley had finished her promenade, Mrs. Gasman left our porch. She wore a flamboyant calico wrapper with a long train. On her head was perched a big flapping, untrimmed hat, such as the Negroes wore in the cotton fields of Louisiana. Black cotton gloves covered her hands, and above her head spread a green cotton umbrella. The effect was ridiculous, but the final touch caused suppressed mirth. From her wrist, as she held the umbrella, dangled a full-sized service revolver, in grotesque imitation of Mrs. Conley's dainty silver-mounted pistol.

Slowly Mrs. Gasman promenaded the front line to the quarters of the Commanding Officer, then equally slowly, she returned to her room. The garrison was convulsed, and yet as she continued these walks, and as Mrs. Conley also continued her promenades, it was a serious matter. Mrs. Conley had red hair and a temper usually imputed to that color, and no one could predict what would happen if the two armed ladies should meet.

Another amusing angle was that officers, passing along the line with peaceful intentions, acquired a habit of making sudden calls in convenient houses, until either Mrs. Conley or Mrs. Gasman had passed by. It was Mr. Conrad, then at the Post Trader's Store awaiting the outcome of his application for appointment as post trader, who succeeded in getting Mrs. Gasman to turn her weapon over to him. So the strain was relieved and the episode became a laughable memory.

MY SIXTH CHRISTMAS

Christmas of 1873 approached. So many officers were away on scouting duty that preparations for trees in various homes were abandoned. It was then that Colonel Merritt and his wife, who had no children of their own, decided to have a Christmas tree in the Commanding

Officer's home for all of the children. There were to be gifts for every child on that tree Christmas Eve, and the families were to bring the home gifts for presentation at the same time.

The Merritts had been very partial to me, and many times had taken me to walk with them. Frankly I always hated walking, and I remember I could not see any sense in walking on the prairie near the garrison when I was accustomed to riding my pony, Dobbin, for miles over the same places. One day, however, we had a real adventure. Colonel Merritt discovered a rattlesnake, and I was permitted to help throw stones until it was dead.

A week before the Christmas tree entertainment, I came in from a ride at an unexpected moment. Mrs. Gasman was in our front room with my mother. In Mrs. Gasman's lap was an enormous doll with china head, legs, and arms. She was making a dress for it. A white Swiss dress with many ruffles edged with narrow pink ribbon. A gorgeous doll, a gorgeous dress. I rushed to her side, demanding, "Are you dressing that doll for me?"

"No," she replied. "It is for Bessie Constable."

I glared at the doll, trying to see some defect in it, and when Mrs. Gasman continued, "Don't you think it is a beautiful doll?" I retorted scornfully, "No, it has three eyebrows."

"But that black mark is its eyebrow, like yours, and the pink line is where it opens its eyes, and the other black line is for the eyelashes."

"I don't like dolls with three eyebrows, but maybe Bessie Constable won't mind it." I left the room hating Bessie Constable. The doll disappeared, but on Christmas Eve, at the big tree in the Merritt's front room that doll was hanging in a conspicuous place. I looked at it, then glared at Bessie Constable, who had no idea how I hated her.

Then the doll was lifted down by Colonel Merritt who was dressed as Santa Claus, and he slowly read, "For Birdie Cooper." My surprise caused a big laugh, for they all knew about the three eyebrows. Too happy to even speak, I held the doll in my arms. Then Mrs. Gasman spoke, "Do you like it?" I replied that it was a wonderful doll, the prettiest doll in the whole world.

"But it has three eyebrows," she went on without a smile.

"I don't care how many eyebrows it has. Dolls ought to have three eyebrows!" Other gifts were handed to me, and among them a beautiful silk scarf that Mrs. Merritt had brought from Paris, and which later was worn as my best sash. So the Christmas of 1872 at Fort Sill, and the Christmas of 1873 at Fort Concho, have never faded from my memory.

A SPECIAL NEW YEAR'S DAY

New Year's Days in garrisons then usually were celebrated by keeping open house, as the officers would call formally in a group upon all the ladies in the garrison. I can see them now, tall, soldierly figures, the cavalrymen in full dress uniform of the familiar dark blue, brass buttons shining, gold cords draped across their breasts, helmets with tossing yellow plumes, and the straps adjusted just above the chin, coming down the line laughing and talking together. To me they were heroes. Knights who rode out to fight, or to die. Even at that age, I understood.

My mother had told Mrs. Gasman that she would not "receive" that day, but just to place a basket on the hall table for the calling cards. Mrs. Gasman made no protest, but what followed has never been forgotten. We heard a bumping on the stairway, and peering out the bedroom door, saw Mrs. Gasman struggling with a life-sized figure of a man. An armchair had been dragged to the center hallway downstairs, and into this chair she shoved the huge dummy.

It was dressed in Lieutenant Gasman's cadet uniform which he had worn at the United States Military Academy. The face was a false face, of the kind used at old-fashioned masquerades. A cadet cap surmounted it, and false hair was twisted about the head. The white cotton gloves, worn by officers on duty, had been carefully stuffed, and these hands rested on a fancy basket supported by the realistic legs. Boots which went up into the bottoms of the trousers completed "the man of our house," who sat there to receive the calls of the officers of the garrison.

We all retreated to the upper rooms. The front door, unlatched, opened, and we heard officers entering. There was a dead silence for a few seconds, then shouts of laughter, which did not cease until the group of callers had deposited their cards in "Hans's'" basket, and the officers went laughing to call at the next house on the line. The story of the day will never be forgotten as long as anyone who was then a child in the old regiment still continues to live.

Later Mrs. Gasman brought her father, a younger sister, and a brother, about ten, for a visit. To provide sleeping accommodations for her father, brother, and husband, hammocks were slung in the upper hall. Daytime the hammocks were looped back, and the hall made a dining room. A tent in the backyard was used as a kitchen, but Mrs. Gasman bewailed the fact that the back window, being a dormer, prevented fixing up a tackle and pulley to hoist the hot meals up to the top floor through the window.

A party, given by herself up there, was a candy pull. The guests assembled without knowing how they were to be entertained, but full of curiosity. Mrs. Gasman never did anything conventional. Curiosity enticed many that night. They were entertained in a totally unexpected manner. Wads of hot candy were distributed and each one, from Colonel Merritt down to the least important person, was told to pull it. There was no way to evade that order, no place to put down the hot, sticky mess. They all began to pull.

Then Colonel Merritt, a major general of Civil War days and fighter on the frontier, lieutenant colonel of the Ninth U.S. Cavalry, and Commanding Officer of Fort Concho, got the surprise of his life. Passing in back of him, Mrs. Gasman smashed a huge wad of soft, hot molasses candy on the top of Colonel Merritt's head!

I was at that candy pull as a special dispensation, for my mother rigidly sent me to bed every evening at half-past seven, but had yielded to Mrs. Gasman's pleas, and my own on that particular night. Colonel Merritt never again accepted an invitation issued by Mrs. Gasman.

9

LIFE WAS NEVER DULL
AT FORT CONCHO

In the spring of 1874 my father at last returned to Fort Concho from San Antonio, and upon his arrival was made post commissary officer. That caused an unexpected commotion in our family. I was always ready to accompany him to the big commissary building in which foodstuffs were kept for the entire garrison. It was like a big store, with the commissary clerk in lieu of a store clerk. Special tidbits that my father would take home with us lured me.

But on one occasion I found a new interest, when I discovered the commissary sergeant about to dump five tiny pink mice into a bucket of water. My vehement protests and loud demands for the mice for "pets" brought my father to the scene. To the amusement of the clerk, my father agreed with me. So the mice were put into a small box and my father and I took them home.

My mother had an absolute fear of mice, but these had no eyes, no fur, and no teeth, so we persuaded her to let me keep them in the box, but in an outside room. The problem of feeding them was easily solved by my father, who really was just a grown-up playmate in my eyes, then, and as long as he lived. A tiny piece of soft white muslin was cut to a sharp point, and twisted to a mere thread. This he dipped into a little milk, warm water, and sugar.

Then holding the mouse gently, and with a slight pressure on the mouth of the tiny thing, he inserted the pointed cloth into the open mouth. The mouse seized it without delay. So we proceeded to feed the mice, day after day, until soft dark fur developed and the bright eyes opened.

My mice were the joke of the garrison, but my mother was firm in ordering the mice to be kept out of the house. Cold weather set in, and I worried for fear the mice would suffer during the nights. Then a brilliant idea occurred to me, which I shared with no one, not even my father. I sneaked the mice upstairs to the bedroom and hid the box. After I had been put to bed, I concluded that my mice would not be warm enough during the night, and looking about for a comfortable place for them, I opened a drawer of my mother's bureau in a corner of the bedroom where I slept.

There I saw a pair of warm riding gloves that were fleece-lined. At once I slipped a mouse into the glove and started it into a finger. Then another mouse went into another finger until I had five little mice, each one in a separate finger of the glove. I closed the drawer and getting into bed, went to sleep, sure that my pets were comfortable for the night. I planned to remove them early in the morning.

Unfortunately I slept late, and still more unfortunately, my mother decided to take an early horseback ride with my father. She dressed in riding habit and hat, then began to put on her warm riding gloves. I awoke when she exclaimed, "What on earth is the matter with this glove?"

With a wild yell, "Oh, you're killing my mice," I started toward her, and she, hearing the awful announcement, began to scream and try to drag the glove from her hand. It stuck. I tried to help, both of us adding to the noise and confusion, until my father appeared, sized up the situation, and got the glove from her hand. She fled from the room.

But the mice did not pursue her. I turned the fingers and five little dead mice fell into my lap.

It almost broke my heart, but my father's suggestion that we could have a military funeral and bury them in the backyard consoled me. We carried out the funeral with every detail possible, though he did not fire his pistol three times over the grave, as I suggested.

MISS HAIDIE'S MARRIAGE

We had moved from the double house where Mrs. Gasman had been with us, and now had quarters in one side of the house where Chaplain Norman Badger lived. He, his wife, and oldest daughter, Haidie, were together. A younger daughter was away at school. The Badgers were charming, old-fashioned people, and I became devoted to Miss Haidie, especially as she became engaged to Lieutenant Levi P. Hunt, second lieutenant of our troop. Brides were always of great interest to me in those days, and this one was going to have a real wedding, which I was to attend. No other child had been invited.

Of course, a new dress from Philadelphia was obligatory, and it came. A lovely blue silk, with lots of flounces. Miss Haidie, her mother, and my mother gathered to try it on me. I was willing, but when my mother held out an affair that looked like a round chicken coop made of white wire and bade me to slip it on over my head, I rebelled. All of them explained that the chicken coop was a "hoopskirt," and my new dress had been made to wear over it. After much coaxing I submitted, and glared at my reflection in a mirror.

On the morning of the wedding, February 24, 1875, I was dressed and instructed how to manage the hoopskirt when I sat down. I paid little attention, and when I sat down in the front room where the wedding was to be celebrated by Chaplain Badger, that hoopskirt flapped up into my face. I squashed it down, but it bulged at the sides. I had only two hands. The hoopskirt required three. I whispered to my mother, "What shall I do with it?" She, with her head bent low, motioned me to keep quiet. Every head except my own was bent and all eyes were closed.

I slipped quietly away. Upstairs I found a pair of scissors, and after taking off the skirt, I snipped every tape so that it could not be put on me again that day. Finally, I realized that new tapes could be sewed onto the wires. I tossed them out the side window, as I dared not carry them down the stairs where the wedding party could see me coming down.

A few minutes later I was out in the backyard, busy with a sharp hatchet at the wood pile. I finished the hoopskirt beyond any possibility of future use. Then, like a punctured toy balloon, I went back to enjoy the wedding. Never again did I wear a hoopskirt.

MY BROTHER AND SPY

Another funny episode happened at this time, yet it is indelibly associated with an official situation that was causing much heart burning in army circles at that date, and for some time afterward. Lineal promotion versus regimental promotion was a constant subject of conversation just then. Under the rigid army regulations, officers of the regular U.S. Army were promoted in rotation to higher rank, according to length of time in service. Thus a second lieutenant of a cavalry regiment advanced by files, whenever a vacancy occurred above him in rank.

A second lieutenant of, say, the Tenth Cavalry would move up a file at a time until he became a first lieutenant of the Tenth Cavalry. Then he advanced in the same way when vacancies occurred through deaths, promotion, dismissal, or resignation from the service. So he advanced to be a captain, but remained in the same regiment until he was promoted to major. That constituted regimental promotion. It was very slow. Men remained in the same grades for years. Some for fifteen and even to the length of twenty-five years or longer, without being promoted even to the grade of captain.

Upon attaining major, an officer was promoted to another regiment, according to the length of time in service. Each regiment had three majors, one lieutenant colonel, and the colonel, who commanded the regiment. That was termed lineal promotion, and was much more expeditious.

Officers, of whom my father was one of the leading spirits, decided to frame a bill asking for lineal promotion for all grades, so that only the length of time in service would be a factor in promotions for lieutenants and captains, as was the case with majors and lieutenant colonels. The promotion of a colonel to brigadier general was entirely at the option of the President of the United States, however.

My father and his friends aroused the interest of officers in other regiments, and so the bill was framed and an attorney employed to "push" the bill through Congress, though army officers of those days were absolutely prohibited to lobby, or use influence of any political nature for any special measure. That may sound like a fairy tale in the present day when political influence constitutes the mainspring of the army and navy.

Chaplain Badger was an excellent cabinet maker, and had a fascinating shop in the back of his quarters. My brother and I spent hours there, and finally at the chaplain's suggestion, my father ordered a fine box of tools for my brother that he might "work" with the chaplain. After many disappointments, the box arrived and was unpacked. I remember it vividly. Shining hammers, chisels, and wonderful things that the chaplain pronounced very good tools. Then I forgot all about it.

Some days later after full-dress parade, the officers in their very best uniforms, and helmets with gorgeous waving yellow plumes, grouped at the front of our house. They were talking earnestly about "lineal promotion." I stood near my father, admiring him and his handsome uniform. A small bit of ground in front of each house had been planted to grass, and wooden posts, four by four, made a skeleton fence to protect the hoped-for lawn. While talking, my father sat down on this support. As the conversation waned, the officers moved away and my father arose to his feet. A sound of cloth tearing violently made them all look back. Then a roar of laughter sounded.

Tacks half-driven into the wooden fence told the story. A great jagged tear in my father's brand new Hatfield trousers that had cost twenty-two dollars explained everything. One of the officers drawled slowly, "Well, Cooper, you ought to have known better than give Harry a box of tools." So the issue of lineal rank became identified in our family, and in the memories of my father's brother officers, with Hatfield trousers, a box of tools, and a package of carpet tacks.

I was the proud owner of a black dog named Spy, a faithful intelligent brute, who fell from grace one day while we were living in the same quarters with the Badgers. Mrs. Badger had dinner prepared, and in order to ensure a juicy, tender steak, she had not put it on the gridiron until everything else was on the table. Old-fashioned stoves in which wood was burned had a projecting front, so that coals raked forward would broil a steak supported by an iron grill.

The steak was sizzling when Mrs. Badger went to summon her husband. When she returned to the kitchen, the steak had vanished completely. Down the back roadway, the chaplain saw the thief, Spy, with the steak dangling from his jaws. Although Spy's mouth was blistered badly, he held onto the chaplain's porterhouse steak and did not return until after dark.

SOLDIER FUNERALS

Dr. William Buchanan was chief surgeon at Fort Concho, while Drs. David Smart and David Hershey were assistant surgeons. The latter were very close friends. Dr. Hershey contracted blood poisoning while operating and died at Fort Concho. My father, other officers, and also Dr. Smart attended the funeral, and Dr. Hershey was buried in the military cemetery at Fort Concho with full honors. I saw the funeral.

Soldier funerals were not rare, but an officer's funeral was more of a novelty to the children in the garrisons. I can safely state that no garrison child, girl or boy, failed to witness such a ceremony. Shortly after the death of Dr. Hershey, Dr. Smart's contract expired, so he said good-bye to the officers and their families, and started to the nearest railroad point at Austin. He was not a robust man, and appeared a victim of tuberculosis. Arriving at a little settlement called Fredericksburg, he was taken ill and died.

The settlement had been established by a few Germans, and the one hotel bore the owner's name—Nimitz. It was built after the manner of small inns of Germany, immaculately kept. My own family has stopped at the Nimitz Hotel in our vicarious journeying. Nimitz' family lived with him, and word of Dr. Smart's death was sent as soon as it was possible to officers at Fort Concho, asking what disposal to make of the body.

The answer was to take care of the body until such time as a wagon could be sent from the garrison to get it. Dr. Smart, so far as known, had no relatives, and no estate was involved by his death. Nimitz was worried. There was no undertaker, no ice, no coffin in the place, and the weather was very warm. Once before Nimitz had faced such a problem. That time a stranger from Canada had died at the hotel, and Nimitz had written to the Canadian relatives asking what they wished done with the body.

Letters were slow in those frontier days, but the reply directed him to embalm the body and ship it to the relatives, who would pay all expenses. No one knew how to embalm a body, so Nimitz, who had a first-class smokehouse where he smoked meats, decided that the body of the Canadian, if left in the smokehouse, would be properly prepared for shipment.

So later it was placed in a crude, coffin-shaped box and forwarded to the bereaved family in Canada. When they opened the box and saw the occupant, changed beyond identification by the smoking process, the family refused to accept the body, and as quite an estate hinged upon this identification, Nimitz was notified that the dead man's brothers were coming to Texas to thrash him for smoking their brother.

It took weeks to straighten out the complicated affair, but finally it ended. So when Dr. Smart died in the hotel and the message bade Nimitz to take care of the body, he was badly worried. No ice, no coffin, no undertaker, and the smokehouse was not to be considered this time. Nimitz, between the devil and the deep, deep sea, resorted to placing Dr. Smart's body (a small man in weight and height) into a huge barrel filled with brine.

But on examining it a little later, Nimitz was aghast. The effect of the brine had been as disastrous as had been the smokehouse process. Nimitz remembered his former experience, and then thought of what might happen when the soldiers and officers at Fort Concho would see Dr. Smart's body. Nimitz did not wait longer. He slipped away from Fredericksburg while his wife remained to explain the situation.

Dr. Smart's body was taken back to Fort Concho, where it was buried in the military cemetery not far from where Dr. Hershey had been interred. Whether Mrs. Nimitz knew the whereabouts of her husband or not, she continued to run the hotel after his disappearance, and the officers and families en route to the railroad at Austin patronized it, we ourselves being among its guests.

BUGLE CALLS

Cut away from any other interests, with mail service limited to a courier, or skeleton buckboard service at uncertain intervals, naturally conversation centered on the conditions around us, past, present, and future. That explains very simply how frontier army children absorbed and assimilated matters which would be almost unintelligible to the average man or woman who lived in civilized sections of the United States, even at the same time. Our very vocabulary was made up of correct military expressions. We learned Indian words, and the time of day or night we children knew by the bugle calls.

From the cannon salute at sunrise, when the flag was raised to the top of the flagstaff that stood in the center of the parade ground, until the sound of taps, the signal for lights out in the barracks, the daily home routine was planned according to official duties of the officers. We children were told to "come home at the first call for stables," or retreat call, water call, guard-mounting, dinner call, fatigue call, or tattoo. The hour of day or night meant nothing to us as a period of time. Bugle calls measured the hours of officers, soldiers, women, and children in garrison life.

Our own regiment, the Tenth Cavalry, had no fewer than forty-two Indian fights in Kansas, Texas, and Indian Territory from August 1867 through 1876. The Seventh Cavalry and the Tenth "cut trails" time and again. The Fourth, Sixth, and Ninth Cavalry also shared the burden of those days, the men scouting, and the women and children passing each other en route from garrison to garrison, changing stations at frequent intervals. Even children identified certain families as "belonging" to the Fourth, Sixth, Ninth, or Tenth.

It may be of interest to know the pay received in those days by officers of the United States Army. A colonel received $291.67 per month; lieutenant colonel, $250; major, $208; captain (infantry, unmounted), $150; captain (cavalry, mounted), $166.67; first lieutenant (infantry, unmounted), $116.67; and the same grade, cavalry, mounted, $125.

From these amounts an officer had to pay for his horse, in fact, he had to have two horses, and thus be prepared for any emergency in case of long marches, or a sick horse. Uniforms were of expensive material, and every article ordered by the War Department had to be bought. Constant moves entailed paying transportation, except for the officer himself. Household furniture or goods were weighed, and every ounce over the allowed weight according to the officer's rank had to be paid by himself.

There were no schools in those frontier days of army life, so the husband and wife had to skimp the best they could to provide for sending the children away to be educated. That problem was faced by my own parents. My brother, sister, and I were all educated in Philadelphia, while our parents continued "breaking trails" for later civilizations.

No one knew when the bugle sounded reveille what would happen before taps that night. Trouble among Indians, hurried mounting of the cavalry in the garrison, good-byes, then waiting for news day after day, heart sick, yet hoping. I shared those waiting days during my childhood. I watched my father's troop ride away, and then when a troop courier brought the news, I stood on the front porch of our home, thrilling as I saw the familiar troop guidon, and then riding at the head of the troop, my father and his captain. Sometimes they were absent for months.

During these years of frontier isolation, the army families in a regiment formed a bond that never was broken in afterlife. Children who played and rode their Indian ponies together became like the children of one large family. In our own regiment, young officers' children were born, and these boys and girls learned to walk and talk, guided by the old Negro soldiers on the back line, and helped by the officers on the front line.

So, from the colonel down to the laundress living on "Suds Row," we were all children of the Tenth Cavalry. We felt that we owned the regiment, and the regiment felt it owned each child. We scorned the infantry children, and we fought other cavalry children who dared claim greater honor for their own regiment.

That spirit has never died. Even today when I meet men who are generals, grandfathers, too, or women like myself who are grandmothers, that same feeling is as strong as ever. Once more we are just "children of the old Tenth Cavalry," living again the days of the old frontier when the names of Miles, Sherman, Sheridan, the Custers, Mills, Crook, Crawford, Lawton, Jesse Lee, and Merritt were household words, mingled with conversations about the turbulent Indians, Sioux, Comanches, Cheyennes, Kiowas, Apaches, and many other tribes.

We children knew the names of them all. We saw famous generals in the garrisons where we lived. We saw Indians stalking along the driveways in front of our homes, or crossing the parade ground for a "talk" at the adjutant's office to voice their grievances against the Indian traders.

❈ 10 ❈

CAPTAIN NOLAN
AND TRAGEDY ON THE
STAKED PLAINS

M rs. Annie Nolan, wife of Captain Nicholas Nolan, died at Fort Concho and was buried in San Antonio. Upon the return of Captain Nolan, he and his two young children, Katie, ten, my own age, and Eddie, seven, one year younger than my own brother, remained at Fort Concho and lived in the set of quarters next to our own. An old colored woman kept house for them, but my mother assumed responsibilities and supervision of the two motherless children, so our home practically became their own, and their problems were our problems.

Texas was rapidly being settled, though ranches were far apart and the towns scattered and small. The subjugation of the Kiowas, Southern Cheyennes, and the pledges of the Comanches in 1875 removed the menace of Indian raids. However, the settlers were keenly alert and promptly reported to the nearest garrison any sign that the Indians had crossed the Red River from Indian Territory (now Oklahoma) into the forbidden area of Texas.

Consequently, the troops were kept on the *qui vive,* as reports, more or less reliable, were circulated. On July 10, 1877, Captain Nolan and my father rode away from Fort Concho at the head of Troop A, numbering about sixty men. They were under orders to make a two months' scout for signs of wandering Indians who had crossed the boundary of the Red River. They were to make a supply camp at some convenient point, maneuver from there in pursuit of any depredating Indians, and protect any settlers they may find.

So "A" Troop marched away. The cavalry guidon fluttering from the lance held by the color bearer was a flag two feet, three inches wide and three feet, three inches long. The upper length was a red stripe half the width of the guidon, while the lower half was a stripe of white. A swallowtail cut of fifteen inches made it fork at the end.

On the upper red stripe the number of the regiment (10) was embroidered in white silk, while the lower white stripe bore the letter of the troop (A) in red silk embroidery. The all-silk guidon was used for special occasions, but a duplicate in bunting, called the service guidon, was carried at other times by the troop to which it properly belonged. Infantry and artillery had similar guidons.

The regimental flag of a cavalry command was of yellow silk three feet wide where it joined the lance and with a fly of four feet. The lance was nine and a half feet long. The coat of arms of the United States was embroidered in silk on the center. Beneath the eagle was a red scroll, with number and name of the regiment embroidered in yellow and yellow fringe. Regimental flags, or standards of bunting, had the same regulations as the guidons. An infantry regimental flag was of white and blue, instead of yellow, while artillery was scarlet.

Any engagement of a troop entitled it to have a silver band with the name of the battle inscribed or fixed to the lance of a troop guidon, but the silver marker is placed on the silk guidon, not the service guidon made of bunting. An engagement by one or more companies, troops, or batteries entitled that regiment to a silver band on its regimen-

Fig. 1: *Travel for army families on the frontier was often in an army ambulance pulled by four mules. It had three seats, could accommodate four or more passengers, and traveled 20 to 25 miles per day. Inside seats folded down, making a comfortable bed for two at night.*

Fig. 2: *Camp Supply, Indian Territory, as shown in the February 27, 1869,* Harper's Weekly. *The* Harper's *correspondent wrote that the post was "one of the most defensible works of its kind on the Plains." Built only three months before, it was occupied by three companies of the Third Infantry, one of the Thirty-eighth Infantry, and detachments of the Tenth and Nineteenth Kansas Volunteer Cavalries.*

Fig. 3: Native Americans on horseback joined throngs of soldiers, civilians, and their families in front of Fort Sill's post headquarters in 1891 as they celebrated Independence Day.

Fig. 4: Comanche chief Quanah Parker poses for a portrait in his home west of Fort Sill about 1897. To the right is a painting of his mother, Cynthia Ann Parker, a daughter of Texas settlers, and her daughter with Comanche chief Nocona, Prairie Flower.

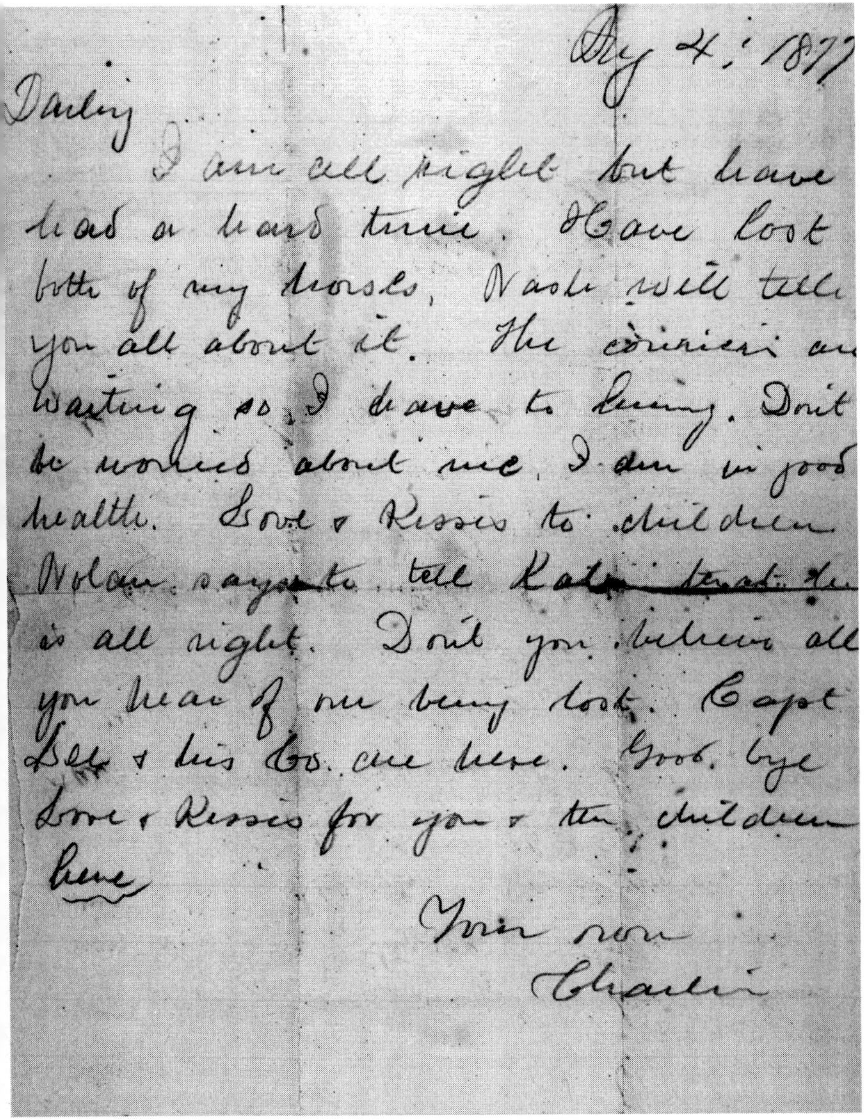
Aug 4: 1877

Darling

I am all right but have had a hard time. Have lost both of my horses, Nash will tell you all about it. The couriers are waiting so I have to hurry. Don't be worried about me. I am in good health. Love & Kisses to children. Nolan says to tell Kate that he is all right. Don't you believe all you hear of me being lost. Capt Lee & his Co. are here. Good bye Love & Kisses for you & the children here

Your own

Charlie

Fig. 5: Lieutenant Charles Cooper scrawled this quick note to his wife on August 4, 1877, after his troop had gone eighty-six hours without water on the Staked Plains of West Texas. Newspapers reported the troop lost, believing all had perished. Daniel Nash rode hard to deliver the letter to Mrs. Cooper at Fort Concho on the morning of August 7. A week later the bedraggled cavalrymen returned to post after their trying ordeal. The letter has remained a family heirloom.

Fig. 6: Fort Davis, Texas, established in 1854 to protect the Trans-Pecos region of the southern route to California. Nestled in the Davis Mountains, the post is shown in the late 1880s. Cavalry and infantry barracks line the left side of the parade ground, and officers' row is on the right. Left of the flagstaff is the chapel, also used for library, legal hearings, and social gatherings.

Fig. 7: A wedding party gathers in the courtyard of the new Fort Grant chapel on August 23, 1888. Lieutenant Powhatan Clarke, with his dog Flash; Dr. and Mrs. W. H. Corbusier (back row, left); Major Anson Mills (pointing at his wife); Lieutenant Levi P. Hunt (top right); Mrs. Hunt (seated next to him).

Fig. 8: Corporal Edward Scott is wounded in an Apache attack in the Pinito Mountains of Sonora on May 3, 1886. Under heavy fire, Lieutenant Powhatan Clarke, top, pulls Scott to safety. Clarke was later awarded the Medal of Honor.

Fig. 9: For three days in March 1886, General George Crook met Geronimo and his Apaches at Cañon de los Embudos, twelve miles below the U.S–Mexican border. Tombstone, Arizona, photographer C. S. Fly was present to capture the surrender conference on March 27: Geronimo faces camera (seated fifth from left); Lieutenant Marion P. Maus (seated seventh from right); General Crook (second from right); and 12-year-old Charles D. Roberts (far right).

Fig. 10: Graduating last in his West Point class of 1884, the dashing Second Lieutenant Powhatan Henry Clarke of Troop K, Tenth Cavalry, would be awarded the Medal of Honor for his valor in a Apache attack in northern Mexico. He is shown in 1891 wearing his medal in Düsseldorf, Germany, while serving as a military attaché with the Eleventh Westphalian Hussar Regiment of the Prussian Cavalry.

Fig. 11: Captain Alexander S. B. Keyes's Troop D, Tenth Cavalry, rests at an army logging camp near Fort Bayard, New Mexico, in 1892.

Fig. 12: Mangus, the Mimbres Apache leader, joined Geronimo in his outbreak in May 1885, but soon separated from that faction, hiding out in the Sierra Madre Mountains of Mexico. In October 1886 he and his followers were captured by Captain Charles Cooper's Troop H.

Fig. 13: Captain Charles Cooper, foreground, and Troop A, Tenth Cavalry, with sabers drawn, at Fort Keogh, Montana, about 1894. Two years earlier the regiment had exchanged posts with the First Cavalry moving from Arizona to Montana. Lieutenant Cooper had joined Troop A in 1871 and became its commanding officer when he returned as captain in 1891.

Fig. 14: Forrestine Cooper Hooker poses for a portrait on December 25, 1910. That year she wrote a short story called "The Lost Troop," based on her father's ordeal with Troop A. Within a decade, New York publisher Russell Doubleday was asking for her memoirs.

tal standard, and when less than half the number of companies constituting a regiment had been engaged, the company letter of each troop engaged was entitled to follow the name of the battle.

The silken regimental standard, used on special ceremonial occasions, can be carried at other times only when ordered by the regimental commander. Any regimental standard, or troop guidon, in need of repair, or unserviceable, had to be passed upon by officers of a board of survey who reports to the Secretary of War if a new flag or guidon should be issued. In such case, the condemned or unserviceable color has to be labeled and sent to the Adjutant General of the Army for preservation when the new silken colors, whether regimental standard or troop guidon, has been received.

It was absolutely obligatory to turn in such a flag in order to receive a new one. We children of the old army days learned these things as naturally as we learned to talk and ride our Indian ponies. In our own estimation we were responsible for the honor and the flag of our regiment, and of our own troop of the Tenth. That was what the fluttering guidon of Troop A, Tenth Cavalry, meant to those who watched it at Fort Concho on July 10, 1877.

Ahead of the troop went the regimental band. It was customary for the band to escort a departing troop out of the garrison. Our band was our pride. At its head rode George Brenner, the band leader, on his black horse. Brenner was a white man and a fine musician. Back of him, on milk white horses, followed the rest of the band—all of them colored soldiers. My father used to delight in quizzing me when I was very small by asking why Brenner rode a black horse and the colored men of the band rode white horses. I never yet have solved that riddle.

BAD NEWS ARRIVES

After the troop had gone, life settled down to its usual routine, with the additional interest of waiting for a courier to come from the troop with letters and news. Katie Nolan was sitting on our porch one evening, just after retreat, when the evening salute from the cannon, and the lowering of the flag from the flagstaff in the center of the parade ground, meant that official duties were over, except tattoo and taps.

She had just noticed a rider and announced, "A courier has just reached the adjutant's office. Maybe he is from the troop and will have mail for us." Officers from different homes hastened to the adjutant's office, summoned by Colonel Grierson's orderly, all of which indicated some unusual condition.

Our house was a double one. Chaplain George Dunbar, his wife, and two children lived on one side of the wide hallway and our family on the other. Colonel Grierson's orderly came to the steps, passed by and into the hallway where he knocked at Chaplain Dunbar's door. The chaplain hurried out and did not speak to my mother in passing. He also entered the adjutant's office.

Later he returned, looking greatly worried, but said nothing regarding the commotion until my mother asked, "What is the trouble?" He hesitated, then answered, "Sergeant Umbles" (who was in our troop) "has come into the garrison and is telling a wild story about the troop, but we do not believe it."

"What is he saying?" demanded my mother.

"That the waterholes were dried up and when he left the command, they had been two days without water."

"I want to talk to Sergeant Umbles myself."

"I would rather you would not see him just now, Mrs. Cooper."

Then my mother faced him and said, "Very well, if you won't ask him to come see me after he gets through at the adjutant's office, though I have never been in the adjutant's office since I have been in the army, I shall go there right now."

It was an unwritten law that no female member of an officer's family, nor of an enlisted man, should enter that official domain. So Chaplain Dunbar took her ultimatum to the office, and Sergeant Umbles was ordered to go to my mother and tell her what he had just been telling Lieutenant Robert Smither, who was acting in Colonel Grierson's place in his absence, and all the other officers at Fort Concho.

"The troop had found an Indian trail," he told her, "and was starting to follow it when a party of buffalo hunters, who had already found the trail, joined them and they took up the trail together in the direction of the Staked Plains." Umbles went on to say that he and two privates with empty canteens started to find water and return to the command with it, but their horses gave out, and they had wandered around until they reached a small ranch where Umbles said he borrowed a horse, and by getting relay horses, had ridden day and night to bring word to the garrison.

The news was wired at once by Lieutenant Smither to Brigadier General E. O. C. Ord, who was in command of the Department at San Antonio. General Ord immediately sent a personal telegram to my mother, saying: "Don't lose heart. I have ordered out troops from Fort Concho, Fort Richardson, Griffin, and Stockton. Everything will be done to bring them back alive. Every available man will be sent out."

Sergeant Umbles had ended his statement to my mother by saying, "Mrs. Cooper, if any man comes out of this alive, it will be because Lieutenant Cooper is in command. He won't lose his head. Before I left the troop, Captain Nolan had broken down and was raving crazy, and we had to tie him on a mule to pack him along with the troop. He'd a died if we hadn't done it."

A LETTER FROM FATHER

So troops were sent from all the garrisons nearest the Staked Plains, and even the Regimental Band of the Tenth, always exempt from scouting duties, rode out from Fort Concho to help find the lost troop. Dr. J. H. T. King (captain and assistant surgeon at Fort Concho) went with medical supplies, and though my mother was not told at the time, Captain Nathaniel Constable, quartermaster, sent out lumber to be used in making coffins for the dead.

A week passed with no news of any kind from the searching troops. Umbles had reached Fort Concho on August 4 after sunset, and the troop had been two days without water when he left it. Relief parties had scattered to locate every known watering place in hopes of finding some of the lost command, but not a trace had been discovered. Not even a body.

Daniel Nash, an enlisted man, who had served his time in the regiment, was employed as a house servant by my parents. His wife, Elizabeth, was our cook. When my father started on the scout July 10, Nash had accompanied him as a personal servant, and was riding my father's extra (privately owned) horse. So it was an anxious week for our family, for old black Elizabeth in our kitchen, and for two little motherless children in the quarters next to our own, where Katie Nolan and her brother Eddie awaited news of their father.

My mother was numb. She did not cry, but seemed frozen. The chaplain and his wife spent most of their time with her, as they lived in the same house. Dumb grief is appalling; tears are relief in suffering. Chaplain and Mrs.

Dunbar were in my mother's room when the sound of a horse dashing into the backyard startled them.

The chaplain rushed down and saw Nash slumped down in the saddle. The man was unable to dismount. Helped by old Elizabeth and Chaplain Dunbar, Nash was lifted from the horse to the ground. He had ridden day and night, begging relay horses at little ranches on the way to carry a message to my mother.

The note, scrawled weakly in pencil, lies before me as I am writing this page. My mother was eighty-two on January 30, 1928. My father lies in Arlington, but that note, in his familiar writing, though the pencil marks are faint, the sheet of paper torn from a book with no envelope, brings back vividly the memory of those days. I have asked my mother to permit me to give that message word for word as she received it.

The chaplain unfolded and read the note as he stood beside Nash and Elizabeth in the backyard:

Aug. 4, 1877

Darling,

I am all right but have had a hard time. Have lost both of my horses. Nash will tell you all about it. The couriers are waiting so I have to hurry. Don't be worried about me. I am in good health. Love and kisses to children. Nolan says to tell Katie that he is all right. Don't you believe all you hear of our being lost. Capt. Lee and his company are here. Good-bye. Love & kisses for you and the children here.

Your own, Charlie

The chaplain read it, then he fainted. My mother heard the note read, saw it really was my father's writing, and that he was safe. Then the frozen grief melted into a deluge of tears that meant the saving of her life. And Captain Nolan's two motherless children in the quarters next door were told that their own father had been spared to them.

Nash, after his ride day and night without rest to carry the message from my father, could hear Elizabeth hustling in the kitchen, singing a hymn, yet breaking off to thank the Lord for His mercies. The record of those days on the Staked Plains I shall give in my father's own words. I have a handwritten copy of Dr. King's report to the Medical Director of the Department of Texas signed personally by Dr. King.

FATHER'S ACCOUNT

Father later wrote his father, James G. Cooper, on the staff of the *New York Daily Tribune*, just what happened. His letter was published with this editorial preface on September 8, 1877, under the headline "A Thrilling Texan Story, Soldiers Suffering for Water":

In the early part of August, intelligence reached this city from Fort Concho, in western Texas, that a company of United States cavalry belonging to the 10th Regiment, under the command of Capt. Nicholas Nolan and Lieut. Charles L. Cooper, while in search of a band of hostile Indians, had been lost on what are known as the Staked Plains—a sandy, waterless region in Northwestern Texas. Later reports said they had made their way to Double Lake in a very exhausted condition, having been four days without water. Following those reports, a dispatch was received from Chicago, August 8, and derived from "official information," stating that a desperate fight had taken place on the Staked Plains between Government troops and Indians, and that the soldiers, who were much exhausted from want of water, had all been killed. It was further added that a list of the killed, consisting of two officers and thirty-one men, would be forwarded as soon as received. Since that dispatch was published, nothing definite has been in the public prints.

The Tribune has now been furnished a letter from Lieut. Cooper, one of the officers of the company, and dated Fort Concho, Texas, August 30, in which he informs his father, a resident of Brooklyn, of his safety, and gives an interesting account of the terrible sufferings of himself and others. The letter is as follows.

Fort Concho, Texas,
August 30, 1877

Dear Father:

You can hardly imagine our astonishment here, to learn of the sensation in the newspaper world our troubles and misfortunes have been the means of causing; and as I can see from the slips you have sent me, that the real circumstances of the case are completely misunderstood, I thought it a good idea to furnish you a brief account of our trip.

Our company "A," 10th Cavalry, left here on July 10, with two officers and about sixty men, for a two months' scout. We were to make a supply camp at some convenient point, and maneuver from there in pursuit of depredating Indians, as [and] also to protect settlers who are rapidly populating this region of the country. Upon our arrival at a place called Bull Creek, about 140 miles northwest from Concho, we found a party of twenty-eight men (buffalo-hunters) who had lost considerable stock on account of

Indian thefts, and who were organized into a company for the purpose of overtaking Indians, and regain their lost property.

Capt. Nolan (who commanded our company) thought it best to establish our supply camp at this place, and go with the hunters, most of them being acquainted with the country, and they having as a guide a Mexican named José, who had been for years in the habit of trading with these Indians, and who became thoroughly acquainted with the country, and knew every "waterhole" and possible camping-place where Indians might be found.

We left our supply camp with forty men and two officers, on the 19th of July. The hunters had twenty-one men all told, so you can see we had quite a party. After marching for several days (and were from the first experiencing difficulty in procuring water, on account of the great drought this year) we found ourselves on the Staked Plains, at a place called Double Lake, where a small quantity of alkali water was obtained. Here we rested on the 26th of July, while José (the guide) and a few men went further west to Dry Lake (seventeen miles) in search of water and signs of Indians.

At 11 o'clock p.m., on the 26th, while we were waiting for José, two of his men came back hastily with the news that though there was no water there, that forty Indians had passed that morning at 8:30 o'clock, and were leisurely going in a northwesterly direction, killing game as they went, and evidently not suspecting that troops were in the country. We saddled up hurriedly, watered the stock, and started for Dry Lake, from whence having arrived about sunset, we immediately started on the Indian trail. This we followed until it was so dark the guide was unable to see it, and then made a dry camp (camp without water for man or beast).

On the 27th, at daybreak, we took up the trail and followed it without a stop until night, and again made a "dry camp." During the day, two of the men were sunstruck, and a sergeant and a few men were left with them to follow us up as soon as they had sufficiently recovered. As for myself, I felt the heat more this day than on any other during the trip, and owing to the intense heat, and having no water to drink, at about 3 o'clock I came near giving up with sunstroke. In the meantime we had, to use a nautical phrase, "boxed the compass" in following the trail, and had wandered all day over a sandy plain with sometimes fresh indications of the Indians having passed recently, and then again completely at a loss to find which way they had gone, as the trails scattered in all directions.

Toward night the guide gave the trail up (feeling assured we could not catch them) and commenced again to look around for water. He had followed the trail with so much perseverance and energy that he had not kept account of his bearings, and we found as a consequence, he, as well as all of us, was lost on the Staked Plains, without water and no prospects of getting any, as we did not know which way to go for it, and from our experience we knew the greater part of the country was as "dry as a bone."

In the meantime our men had been dropping from their horses with exhaustion, as we had now been nearly two days without water, and we were retarded greatly in endeavoring to keep the men together; this, too, at a time when every moment was precious to us. We made another dry camp after dark, and endeavored to forget in sleep the sufferings we all endured; the guide in the meanwhile keeping on in search of water, followed by eight of our men with all the canteens of the command, so that in case they should happen to reach water they could fill the canteens, and returning to the command, help us.

That is the last we saw of the guide and the eight men, until we got back to the supply camp on the 6th of August. The next morning, having had no news of the guide and men, we saddled up and attempted to follow in the direction we supposed they had gone, but having nobody to guide us, being in an unknown country, we did not better our condition. After marching nearly all day in a northeast direction, Capt. Nolan and I conferred together, and finally concluded to push back to Double Lake, the direction of which we did not know, but reckoned it to be about southeast.

We marched until it was very dark, and then halted to wait for the moon to rise to enable us to proceed. We had now reduced our little party to eighteen men, two officers and one buffalo-hunter, and you can imagine we were all in a bad condition. The men were almost completely used up, and the captain and I were not much better. Our men had dropped back, one by one, unable to keep up with us; their tongues and throats were swollen, and they were unable even to swallow their saliva—in fact, they had no saliva to swallow, that is if I [am a] judge of their condition from my own. My tongue and throat were so dry that when I put a few morsels of brown sugar, that I found in my coat pocket, into my mouth, I was unable to dissolve it in order to swallow it.

During this time while lying on the ground, one of my private horses showed signs of exhaustion, staggered and fell; so, in order to relieve the men, I had his throat cut, and the blood distributed amongst them. The captain and I drank heartily of the steaming blood, and though it aided for a time to relieve our intense suffering, nevertheless in a short time we were in a worse condition than before, for the horses, having suffered so much from thirst, as well as we, their blood had naturally become diseased, and as we had partaken freely, we were soon attacked with "blind staggers," with the same symptoms as the horses.

We left our resting place at 11 o'clock the next morning, when, owing to the intense heat, our famished condition, on account of want of food and water (for, although we had plenty of rations with us, not one mouthful could we swallow; I tried to do so by soaking a hard tack in horse's blood, and masticate it that way, but I nearly strangled in the attempt), and the fact that the horses were giving out, one by one, we laid down on the open prairie and endeavored to obtain such shelter from the fearful heat as a woolen blanket thrown over a small mesquite bush would afford.

This, our fourth day without water, was dreadful. A picture of the infernal regions, and the rich man begging for a drop of water to cool his tongue, could not have been more fully portrayed, as to his agony, than it was to us during that eventful day. Men gasping in death around us; horses falling dead to the right and left; the crazed survivors of our men fighting each his neighbor for the blood of the horses as the animals' throats were cut. Prayers, curses, and howls of anguish intermingled came to one's ears from every direction. There was rain, apparently, in the far-away distance, yet never a drop for us.

Can you wonder that the minds of men, under the circumstances gave way, and that, instead of having with us the forty rational men who left camp with us, our party now consisted of eighteen madmen. As night came on, I made a brief sort of speech to the poor fellows, showing them our plan which was to drive the horses as far as we could, killing them for their blood when required; and, by travelling by night and resting by day (thus avoiding the intense heat), endeavor to reach some of the streams to the east of us—thus perchance, to find water, and also run a chance of being picked up by a possible relief party from the Fort.

Some of the men understood me, and said they would follow. At this camp, being utterly exhausted, we abandoned all our rations and every unnecessary article, taking our guns and pistols, in case we were attacked, and also to enable us to kill buffaloes for their blood. Every horse we had but two, finally dropped dead before we left that camp; and, as Capt. Nolan and myself had lost all our horses (my second one dropping dead here), we mounted pack mules, and the men followed us on foot. We left camp at 8 o'clock at night, and travelled until about 3 the next morning, when, as we were marching along, we came across what seemed an old wagon-trail. As soon as I saw it and had hopefully travelled it a little way, it occurred to me where we were. I at once made the good news known to all, and such wild hurrahs and firing of guns you never heard in your life.

The captain and I travelled some five miles on that blessed trail, and finally reached Double Lake, completely exhausted. We found here six of the men of our company, whom we had missed, and immediately started them out with canteens of water for their suffering comrades. Our loss on the trip was four men died from thirst; also one citizen died; and twenty-three Government horses and four mules. At Double Lake we came across Capt. Lee, of our regiment, and eleven Tonkawa Indian scouts—the relief party sent from Fort Concho in search of us.

This, I suppose will in a measure account for the statements in the Eastern papers (since seen by me) that we were attacked by Indians, and, being all nearly dead—our horses quite so—had been massacred. The exaggerated reports about us, it seems, were circulated by some of the men left behind, who managed to reach water first, and, believing us all dead, came into Concho and told the stories that have since been going over the country, and which nearly deprived my dear wife, at the Fort, of her reason.

FATHER TELLS MORE LATER

Some time later father explained to my mother more of what had occurred in that desolate wilderness. Some of the men would stop and almost bury their faces in the sand, believing they might smell water in that way. Even during the hours when they rested, hoping for sleep, but only in a semi-stupor, they saw water, green trees, and rain falling about them in torrents. Banquets of rich food, and water, water, water everywhere, he said. In his dreams when he stooped down to drink, or to plunge hands and face into the water, it would recede from his lips and he would awaken to realize that he was biting the hot, dry sand, as they could see the other poor devils doing in their semi-delirium.

George Clark, a faithful old Negro soldier of A Troop, had followed father every step, like a faithful, dying dog. The last few drops of water in his own canteen he had shared with him, though Clark tried to refuse to take one drop. Back of them struggled what was left of the command. No one spoke. It was agony to even breathe. Their faces were ashy gray and covered with the alkali dust of the desert; eyes sunken back in sockets, lips tightly closed, and each breath, drawn through nostrils, prolonged to avoid the suffering of the air passing between the dried membranes of the throat and lungs.

A white froth had dried on their closed lips, giving an appearance of men who were already dead, and whose lips would never again open to speak. Fingers and palms of their hands were shriveled and pale; dizziness, vertigo, and deafness affected them all.

When father thought he saw the old wagon trail, he dared not trust his eyes, fearing it was another hallucination. As he rode on, the wagon tracks seemed more distinct.

He turned to old George Clark and forced himself to speak in spite of the agony it cost.

"Clark, do you see a trail?"

"Yes, sah, but I feared it was fooling me."

They did not speak but continued on, each fearing disillusion, but watching the faint wagon trail in the soft sand until sure beyond any doubt. Buoyed by hope, they dragged on until they realized they were following a trail that had been made by their own command and they were near Double Lake. At last when they came in sight of Double Lake and knew they had found water, just at the time their last atom of strength and endurance had been reached, they collapsed beside the alkali pool. In that pool was a decomposed carcass of a dead buffalo, but they paid no heed to it.

The utmost self-control was necessary, for the men, almost crazed at the sight of water, wanted to drink to repletion. The officers had to make them contain themselves, and yet even the few drops drawn through their dry lips caused nausea and pain. Their systems were drained of moisture, increased by the dry, hot air of the Staked Plains. So they lay there, almost unable to help themselves while their supply camp was fifty-five miles away. All rations had been abandoned and they had no food of any kind, even if they had been able to eat it then.

Again and again they sipped water, lying face down, but it was impossible to alleviate the agonizing thirst. Every pore of the body was drained of moisture, and the stomach rejected water when they swallowed a few drops. Then from the distance, figures moved toward them. They were Indians. Not one man had the strength to resist an attack. The Indians halted, and fired into their group.

Then father realized the Tonkawa scouts had mistaken them for hostile Indians. Unable to get onto his feet, he dragged his saber from its scabbard, and tearing the dirty handkerchief from his neck, he lay on his back and held it up on the point of the cavalry blade, hoping it would be understood before the bullets from the guns of friendly Indian scouts killed anyone.

The glint of sunlight on the blade was seen by Captain Phil Lee, and the firing ceased. Captain Lee had barrels of fresh water with his command, and hot coffee was at once prepared. It was the only thing that revived them, but for six days they remained at Double Lake, too weak to be moved toward their supply camp.

They reached the camp August 6, but father had already written a note to my mother on August 4, which was carried to Nash at the supply camp with instructions for him to ride night and day until he had delivered it to Mrs. Cooper at Fort Concho, so she would know they were all right. Nash reached the post on the morning of August 7, carrying the note to my mother, who was eternally grateful to him.

Captain Nolan and father and their haggard command arrived back at Fort Concho at 9:00 o'clock on the morning of August 14. Four men were lost: two who died and two who remained missing. Twenty-five horses and four mules were also lost. At last their ordeal was over.

❧ 11 ❧

PHILADELPHIA FOR
SCHOOL AND RETURN
TO FORT SILL

Our troop was ordered back to Fort Sill while I was at school in Philadelphia, and living in the old house on South Third Street where my mother had been raised and married to my father. Too close confinement within the boundaries of city streets resulted in a nerve condition that defied ordinary treatments. Auntie Mary Green took me with her to visit "an old friend" one day. I became so interested in looking at books in the bookcase, that I paid no attention to what the tall man was talking about. They had greeted each other as old friends.

At the end of that visit, the man, whom she addressed as "Weir," while he called her "Auntie Green," had a chat with me about books. I confided to him, with the gravity of twelve years' experience in life, that I wrote stories when I hadn't any new books to read. Auntie objected to my scribbling, and commandeered any penciled pages. They were fairy tales, which she classified as nonsense and lies, because there were no such things as fairies.

The result of that chat was permission to write my stories, and then Weir Mitchell said, "Maybe when you are grown up, you will write a story and I shall read it, and maybe I shall write a story and you will read it." So, seriously enough, I gave the promise.

Dr. Weir Mitchell's prescription was that I was to go back West to the regiment, ride my pony again, and forget about music lessons and school rooms. Later I learned that Dr. J. K. Mitchell, the father of Weir, had been a warm friend of Captain John Green, and more than once had accompanied him on a long voyage on one of Captain Green's sailing vessels.

Captain Green owned a fleet of sailing vessels and traded with the Orient as well as the West Indies. After having served through the War of 1812, he married Mary Curl, who was born in 1800 and lost her father during the fighting of 1812. She was fifteen when she married Captain Green, and sailed with him on many long voyages to the West Indies, the China Sea, and the Mediterranean. Voyages in those days frequently consumed twenty-four months, as it required a year each way, even with favorable winds.

Auntie told stories of fighting pirates at the "Hole-in-the-Rock," where she acted as "powder monkey," carrying ammunition to the sailors, and loading guns with powder and ball while the men were fighting, finally driving off the two pirate boats. I listened, enthralled by her tales of how the Brig *Mary* had been bought from the United States government at the close of the War of 1812, and how it was refitted and named in honor of Captain Green's young bride, who christened the ship by breaking a bottle of champagne on its bow.

I listened to how the sailors mutinied off the Spanish coast and ran the boat onto the rocks, where she pounded to pieces and sank, but Captain Green, a young boy and the first mate, escaped, and saved the fifty thousand dollars in Spanish gold doubloons that the crew had planned to steal. They drifted in a lifeboat until picked up by a passing vessel. A long gold chain was made for Auntie Green by the Dubois Brothers, the first manufacturing jewelers of Philadelphia, out of some of those very coins. That chain was placed on my neck by Auntie when she told me the story. I still cherish it and the memory it brings back.

Then came the story of how Doc or J. K. Mitchell, after Uncle Green had retired, remained a friend and the family physician. No children had come to the home of the Greens, and Auntie Green brought her first cousin, my grandmother, Mary Ann Wallace, who was then a young lady, to act as a companion during the loneliness imposed by Captain Green's trips. But Mary Wallace soon married a handsome young lawyer, John Koehler.

Though there were no babies in the Green home, many came to the house next door, boys and girls, all unusually handsome. Grandmother's and Auntie Green's houses were like one, with a common garden at the back, and a passageway between the two houses on the second floor. So when my own mother was born, Captain Green and Auntie wanted to adopt her, but grandmother refused.

It remained for an old servant of Auntie's to settle the matter, which she did by going into grandmother's room and picking up the baby, a little over a year old, and carrying her through the passageway into the home of Auntie Green. From that day until after Auntie Green's death when I was thirteen, my mother never slept again in grandma's house, yet she was never separated from her own mother or her brothers and sisters. In that house of Auntie Green's, I was born.

My mother laughs when she tells how as soon as I had been dressed in my first clothes, Auntie collected all the jewelry and money in the house, piled it upon me, then carried me upstairs to the top floor. "Now she will go up in life, no matter how many times she may go down. She is sure to go up at the end and stay up." It was an old Pennsylvania superstition, I have since been told.

When my mother was five years old, Uncle Green became ill, and was operated upon in the same home. Dr. Pancoast, the famous surgeon, was assisted by Dr. J. K. Mitchell. Young Weir Mitchell was a medical student at the time. There were no trained nurses in those days and because of the close friendship, Weir Mitchell stayed all the time, day and night, with Uncle Green. Another student came during the day, but Weir Mitchell remained in the house, and took charge of the sick room at night.

About midnight a tray with hot coffee and tempting food was brought to Weir. He would wait until the maid had gone downstairs, then sneak up the flight to the upper rooms, calling softly, "Puss-in-Boots, are you awake?" So the five-year-old child, in nightgown and with long dark curls, would peep over the banister, and then sit down beside Weir Mitchell, who drank the coffee himself, but gave her the other things to eat.

After that she slipped back into her bed, and he carried the tray, minus any scraps of food, back to the lower floor. In spite of all their efforts, Uncle Green died. So that was the "family friend" to whom Auntie Green took me that day, and to whom I gave my promise to write a story when I had grown up.

Doctor Weir Mitchell at that time had been writing scientific articles, but was not known as a writer of fiction, though he really was having fiction accepted and published under a nom de plume. I met him in 1880. His first fiction under his own name was published in 1881, I believe.

I never saw him again, but that encouragement of a child's dreams had its influence on my life. So I was taken back to my parents and the regiment at Fort Sill in 1880. I never returned to the old home to live, for Auntie Green died shortly after I started for Fort Sill.

FRIENDSHIP WITH QUANAH PARKER

Quanah Parker had become a personal friend of the officers stationed at Fort Sill, and visited them in their homes. My father and he were very close friends, and when there were hardly enough well men, officers or soldiers to "mount a corporal's guard," owing to the malaria, Quanah came each day to our house, walked softly through the hall to my father's room, and sat down at the bedside. Not one day did he miss until my father had passed the danger point.

I remember Quanah well. He was frequently a guest in our home at Fort Sill, so what I relate of him is not hearsay, but gathered from family memories of my mother, my father, and my own vivid recollections of him, ranging from a very early age until almost eighteen.

Quanah's father, Peta Nocona, was chief of the Quahada branch of the Comanches. They were known as the Antelope Eaters of the Staked Plains or Llano Estacado. Peta Nocona was known as "The Wanderer." It was the middle of May 1836 when Nocona, at the head of his band, swept down on Parker's Fort in central Texas, then a tiny settlement of thirty-plus people—men, women, and children—where the Parkers and others had located.

After the fight with Nocona's band, the nine-year-old daughter of Silas and Lucy Parker, Cynthia Ann Parker, was carried away as a captive. She grew up among the Quahada Comanches and was treated with every consideration, and finally became the wife of Chief Nocona. Two sons and a younger child, Prairie Flower, were born. During the fall of 1860, when Prairie Flower was still a babe in arms, Cynthia Ann was thirty-three years old, and Quanah, the oldest son, was about eleven, Peta Nocona led the Quahadas in a raid through central Texas.

In retaliation, the Texas Rangers under Captain "Sul" Ross (later governor of Texas) followed Nocona's band and engaged in a fierce fight. Cynthia Ann, holding Prairie Flower in her arms, was captured, but Quanah and his brother escaped. Peta Nocona, mortally wounded, dragged himself to his feet, and braced against a tree, sang his death chant to the Great Spirit. His right arm hung broken at his side, in his left he held a spear. Called upon to surrender, he held the spear ready to fight to his last breath. Thus he continued his death chant until the order was given to "finish him," and the death chant was silenced.

Cynthia Ann and Prairie Flower were held prisoners, but the identity of the woman as Cynthia Ann Parker was established beyond question. Unable to learn anything about her sons, or the people she loved as her own, she grieved constantly. Her sorrow was intensified when little Prairie Flower sickened and died shortly after the captives reached a "home" among white people. Two years after Nocona's death, the lonely captive was laid to rest beside her little daughter. Quanah, unable to learn anything about his mother or sister, would eventually become chief. And so the grandson of Silas Parker led the Quahada Comanches in their struggle against the white people.

In 1867 the Medicine Lodge Treaty took place when the Cheyennes, Kiowas, Arapahos, Apaches, and all the Comanches except the Quahadas under Quanah were assigned to reservations. Quanah and his followers absolutely refused to be a party to this treaty, and as a consequence they wandered free until the winter of 1874–75 in their familiar haunts of the Texas Panhandle and the Staked Plains. Subsisting on game as in decades past, but granting no allegiance to the white people or the United States, they kept aloof from all reservations and practically cut themselves away from every tribe of Indians, including other branches of their own people.

The Staked Plains was a desert practically devoid of watering places, and only the Quahadas ever ventured there for any length of time. Sandstorms obliterated trails within half an hour, and the contour of the low mounds constantly changed with action of the winds, thus destroying what might have been a landmark for a lost traveler.

Many years later my father asked Quanah where water had been found by the Quahadas in their wanderings on the Staked Plains, for it was agreed by the officers that they were able to get water in some mysterious manner that no white man could explain, other than secret watering holes or springs. Quanah answered, "We carried water with us in skins, and kept them filled." A system of couriers on swift ponies showed Quanah's remarkable executive ability as a leader, in this one matter of water supply.

Quanah lived on the reservation in a good house. Ordinarily, he dressed in well-tailored conventional clothes of fine quality, but when he came calling on officers at Fort Sill, he wore the uniform of a captain of cavalry, as a compliment to the men he knew were his staunch friends, for the Tenth Cavalry officers were all his friends.

He wore a handsome pin in his scarf, shaped like a tomahawk, a gift to him from other white friends. His gold watch was worn on an unostentatious chain. In fact, Quanah instinctively avoided anything that was not in good taste or that lacked refinement. He carried himself with easy dignity, but had a keen sense of humor—a trait my own father had in common with Quanah.

Once in 1880 my mother invited him to bring his little girl with him to lunch. We called her "Little Quanah" as we did not know her Indian name. She was dressed in the same kind of clothes that I wore, for Quanah always asked the advice of the officers' wives on such matters.

He always said that he wanted his daughter to grow up and be educated like the daughters of the army families, whom he knew so well. "Little Quanah" was a pretty, shy little thing, several years younger than myself, but she, my brother, and I were able to play nicely together companionably, though she did not know a word of English, nor we one word of Comanche.

At the lunch table we had waffles and syrup. The last drop on the lip of the syrup pitcher was always my Waterloo. That day I demurely passed the syrup pitcher to Quanah, and watched slyly to see what he would do with that lingering drop. Quanah evidently read my mind. He thanked me, accepted the pitcher, and poured the liquid slowly. Then he glanced at me with twinkling eyes as he calmly tipped the pitcher so that the drop fell back inside of it. But he smiled openly, when my parents burst into laughter at my expense. I never see a syrup pitcher without recalling my chagrin that day.

After luncheon, we sat on the front porch where I heard Quanah relate in detail to my parents the full story of his life, the stampeding of the horses of the Fourth Cavalry, his fight with the buffalo hunters, and the final battle when the ponies were all shot by Colonel Ranald Mackenzie's command. Some things he told my father were sacredly confidential, and I cannot reveal them.

The sun was setting. The soldiers assembled at the bugle call for retreat. Bugle notes floated across the prairie, then the cannon fired its salute as the flag slipped down from the top of the flagstaff. Quanah watched the flag in silence. Something shone in his face that I have never forgotten all these passing years. He, too, was an American. It was his flag, as well as ours.

After "retreat," we children were playing with bows and arrows, shooting at marks. Quanah called for a bow and arrow and a target. We hung a straw hat belonging to one of the boys at a good distance, confident Quanah could not hit it. But the hat was impaled. Then coins were tossed into the air, and again he proved his marksmanship with bow and arrow, while officers grouped about him applauded his wonderful skill.

A LESSON IN POLITICS

During 1880, Quanah received his first lesson in the great American game of politics. Having learned that it was more efficacious to make a trip to Washington rather than don war paint and feathers when a grievance arose, he decided to follow the advice of my father and other officers at Fort Sill who were his sincere friends.

They told him to see the Commissioner of Indian Affairs in Washington and personally report to him about the shortage of rations and annuity goods at the Fort Sill agency. Conditions had become so bad that indignant army officers were actually helping to feed the hungry Indians, and having extra articles of food charged and paid for themselves at the Post Commissary—a shameful situation.

Washington was in the throes of a national election in 1880, when James A. Garfield was the Republican candidate for President. The train on which Quanah was traveling stopped at Fort Worth, Texas, for a few hours and Quanah, sightseeing, discovered an elaborate display of campaign buttons and badges. He was totally ignorant of party affiliations, so selected insignias that seemed most attractive to him. The Democratic buttons were the most elaborate.

Quanah pinned them on his coat in profusion. He noticed that the street decorations and the majority of citizens displayed these same decorations. Texas was red-hot Democratic in politics, but Quanah knew nothing of that angle. Still decked with the buttons and badges, he reached Washington and obtained the desired appointment with the Commissioner of Indian Affairs, but received a curt and frigid audience and peremptory refusal to his pleas. Puzzled, but still hopeful, he next called upon the Secretary of the Interior and met with the same experience. Thoroughly humiliated and demoralized, he returned to Fort Sill. Once there he lost no time in relating his experiences to my father, who looked at the campaign buttons pinned to Quanah's coat.

"What are you doing with those buttons, Quanah?" he asked suddenly.

"Oh, nothing, I bought them at Fort Worth."

"Did you wear them in Washington?"

"Yes, they look pretty. All the men in Washington wear ribbons and pretty buttons," was the Indian's guileless answer.

My father explained the bitterness between political factions, and Quanah listened intently. Then he realized that the buttons he had flaunted were those of the rivals of the party at that time in power at Washington, as Rutherford B. Hayes, Republican, was still President.

"It's like an Apache coming into a Comanche camp with fresh Comanche scalps," commented Quanah. "Now I understand." After mediating a few seconds, he looked up at my father, then with a twinkle in his eye, Quanah announced, "I am going back to Washington."

He did so. Long before he had reached the National Capitol, Quanah discarded the Democratic emblems and was even more profusely decorated with Republican buttons and badges. He was received with open arms, where he had formerly been repulsed. The complaints were heard courteously and satisfactorily adjusted. Quanah had learned his first lessons in American politics.

Later his qualifications as politician and diplomat were evinced in the manner he handled the affairs of his people. During his frequent visits to Washington, he became well known among prominent officials from all over the world. But his greatest delight was to renew friendships with the army officers at the old Ebbitt House, which was practically their headquarters. Quanah always registered at this hotel himself.

~❧ 12 ❧~

FORT CONCHO, GRADUATION, AND OFF TO FORT DAVIS

My father transferred from "A" Troop to "M," which was stationed at Fort Concho, so once more we started on that trail. The date was May 31, 1880. This time, owing to shortage of transportation, and the necessity of moving government property for other troops at Concho, we had ox teams instead of the usual government mules to haul the big canvas-topped prairie schooner wagons. A detachment of mounted soldiers accompanied us as an escort for protection against any Indian attack, and my father rode his own horse. We had our own big carriage and horses.

In our vehicle was my mother, myself, my brother and sister, two canaries in cages, a pasteboard box with horned toads of assorted sizes, a spotted black and white cur pup named Prince (my own property), and Elizabeth, our colored cook, the wife of Nash. In Elizabeth's lap reposed an accordion, the pride of her heart, and on that trip her "tunes" enlivened the monotony of prairie travel. It was small wonder that the officers at Fort Sill, gathering to say last farewells to us all, dubbed our outfit, "Cooper's Menagerie."

The ox-train drivers were called bullwhackers. It was fascinating to watch them hitch up the teams of oxen until they stood in pairs, heads bowed meekly under heavy wooden yokes. The long blacksnake whips cracked like pistols, and the bullwhackers' calls, "Gee," "Haw," "Whoa," soon became familiar to our ears.

It was slow traveling. Ten to twelve miles a day was called a good march with the ox train, whereas the mules and our cavalry troops covered twenty-five miles each day. But there were compensations. From the hand-drawn map of the route, we knew the exact location of the next stop, and sometimes Nash drove us on ahead, while at other times, the ox train went on its way while we loitered in a pleasant spot, and then caught up with the rest of "Cooper's Menagerie."

That was the only time in my life I ever traveled with prairie schooners drawn by oxen. It was like traveling with a circus caravan, but eventually we landed once again at Fort Concho, where my father reported to his new captain, Stevens Thomson Norvell, commanding Troop M of the Tenth Cavalry.

FREE AT LAST

I was graduated at a private school near Philadelphia the last of June 1884, when I was barely past my seventeenth birthday, and went with my parents, brother, and sister to Fort Davis, Texas, where the Regimental Headquarters of the Tenth Cavalry was then stationed. Regimental Headquarters meant having the band at our garrison. I eagerly anticipated my return to the old regiment in which I had practically spent my life.

From my parents, as well as the *Army and Navy Journal*, I knew exactly who was at Fort Davis long before I reached it. Most of the names and faces had been familiar to me from earliest childhood, but there were a few younger officers whom I did not know.

Marfa was the nearest railroad point from Fort Davis on the Southern Pacific Railroad. When we stepped from our Pullman, there was just an expanse of prairie, and one low red building which was the station and freight, also telegraph office. Marfa had no population whatever. On a sidetrack stood a tank car that contained water. There was no other way of obtaining water at Marfa in the fall of 1884, except by tank cars from other railroad points. However, I was accustomed to "dry camps" and unsettled sections of Texas, Kansas, and Indian Territory, so I accepted the situation as a matter of fact. Over twenty miles of smooth hard road we were carried in a government ambulance by four trig mules at a spanking trot, though we went steadily uphill toward distant peaks. At the foot of these peaks lay Fort Davis.

The garrison was laid out in the regulation square, a line of quarters for the officers, opposite the low, long barracks for the troops. Back of the barracks were the cavalry stables. Quartermaster, commissary, and adjutant's office grouped at a third side of the big parade ground, and on the fourth side was the trader's store, officers' club, and mess.

Only an army girl of seventeen, coming back "grownup" could understand my own feelings as we drove along the front line, and I saw familiar faces, men and women, on the porches, smiling and waving a welcome to us. Colonel Grierson, who had known me in my baby days, and whose own children had been my playmates, including his only daughter, Edith, who had died [1878] at Fort Concho some years before my graduation, had shared those days of my childhood. Colonel Grierson, on his front porch, smiled, and waved greetings.

Then came a yelp from Prince, my spotted black and white cur. He had not forgotten me. I think that was the happiest day of my entire life, as I look back on it now at the age of sixty-two [1929], more child than woman,

> "Standing with reluctant feet, where the brook and river meet, Maidenhood and childhood sweet."

FATHER IS PROMOTED

My father had been promoted to captain of Troop H in 1883. When he had been a junior first lieutenant, he always envied Captain Louis H. Carpenter, who commanded that troop, and hoped that someday he might command it. To his great joy, that hope had been fulfilled when Carpenter was made a major of the Fifth Cavalry, after having commanded "H Troop" of the Tenth for seventeen years, or since it was formed in 1866.

It was H Troop that had ridden with Carpenter to the rescue of Major "Sandy" Forsyth and his detachment in their desperate fight against Roman Nose, while Jack Stilwell and Pierre Trudeau made their desperate attempt to go for help. Some of the soldiers who had ridden with Carpenter that day were still serving in the troop. Seventeen years it had been "Carpenter's Troop," and then it was known as "Cooper's Troop of the Tenth Cavalry" until he became a major of the Fifth Cavalry in 1898 at the time of the Spanish-American War.

Officers and soldiers of those past days and times remained in one regiment so long that their names were always identified with it, though they might become brigadier generals, or even command the army. Pride in his own troop, and the honor of the regiment, ruled every officer and man who was a soldier at heart.

Our house at Fort Davis was at the very end of the line, and back of it sloped a mountain. Not a tree was in sight.

The country was rocky and bare. Below the post were two small settlements. One was called Chihuahua, as many Mexicans lived there, but Newton or Newtown, nearer the garrison, was a thrifty place with good stores and many delightful people. Riding horseback, frequent garrison dances, and informal visits from house to house filled the time of the officers' families, while the men were kept busy with official duties. I never found a dull moment.

OUR WEST POINT GRADUATES

Two young lieutenants were graduated from West Point the same month and year that I finished school in Philadelphia in June 1884. Upon our arrival at Fort Davis, we learned that owing to shortage of quarters these two officers had been assigned temporarily to rooms on the second floor of our own home. My brother, then a boy of fifteen, had the other room upstairs. This left the lower part of the house for my parents, my sister, and myself.

With a common front hall and stairway, the only exit except through our dining room, and the very informal manner of living in a frontier army post of those days, it did not take very long for a girl of seventeen and two youngsters, aged twenty-one, to become close friends. Lieutenant Powhatan H. Clarke, like his classmate and bosom friend James B. "Jim" Hughes, were both Southern born.

Though different types in appearance, both were handsome and magnetic, and both were of the best type of Southern gentlemen. In a short time they were the most popular young officers in the regiment, and though older men laughed at their boyish pranks, they agreed "there is good timber in them for officers." Though I had known how to ride from my babyhood, I had never been taught to dance, so that deficiency was remedied very soon when both young officers began to teach me "how to step" without treading on my partner's toes. I consider they were martyrs to a sense of honor.

My father came into our quarters at Fort Davis, smiling broadly as he announced that Quanah Parker and George Fox had just arrived in the garrison. "I have asked them to come and stay with us. They'll be here in a little while," he said.

We were all as much pleased as he was when Quanah and Fox appeared. It was a happy reunion of old friends. Quanah explained that a root used by the Comanches to counteract malaria had entirely disappeared in the vicinity of Fort Sill, either having been used up or destroyed. Realizing its value to his people, he obtained permission from Washington for himself and a select body of Comanches to leave the reservation and go to mountains in southwest Texas where he knew they could procure the roots to start new plants.

George Fox, the nephew of a former mayor of Philadelphia, accompanied Quanah on the trip. He, too, was an old friend of our family. Fox, because of weak lungs, had gone to live in Indian Territory, and while there became a friend of Quanah. Through Quanah, Fox was adopted into the Quahada tribe and thus had a legal right to live on the reservation. Fox was an educated man and a gentleman by birth and manner. On this trip he was acting as secretary, interpreter, and confidential advisor.

The position as interpreter was rather amusing at Fort Davis. Quanah, learning that Colonel Grierson, whom he knew very well, was absent, and that Major Anson Mills, a newcomer to the Tenth from the Third Cavalry, was in command of the garrison, at once instructed my father and Fox not to divulge the fact that he could understand or speak

English. As a result, Mills was rather disinclined to listen to Quanah's interpreter.

Quanah had authority from Washington to request an officer and detail of soldiers in order that citizens in Texas might not mistake his party for a "war party," and open fire upon them. Fox urged, and Mills became rather plain spoken, about having an officer and soldiers trailing around with Quanah. However, he finally gave grudging permission.

My father and Fox arose to go, and then Quanah, in perfect English and with impassive face, said politely, "Thank you very much for your courtesy, Major Mills." They departed leaving Mills speechless. On returning to our home immediately after this interview, Quanah related the incident, acted it out to perfection, and enjoyed the joke on Mills as much as the rest of us.

When Quanah requested an officer and detail of soldiers from Mills, it was Lieutenant Powhatan Clarke who was ordered to accompany Quanah and Fox. Probably Powhatan had seen Indians previously, but I know this was his first duty in connection with Indians. He hurried to our quarters at once to meet Quanah and Fox, and discuss plans for the trip with them.

Quanah studied him quizzically, watching the impulsive, boyish mannerisms that were characteristic of the young officer. It was a delightful evening for us all, filled with laughter and jokes. After Powhatan had left, Quanah smiled at my parents, as he said dryly, "Boy Clarke."

I was up and saw them start from our quarters that morning at reveille, after a daybreak breakfast which Powhatan shared with us. They were absent over ten days, then Quanah and Fox again were our guests for a couple of days before returning to Fort Sill. The coveted roots were found, dug up, and carefully packed for the return trip to Fort Sill, where they were to be planted and cultivated.

Quanah had many jokes to tell on the young officer, one of which was his falling asleep near the campfire, and when his cap rolled near the fire, it began burning. Quanah and Fox discovered it too late. Only the patent leather visor was left, and so Powhatan rode back to the garrison with a large white silk handkerchief tied about his head like an old lady's hood. On another occasion the Indians had found a root which they used for an eye lotion. Quanah showed it to Fox and Powhatan, explaining its valuable properties, but telling how poisonous it was if taken internally.

While they were chatting, Powhatan, absentmindedly, picked up a bit of this root and chewed it. Only when he was taken violently ill did anyone realize what he had done. Quanah's knowledge of herbs and roots, and his supply of such emergency aids in camp and on the trail, prevented a serious ending to the episode. But when Quanah returned and Powhatan came to our house that evening, the story of "Papoose" Clarke, who wore a baby cap, and chewed things like a baby, was told to us all. However, it did not in the least worry or embarrass the young officer, who enjoyed the jokes at his own expense.

Quanah always called me "Cooper's Girl." That night he opened our piano and turning to me said, "Play for me, Cooper's Girl. Play the Thunder music." I was surprised. Five years previous at Fort Sill I had played a piece of music that Quanah called "Thunder music," but I had almost forgotten the occurrence. However, I had the music and so I played it.

Then I played other music for him as he sat back in a big Morris chair with one of my father's special cigars, almost forgotten at times in his fingers. I could see his face from where I was sitting at the piano, and I wondered then, as I do now, whether his memory had not carried him away to the days when he had ridden as a lad beside his mother and father across the plains of Texas—his father's heritage and his own from generations past.

Quanah's great passion in his life was the memory of his blue-eyed, white mother, Cynthia Ann Parker. His big ambition was to find her body and bring her and his baby sister, Prairie Flower, back to sleep among "her own people—the Quahada Comanches." He often spoke of this to my father and to George Fox. Not until Quanah came to live on the Fort Sill Reservation did he know that his mother and sister had died soon after they were taken captives in the fight with the Texas Rangers.

That evening at Fort Davis, while I sat at the piano, Quanah, standing near me, lifted one of my very long and heavy braids, saying, "You have a very fine scalp lock, Cooper's Girl." I swung around on the revolving stool, and with the assurance of seventeen, retorted, "Where is your scalp lock, Quanah?"

My mother was shocked at my impudence, but Quanah smiled, slipped back his coat and displayed a very thin braid, hidden by his other shorter hair, and then twisted around his arm a much longer scalp lock than my own. He explained that he did not cut off the scalp lock because his people would not wish it done. Quanah and Fox returned to Fort Sill, and a few weeks later my father received word from Quanah that Fox had died. The tubercular trouble that he had fought for years had finally made him its victim.

Our regiment was ordered to Arizona in early April 1885, and neither of my parents nor I ever again saw Quanah Parker, but we knew what was happening to him all those years, for my father and he kept in touch with each other until Quanah's daughter wrote us of her father's death on February 23, 1911.

CHRISTMAS AT FORT DAVIS

Christmas 1884 was celebrated at Fort Davis by everyone in the garrison, from the colonel of the regiment down to the smallest pickaninny on "Suds Row," where the wives of the colored soldiers constituted a colony of laundresses, sometimes depleted by excursions into kitchens of the officers' families as cooks. Each troop vied with the others in having the most elaborate dinner, and the officers and families went from one mess room to the other inspecting the decorated feast, and deciding which one excelled.

On officers' row, individual celebrations gave way Christmas Eve to a general gathering at the library. There a great tree had been decorated by the officers' wives and every child in the garrison had been remembered by a gift on that tree. After receiving the gift, children were to be sent home and a dance continued the festivities for the officers and their families.

I was considered too young to be classed as grown-up, and was not to be allowed to attend any dances until my eighteenth birthday, much to my chagrin, now that I had actually learned how to dance, thanks to Powhatan, Jim Hughes, and Bob Grierson, who had struggled nobly to attain that end. My mother was firm. I could go to the tree and remain till nine o'clock, then I must go home.

Mrs. Robert Smither, Mrs. Alexander Keyes, and others interceded for me, including my three dancing teachers, and finally won consent. I was arrayed in my white silk graduation dress, but my hair hung in its two usual long braids ending in curls, as I wore it every day. It was a brilliant moonlight night. The tree was a great success, and from it was handed a gift for me as one of the children of the garrison. Powhatan and Jim enjoyed my confusion until they, too, heard their names announced by Chaplain

Francis Weaver, and each of them also received a toy as garrison children. So I had my revenge.

We helped the younger children play "Blind Man's Bluff," and others "Hide and Seek" for toys and small boxes of candies, and really became the ring leaders, deciding we might as well have the game as the name of garrison infants. The uproar was deafening, and I avoided my mother's eyes.

Two tables at the side of the room were arranged with the feast; one for the adults, the other for the children, who were to go home after the supper. My two companions had been augmented by a third, Lieutenant William E. Shipp, second lieutenant of my father's troop. He had been in the class of 1883 from West Point, and was a tall, bashful chap, very easily embarrassed, so I was rather surprised when he joined our group of fun makers for the children.

At the signal, which was "mess call" on a bugle, the children started toward their table, the adults toward the other. Naturally, the four of us went to the table for grown-ups, but I met my mother there, and she told me that since I had behaved like a small child, I must go to the children's table, and after supper go home. I meekly obeyed, but with me went my three loyal companions. The children were delighted, the grown-ups were in gales of laughter as we four sat down. A chair, the best seat, was given to me.

A vacant chair on either side at once was appropriated by Lieutenant Hughes and Lieutenant Shipp, who grinned at Powhatan as he realized he was "cut out" by them both. He tried to "transfer," offering various inducements, but failed. A child opposite me called out, "You can have my place, Lieutenant Clarke."

So he accepted it with thanks and then announced triumphantly that he had the best place after all, as he could look straight at me all the time he was eating. Then he proceeded to make life miserable for poor Lieutenant Shipp, who did not know me as intimately as the other two.

Powhatan seemed satisfied where he was, and later turned and glanced back of him toward the grown-up table. Suddenly he excused himself, saying, "Your mother wants me for something." I expected a message bidding me to behave with more dignity. I forgot to say that my mother was very dignified and handsome, with dark eyes, and masses of pure silver hair. That hair was the result of the mental strain during the terrible week of the Staked Plains scout. Powhatan returned soberly and said, "I was mistaken. Mrs. Cooper wants to speak to you, Shipp."

At once the other man hastened to my mother. I saw him speak to her, and her glance of surprise and negative shake of her head. Shipp turned around perplexed, and just then I heard Powhatan's chuckle at my side as he sat down in the vacant chair. "Worked, didn't it?" And there he remained while Shipp was forced to occupy the seat opposite. The children went home, but I stayed on till the very end of the "Virginia Reel," in which everyone joined, young or old, and after that came the "Home, Sweet Home" waltz by our string band.

One incident stands out above the others. Near midnight, Mrs. Keyes told me Mama had consented to have me accompany her and Captain Keyes down to Chihuahua as there was to be Midnight Mass in the little adobe Catholic church. I had been graduated from a convent, though my parents were not Catholic. Many army girls were sent to such schools.

So we left the dancing and music and entered the ambulance at the library door. Powhatan was with us, as he was a Catholic, as was Mrs. Keyes. The moonlight was beautiful and when we reached the little, one-story adobe building, all windows and the wide door were opened so that rays of light from within the church lighted up figures, men with bared heads, and Mexican women draped with black shawls, who unable to get into the church, were kneeling outside in the roadway.

We got down from the ambulance, but could get no nearer than the kneeling figures. Then, the courtly Sir Walter Raleigh, Powhatan, unfastened his blue cape, lined with cavalry yellow, and lay it on the ground for me to kneel upon. So we heard that Christmas Midnight Mass. I have never forgotten it.

When it was over, we were driven back to the hop room to the music, bright lights, dancing, and laughter, and soon my Christmas was over. But when my parents started to walk home with me, Powhatan and Jim went along, and Lieutenant Shipp went, too. I had another and unsuspected admirer that night, a little boy, ten years old, the son of Captain Robert Smither.

Just a few weeks ago in Washington, while Brigadier General Henry Smither, himself a grandfather, was talking to my mother and me when we were spending an evening with him and his wife and children, he suddenly said, "Bird, did you ever know that you were my first love?" It was a surprise and I laughed, "Never, when was that?"

"At Fort Davis, when you came out from school. You were seventeen, I was ten. I used to watch to see you come along the line, and I was wild with jealousy of Jim Hughes and Powie Clarke." It was that same little boy, aged ten, who gave up his place opposite me at the Christmas supper table for "children only."

So we all laughed over the confession, but there were tears in the laughter. Tears and memories of those who have gone from us all since that night, forty-four years ago when I was seventeen and he was ten.

Both Jim and Powhatan were unusually fine riders, and when the three of us rode together, I was the audience while they tried new "stunts." It was a regular Wild West Show, plus West Point Riding Academy tricks. So life ran carefree and joyously for us all.

✺13✺

THE TENTH CAVALRY
MOVES TO ARIZONA, AND
WE GO TO FORT GRANT

———

Then came orders. The entire Tenth Cavalry was to change stations with the Third Cavalry. We were to move to Arizona Territory while the Third Cavalry was to come to Texas. The regiment, with its property, was to march to Arizona, though many of the families decided to go by rail to avoid the thirty-day trip, camping each night.

When the orders were given to various troop commanders as to their particular destination in Arizona, we learned that Captain Smither of "B" Troop was to go to Whipple Barracks with regimental headquarters. Lieutenant Jim Hughes was in that troop. My father's troop was to go to Fort Grant. Captain Thomas C. Lebo's Troop K, and Lieutenant Powhatan Clarke were also to go to Grant. So the "Triple Alliance of the Regimental Infants," as Mrs. Keyes had nicknamed the three of us, was doomed to be dissolved.

The regiment gathered at Fort Davis where a farewell hop was given, and the next morning I watched the whole regiment, headed by the band, march out of the garrison. It made its first camp about ten miles distant, so that evening many of those who waited to make the trip by railroad later drove out to the camp and had dinner there. I was among those present. So I said good-bye to those who would be stationed at other garrisons than Fort Grant, our own destination. Many I never saw again. Others I did not meet again for years.

The regiment had started on April 1, 1885, for Arizona, so my mother and several other ladies timed their arrival at Fort Grant a day or two ahead of the troops. On our trip by rail, we knew about where to expect to see the regiment, so watched until it came into sight. At once, Mamie Beck and I hurried to the rear of the train and the observation platform, waving handkerchiefs, as we were recognized by the column of riders.

They were coated with alkali dust, while many wore handkerchiefs over noses and mouths. But as the train rushed past, two officers galloped beside the track, waving their campaign hats and whooping like Indians. Powhatan and Lieutenant Leighton Finley kept up their losing race as long as they could, and then with a final whoop, gave it up.

The regiment reached El Paso, only to discover that the Rio Grande was so badly swollen that it was unfordable. The only bridge over the river was three miles below the New Mexico line and that bridge crossed into Mexico. American soldiers, according to international law, could not cross into Mexico unless by consent of Mexico and the United States authorities. So for one week the regiment camped there while red tape of Mexico and the United States was being unwound to permit the crossing of that solitary bridge.

The next event in that trip was at Deming, New Mexico, where the Tenth Cavalry met the Third. My father then again saw his old friend, Captain Emmet Crawford, who had been at Ship Island when I was a baby. Another interesting incident at Deming was that Major Anson Mills, who had been promoted to the Tenth from the Third, again contacted officers who had formerly served with him during the Sioux War in 1876. Major Frederick Van Vliet, also promoted to our regiment from the Third, found familiar faces at Deming.

Major Mills, Captain Crawford, and Major Van Vliet were three of the five officers of the Third Cavalry who had been in the Sioux fight on June 17, 1876, a week before Custer was killed. Those same officers the following September 8 had recaptured Captain Miles Keogh's guidon at the Battle of Slim Buttes, Montana, when General George Crook was Department Commander in that country. Now Crook was the Department Commander of Arizona, where Mills, Van Vliet, and later Crawford were to serve together once more in the Apache campaign.

Deming was about a hundred fifty miles from Willcox, Arizona, and when we reached that little town, typical of the old frontier days, we found that Colonel William R. Shafter, commanding the First Infantry and also Fort Grant, had already sent down transportation for our party of women and children. Fort Grant was twenty-seven miles north of Willcox in the Sulphur Spring Valley.

FORT GRANT AND THE APACHES

The garrison was located at the base of the Graham Mountains, the highest peak of which was Mount Graham towering 10,600 feet above sea level, while the garrison itself was at an elevation of about 7,000 feet. Across a fertile valley facing the garrison was a beautiful range of mountains, the Galiuros, and between the two mountain ranges forming the valley, thousands of cattle grazed as though in an immense, unfenced green pasture.

Ranches could be seen here and there in the valley, and groups of cottonwood trees near the watering places added to the attractive scene we first saw from the front porch of Colonel Shafter's quarters, where we had been invited for our first meal at Fort Grant. As the troops were not due for several days, Colonel Shafter had arranged every possible convenience for our whole party in a set of vacant quarters, and we arranged to have our meals at the officers' mess, which adjoined the club and Post Trader's Store.

Arizona's first railroad, the Southern Pacific, was laid in 1880, and when we arrived in the spring of 1885 the country was very far from being settled. The Apache menace was ever present. General Crook, in command of the Department of Arizona, had been struggling with the problem for many years, but during a period of over thirty years the Apaches had played a game with the authorities over them.

Surrenders, acceptance of terms, returning to the Indian reservations, collecting supplies of guns, ammunition, and food. Then waiting till there was ample grass and water, and once more sneaking away across the border into the mountains of Mexico, plundering, stealing, and slaughtering until ready once more to "surrender."

The Apaches could live where a white man would have died, and their runners have been known to cover a hundred miles afoot in a day over mountains that were practically impassable. Thousands of canyons afforded hiding places when the soldiers pursued them. The Third Cavalry knew these Indians and their trails, but our regiment had served entirely in Texas, Indian Territory, and western Kansas since 1866 when it was organized. So when the troops reached Fort Grant, and the other Arizona garrisons to which they were assigned, they were in a totally unfamiliar country, their horses foot sore and leg weary from the trip of more than thirty days during their march from Fort Davis.

Five troops arrived at Fort Grant: D, commanded by Captain Alexander Keyes; E, Captain Joseph Kelley; F, Captain William Kennedy; K, Captain Thomas Lebo; and H, my father's troop. The next day after their arrival, news was flashed from Fort Apache in the north that Geronimo, Mangus, and Natchez, with a picked band of 125 seasoned Chiricahua Apaches, had "jumped the reservation," and eluding pursuit, were supposed to be on their way to Mexico.

The Fourth Cavalry and the First Infantry were also stationed in Arizona, and at once, the Fourth and the Tenth took up the trail of Geronimo. Two troops of the Fourth, aided by Indian scouts, had an encounter with the Apaches on May 22 at Devil's Creek in the Mogollon Mountains of New Mexico. The next news we had was that Captain Charles Hatfield of the Fourth had an engagement with Geronimo's forces, or a part of the band, on June 8 at Guadalupe Canyon near the border with Sonora.

The Apaches, pursuing their usual tactics, were hidden in the cliffs and boulders that lined the canyons of Arizona and Mexico, and thus were protected and invisible when making an attack. During the fight, Hatfield's command lost quite a bit of its property, the most important item being guns that had been issued to only one troop, Hatfield's, for experimental purposes. These guns had what was later known as pistol clutch stocks.

At Fort Grant and the other garrisons where the Tenth was now stationed, every one of the men and officers were eager to "jump in" on the campaign. The old rivalry between the Fourth and the Tenth that had burned so fiercely in Texas and Indian Territory during the Comanche, Kiowa, and Cheyenne troubles once more blazed up. Most officers of the two regiments, and many enlisted men of both, had served in the former campaigns, so now each command was determined to have the glory, and also the work of conquering Geronimo's band of Chiricahua Apaches.

Geronimo, though credited as the head of these Indians, was merely a Medicine Man, and a self-constituted war chief. The real chief by hereditary right was Natchez, son of old Cochise. Second to Natchez in tribal rank was Chief Mangus, son of Mangus Colorado (or Red Sleeve), who in the preceding generation had terrorized Arizona, New Mexico, Texas, and northern parts of Mexico. Natchez and Mangus were men of superior intelligence and courage, worthy of their blood chieftainship.

They were men capable of planning an extensive campaign and were quick to grasp the ideal moment for their break, when they knew that the Third Cavalry, with its knowledge of trails and Apache warfare, had just been replaced by new troops, Negro soldiers, whom the Apaches had never seen before, and those soldiers mounted on worn-out horses. Further, the winter rains and snows had been plentiful, so grass was abundant and normally dry creek beds were full of water. Hidden rock tanks that only the Apaches knew were also overflowing.

That was the biggest problem of all—water and grass. The Apaches were never worried about obtaining horses, food, or blankets. Isolated ranches, freighters, prospectors, and men on lonely trails were easily shot from ambush and their belongings appropriated. Guns and ammunition also were obtained in that way. The cavalrymen had no way of getting fresh horses, their supplies of food were issued for a specified time, yet the trail could not be abandoned as long as it was hot.

The Chiricahua Apaches were the smallest band, but the most dominant. On their reservation at Fort Apache they lived with the Warm Springs Apaches, who were friendly to the Chiricahuas. The two bands were estimated at four hundred. The White Mountain Apaches also lived on the same reservation, but were at enmity with the Chiricahuas. They feared the Chiricahuas. There were forty thousand Indians in Arizona and New Mexico at the time our regiment arrived in Arizona, and as in any such aggregation of people, white or red, there were always individuals ready to join in plunder, slaughter, and outlawry. Between Fort Grant and Fort Apache was the San Carlos Indian Reservation lying forty miles south of Fort Thomas. The Yuma and Mojave Apaches were all friendly to the Chiricahuas, and consequently furnished them with supplies, ammunition, and information as to the movements of the troops, when not actually furnishing small bands of recruits.

During those summer months, detachments of different troops were constantly on the move, and no one knew when reveille sounded what would transpire before taps. My father went and came; so did the other officers and soldiers. Sometimes a command from another garrison, or possibly officers of the Fourth Cavalry would be in the garrison a few days for supplies and to make special reports.

At Fort Bowie, about forty miles from Grant, General Crook had established his field headquarters, and every young officer in our regiment was imploring and beseeching to be sent out on field duty, instead of "kicking his heels in the garrison."

Among those, we learned through letters of the chagrin of Lieutenant Jim Hughes, who practically trod on General Crook's heels when that old soldier was at Whipple Barracks a few days. The persistent request to be sent out on Indian duty met with refusal that enough were already in the saddle. Then, desperately, the young officer begged, "Well, won't you send me out to guard a waterhole, if there is nothing else for me to do?"

General Crook's reply was final: "There are more second lieutenants now than I have waterholes to guard." That settled it. Down at Fort Grant, Lieutenant Powhatan Clarke's troop, under Captain Lebo, was still inactive and the young officer was fretting at not being in the field. Several times he went to Fort Bowie, only to return with the same information as Crook had stated to Lieutenant Hughes.

LIEUTENANT CLARKE
AND THE FROG RACE

It is said that a certain individual in the "lower regions" finds works for idle hands, and I might add, trouble for inactive lieutenants during Apache troubles. As this also concerns the late Major General William R. Shafter, and was known only to him, Lieutenant Clarke, and Lieutenant Levi P. Hunt, as well as myself, I shall tell the amusing incident now for the first time publicly, just as it occurred that summer in 1885 at Fort Grant.

My father's troop was out in the field, as we termed scouting, so my mother, my brother, age fifteen, my sister, twelve, and I occupied our half of "The Folly." It was the only house at Grant that boasted an individual name apart from being "Coopers' quarters." It was a double house, the hallway having been partitioned to make two sets of quarters. Captain and Mrs. William Dougherty, of the First Infantry, lived in the other side, but we had a common porch. This house was reputed to be haunted.

During an absence of Captain Dougherty, as well as my father, Mrs. Dougherty rushed into our home one night, declaring she had heard the ghost. It was moaning horribly and clanking chains. She remained in our side of the Folly that night, and in daylight no signs of the ghost could be found. Later, however, the officer of the day came along and explained that during the night, one of the sentinels had discovered a drunken infantry soldier at the side of her house, and had taken him to the guardhouse in irons. That drunken soldier had been Mrs. Dougherty's striker, who in his maudlin condition had wandered to her quarters instead of to his barracks for the night. So our ghost story was spoiled.

I was in my own room one afternoon about half-past three, when my brother and sister invited me to go down to Grant Creek with them, as my brother had made a water-wheel with some special feature which was to be installed in the little stream that flowed near the post. With us went old Amelia, our colored cook pro tem, a kindhearted, simple old woman. Then as an escort for the waterwheel followed Lucy and Max Keyes, and the four boys of Dr. William H. Corbusier, all of whom were younger than my sister.

We went down the back line passing the trader's store to cross the bridge, as some particular spot had already been selected to set the waterwheel spinning. Lieutenant Clarke popped out the door of the club room, demanding to know what was happening and where we were going. That explained, he joined the caravan, and finally with Amelia as chaperon, we reached the place and installed the water-wheel. At least, everyone helped except me. I superintended, though I knew nothing whatsoever about waterwheels.

It worked beautifully, and while we all were sitting there watching it, Powhatan discovered a "queer" rock nearby and investigated. It was covered thickly with small brown frogs. It took only a minute or two for the children to follow his suggestion of having a "frog race." Each one, including old Amelia and me, found a bit of wood, or broke it from a branch of the sycamore trees that bordered the creek. Then a frog was placed on the "boat" and at the count, released.

Each of us watched our own "entry" in the race. Some frogs deserted at once; others stayed staunchly by their ship or were wrecked, until finally only one boat and one frog remained, it being the winner. The races continued enthusiastically when the report of the cannon awoke us to the time. It was after retreat.

That did not worry me, nor even Amelia, for she had her supper almost ready before we had started. However, Lieutenant Clarke started to his feet and exclaimed, "Retreat! By jove, I'm officer of the day and I've missed it!"

Amelia and the children were hurrying toward home and we two followed quickly. I was worried, too.

"Where's your saber?" I asked.

"I took it off in the club. That's how I forgot about retreat. I would have remembered if I had worn my saber."

"And I would have thought about retreat if I had seen it," was my only chance for sympathy or help.

In answer to my query as to what would happen, he grinned and said, "Shafter will court-martial me and have me shot at sunrise, I guess."

I did not consider it a joking matter. My father was punctilious about the least important official duty. However, Lieutenant Clarke told me not to worry over it, that he'd report to Colonel Shafter that he had missed retreat while officer of the day, and probably Shafter would "give me a dressing down," and that would end it.

The next morning old Amelia came to my room, her eyes popping like huge white marbles on a stick as she said, "Oh, Miss Birdie, Kunnel Shaftah done put Leiu'tnat Clarke in arrest and he's done confined him to quarters. Lively jes' done come and tol' me."

In passing, I would add that Lively was a soldier in K Troop under Captain Lebo and Lieutenant Clarke. Also Lively was "makin' up" to Amelia and did his courting in our kitchen back of the house. So I did not doubt the truth of Lively's information.

My father was away, but Lieutenant Hunt was in the garrison. I had known him from the time I was a baby, and had also attended his wedding to Miss Haidie Badger, when I had chopped up my hated hoopskirt. Probably our family was a bit closer because of the old days, and that Haidie had died long ago. Anyway, I felt at liberty to look for Lieutenant Hunt and I found him coming slowly along the line, wearing his saber, and I knew that he was the officer of the day.

He was the smallest officer who had ever been graduated from West Point, and the nickname of "Dad Hunt" always clung to him. I asked why Lieutenant Clarke was under arrest, and he replied, "Absent from retreat while officer of the day, and he refuses to give a satisfactory explanation to the commanding officer."

Then I told the whole story and offered to go with Lieutenant Hunt and explain it to Colonel Shafter.

"You keep out of official matters, young lady," ordered Hunt. "Clarke evidently does not want you dragged into this. Go home. I'll see Colonel Shafter myself."

That afternoon I was on the porch when Powhatan came whistling down the front line and turned toward our steps before he saw me there.

"Colonel Shafter just released me from arrest," he announced cheerfully.

"For being absent last night?" I tried to look innocent.

He stared at me rather quizzically, and asked, "Did you say anything to him?"

"Certainly not. I never meddle in official matters. I know better."

Then he went on, "Old Shafter's not so black as he's painted. He just sent for me, and when I got there he gave me a stiff dressing down about neglect of duty, then released me. I thanked him and started out when he called me back, and this is what he said: 'Oh, Mr. Clarke' (he was mimicking Shafter's voice to perfection), 'hereafter when you are officer of the day, I want you to remember that you belong to the army, and not to the navy.' So if you didn't see him, how the dickens do you suppose he knew about that frog race yesterday evening?"

Shafter never referred to the frog race in any way to either of us. Neither did Lieutenant Hunt ever tell the story of my part in official business.

A RUNAWAY HORSE

Another episode that was not so amusing, and nearly became a tragedy, occurred one afternoon when Lieutenant Clarke and I were riding. My horse, Don, was a fractious animal and hard bated. He had been a gift to me from my father on my sixteenth birthday, and it seemed impossible to ever thoroughly break him. But I enjoyed Don's unexpected tricks. It prevented monotony in my rides and I never knew what he would do at any moment.

A narrow lane with five strands of barbed wire on either side of the road near the limits of the military reservation faced a store. Just before reaching the middle of this lane, with room for one wagon to pass a well-managed horse, Don decided to run away. I did not mind that. It was always a part of my rides.

But a half-drunken Mexican had started toward us in the lane, and suddenly he began to whip his team. They bolted toward us. I could not stop Don, and the Mexican could not stop the team in time. It meant a crash of my horse into the team, or my being dragged into the barbed wire fence.

I was not really frightened. I had not time to be, when I heard Powhatan call out, "Sit steady! Drop your stirrup!"

I was riding a sidesaddle with slipper-stirrup. He crowded up beside Don, and then said, "Ready, let go!"

I did it. Don went on without me, passed the wagon. Somehow I was hunched on the other horse in front of Lieutenant Clarke. He stopped and let me slip down to the ground. Then he proceeded to "cuss out" that Mexican in first-class greaser language. While I stood there, he started on a wild chase after Don and finally caught him.

A slight scratch on Don's flank was the only evidence of what had happened. So after my saddle had been cinched firmly, I went on with the interrupted ride, and that incident was another "secret" we did not tell. It would have been the end of my horseback rides, or else having to ride like a beginner, towed along by some sedate escort and a lead line.

Shortly after this, my father came to my room one day and bade me to "cut" Lieutenant Clarke, but would give no reason for his command. I had never disobeyed my parents, and my father and I had been real "pals" from my babyhood days. But a sense of unfairness always rankled me, and I refused to do as he asked unless he would give me his reason for it. He considered his demand should be sufficient and I became angry and stubborn, so he left the room.

I could not understand the sudden change of attitude toward the young officer, who had always been privileged to come in and out of our home informally. However, I concluded that it would soon "blow over" and everything would be as usual. The Geronimo campaign was getting on the nerves of officers who were kept in the garrison, inactive. The younger officers were bombarding their superior officers and also General Crook with requests to be sent "out in the field."

I understood all this, but I was not prepared to have my father go to Lieutenant Clarke that afternoon at stables, and state that the young officer should stop calling at our home and that he was not to connive at meeting me elsewhere, as his attentions to me were obnoxious to my parents.

"Suppose I do come?" Clarke asked coolly.

"If you will not comply with my demand as a gentleman should, I will kick you out like a cur."

Luckily the hotheaded young officer kept his temper and merely replied, "You wear a pretty good-sized boot, captain. I will not invade your home, but I will not make any attempt not to meet Miss Birdie elsewhere in an honorable manner unless she forbids it herself."

No further words passed between them, and the very next morning H Troop, with my father riding at the head, left Fort Grant to take its part in the campaign. That was the latter part of April 1885 and H Troop did not again return to Fort Grant until May 4, 1886.

Shortly after my father left Fort Grant, Lieutenant Clarke stopped at our porch steps one day and announced, "I'm not officer of the day this time, so come on down to Frog Headquarters with me." The frogs were ahead of us, covering the huge boulder. It appeared truly a frog convention. Over the rock two immense sycamore trees formed a perfect arch of interlacing boughs. The twisted white roots were bare under the ripples of Grant Creek, and reflections of roots and trees so distinct as to appear four trees growing from a single base.

As we sat there talking, Powhatan told me that he had obtained permission from General Crook to get into field duty, and that he would start to Fort Bowie the next morning before daybreak. Then on the smooth white bark of one of the twin sycamore trees, he carved a monogram of our initials intertwined, after we had an animated discussion and worked out the letters by drawing various designs in the soft earth until satisfied with the result. When the monogram was completed, he cut the outline of a large heart surrounding the letters.

"Someday we will come back to our tree," he said. "Promise it." I promised. Then we said, "*Au revoir*," instead of "Good-bye," and walked back to the garrison. The next morning I was up and dressed by the time he rode past our house, though it was not quite dawn, and he jumped from his horse to say a farewell word. "I don't know when I'll get back. Don't forget our tree."

The garrison was rather stupid those summer months, for only a few officers were there, except Colonel Shafter and Lieutenant Thomas Barry, who was adjutant of the First Infantry under Shafter. I was the only girl at Fort Grant among married women and mothers of families, so Don and I rode alone over the valley and up the trail of the Graham Mountains back of the garrison.

CAPTAIN CRAWFORD'S VISIT

My brother and sister were to be sent to school in Philadelphia, and just previous to that time, my father was given permission to come to Fort Grant for a few days. While he was there, he came in with the news that Captain Emmet Crawford was in the garrison, en route to Fort Bowie. Although Crawford's regiment, the Third Cavalry, was still stationed in Texas, Crawford's experience with the Indians in Arizona had made him invaluable to General Crook, so the latter had requested that Crawford be detached from his own regiment and return to Arizona to assist in the Geronimo campaign.

That evening Captain Crawford ate dinner with us in the Folly. He was to leave Grant at daybreak the next morning and report to General Crook at Fort Bowie. He had not seen me since as a baby he had carried me about in his arms, and helped me take my first steps and speak my first words at Ship Island in the Gulf of Mexico. After the meal he sat in our front room before the wood fire that blazed cheerfully.

The conversation was of mutual friends and memories of days at Ship Island where he and my father had been stationed as young lieutenants in the Thirty-ninth Infantry previous to the reorganization of the army in 1870. Then it veered to the Apache campaign, the habits of Apaches, the trails with which Crawford was thoroughly familiar, and of which my father was practically ignorant at that date.

Crawford said he was very tired and had hoped for a rest, that the whole problem seemed so futile. He added very slowly, "I hoped when I went down to Texas that I was through with it here, but I had to return. Somehow I have a feeling that when I go down into Mexico I will not return."

That was a mood entirely foreign to Crawford, and my parents were surprised at his words. He went on talking freely. It was a compliment for Crook to ask for him. It was not an order, but a request, and Crawford could not very well decline, though he could have done so. Two companies of friendly Indian scouts of fifty each were to be commanded by Crawford, and included Warm Springs Apaches, White Mountain, and some loyal Chiricahuas. Their orders were to follow "hot foot" after the hostiles under Geronimo, Natchez, and Mangus, until the band had been captured or surrendered unconditionally.

Lieutenant William Shipp, second lieutenant of my father's troop, had been assigned to go with Crawford, also young Lieutenant Marion P. Maus, of the First Infantry, who was stationed at Fort Grant. Lieutenant Samson Faison, also First Infantry, and one other officer, Dr. Thomas Davis, whose brother, Captain William "Bill" Davis, Jr., was in our own regiment. Captain Davis had a very powerful voice, so was nicknamed "Whispering Bill."

A second organization of a hundred Indian scouts was to be under Captain Wirt Davis (no relation to Whispering Bill or Dr. Tom Davis). Captain Wirt Davis was in the Fourth Cavalry and was to have his own troop, as well as the hundred scouts. Crawford's command was to operate in Sonora. Davis was to scout in the state of Chihuahua in Mexico, confining his activities south of the border between Arizona, New Mexico, and Mexico.

The Apaches had ducked back and forth from Mexico to Arizona, and Mexican troops pursued them to the border, but could not enter Arizona, while the U.S. forces were in the same predicament. This led to an agreement between the two countries that American soldiers, when on a "hot trail," could cross into Mexico. They would follow the plan of General Crook to keep Indian scouts under regular officers of the United States Army below the border to harass the Apaches, and force them into the arms of the Mexican soldiers, or across the border where the American soldiers could nab them.

The drawbacks were serious. Loyalty of the Indian scouts to their American officers when far from any habitation was questioned. And the fact that the majority of Mexicans in rural districts could neither read nor write, and had no knowledge of an agreement, added to their problems. The latter were distrustful and antagonistic to Americans who were in Mexico. It would be especially dangerous to try to convince them that armed Indians commanded by officers of the United States Army had no sinister aim on Mexican soil.

If any Mexican fired a shot, the Apaches might become uncontrollable and retaliate, despite the commands of their officers. Such a situation would involve national complications, the end of which could not be foretold. Captain Crawford realized this when he said good night and good-bye to us all. Four white men against a hundred armed Apaches who might turn traitor in the heart of an unfriendly country. It was a serious problem for any officer to face.

After Crawford left our quarters that night, my mother investigated as to why the dessert course had been tardy arriving at the table. The reason was frankly given by Amelia. When she went to the kitchen, which was located quite a distance from the house and reached by a porch, she found a skunk which was evidently determined to stay there. To disturb the creature or even shoot it would have ended our dinner, and certainly deprived us of the dessert which was waiting on the kitchen table.

With rare courage, Amelia dashed a bucket of water on the skunk, then seized it by its long tail, holding it downward, and carried it into the backyard while holding it at arm's length until the animal had been shot by our striker. Crawford never knew how nearly that dinner had ended without dessert.

⚜ 14 ⚜

WE JOIN FATHER
AT CAMP BONITA

Captain Crawford's command left Fort Bowie in late
November 1885. My brother and sister had gone East,
leaving my mother and me alone in our side of the Folly, as
my father was then at Camp Bonita Canyon with his troop.
My mother decided to risk a trip to his camp and eat
Thanksgiving dinner with him. Strict orders had been
issued prohibiting the families of officers or enlisted men
from visiting any camps, but my mother ignored this when
she made her plans.

She wrote to my father, telling him of her intention, and
before he received her letter, she had one from him saying
that General Crook had informed him that Bonita Canyon
was to be a permanent winter camp, and that my father's
troop, as well as Troop E of Captain Kelley's, would remain
there during the winter, scouting from that point when
advisable. Troops were stationed to guard permanent
watering places, and thus prevent the Apaches from stopping for water during their raids.

My mother at once began preparations, as the permit
included old Jenny Miller, wife of Sergeant Girard Miller
of our troop, and me. So we drove to Bonita Canyon, stopping one night at Willcox. It was twenty-seven miles from
Grant to Willcox, and about sixty-five from the fort to the
camp at Bonita Canyon which we reached the evening of

the second day. North of Camp Bonita was Apache Pass, noted for the many murders by Apaches, as it was narrow, rocky, and twisting.

The camp was sixteen miles from Fort Bowie where Crook had his headquarters. We were in a rugged narrow canyon with the two troops in tents. The stables constructed of logs and brush afforded excellent shelter for the horses. Our own quarters consisted of a two-room house, or rather one large room that opened into a lean-to. It had been built by a man who was taking up land by "squatter's rights."

That meant the ground had not yet been surveyed by the government, hence no title could be acquired except by actually living on the ground. To leave it unoccupied was an invitation for any person to take possession and thus acquire all right and title unless he, too, vacated. The fellow had gotten tired of picking up and getting into Fort Bowie because the favorite trail of the hostiles led through Apache Pass and Bonita Canyon, where there was an excellent spring of permanent water. So he gladly accepted fifty dollars from my father and moved into Fort Bowie with his wife and child.

HOME AT CAMP BONITA

The front room had a large window, wood floor, open fireplace, and mantel. The walls were covered neatly with newspapers. An open space, minus a door, led into what had been a kitchen with a dirt floor, and one tiny window that slid sideways to open. A large wall tent was erected at one side of our house, a board floor laid, and that made our dining room.

The old conical-shaped Sibley stove, placed on an earth foundation or a deep box of earth, gave ample heat in the coldest weather. Back of our dining room another wall tent was arranged for the kitchen, and beside it a smaller tent made Jenny's living quarters, also equipped with a Sibley stove.

In the small house my mother hung curtains of unbleached muslin bordered with two-inch bands of turkey-red calico. A drape of the same crossed the top of these curtains, which were caught back by bands of the plain red. Bright Navajo rugs were spread on the floor. A table with a red cover and Rochester coal oil lamp in the center of the room, comfortable chairs, and a tall screen hiding the bed made a very pleasant and attractive room, despite the newspapered walls. In fact, as only finely printed pages had been used, the effect was of mottled gray and restful.

Curtains hung at the doorless opening into my room. Hay strewn on the dirt floor was carpeted with gray army blankets, and over them a big buffalo robe. A Sibley stove stood in a deep box of earth, bed springs supported on trestles, and the trestles or sawhorses hidden by a deep flounce of bright cretonne. Boxes were arranged to form a dressing table, draped with cretonne, and my desk was a large wooden table with a cloth and big blue blotter. It was really bright and inviting, as well as comfortable.

But when the rain began, I discovered my roof leaked. The soldiers spread canvas on the roof, but the leaks persisted. Then I hit on the original plan of stretching heavy cords from side to side just below the low ceiling, and from these cords I suspended empty tomato cans. The cans had been opened by crosscuts of a hatchet and the four points bent backward from the middle. This trolley enabled me to slide the cans to any point that began to leak. I was happy and dry. But I neglected to empty the cans and failed to remember that the tin edges would fray the cord.

As a result, one night when no clouds were in sight, and no rain falling, the deluge struck me. Tin cans of muddy water simply rained on me in my bed, and roused my parents who called in alarm. I got up and surveyed the tin cans and broken strings, while dirty streams trickled over the bed clothes, my nightgown, and from my hair. The next day we strung wire across the room, and Jenny assumed the responsibility of dumping water from the cans after each rain.

It was not lonesome for me in Camp Bonita, for I had Don to ride and had discovered Louis Prue's Ranch just outside the canyon a mile from our house. Three miles farther was the Brannick Riggs Ranch, father, mother, two daughters, Rhoda and Martha, older than myself. Then there were younger children, a married son, and two other grown sons. I always found a welcome at these two places on my rides and shared many ranch dinners.

The Riggs had an old-fashioned small organ, and when it was known that I had received a first-class musical education and loved to play and sing, I was always asked to give them music. The Riggs girls were expert cowhands, but rode sidesaddles and wore long riding skirts over their other skirts. I could ride, of course, but had no experience riding after cattle before I was married. So when my father asked me to see if Mr. Riggs would "rent a cow," the old man agreed promptly, provided I would drive the cow myself, unaided, to the front door of our cabin home. The other stipulation was that I should sing and play each time I visited the Riggs Ranch. Further than that, no payment would be accepted for a first-class milk cow during the time we were in the camp.

I was delighted. The cow was turned out of the corral and I began to drive her toward the camp, a distance of three miles. Until sunset the cow and I fought. She ducked, dodged, darted, then raced, and Don, getting fractious, frequently raced ahead of her, instead of at her tail. When we reached the mouth of the canyon, she simply climbed the side, and I followed after her, determined to make her go down into camp.

It was then that Sergeant Charles Faulkner saw a cow racing on the top of the bluff, and back of it a figure with streaming hair. Knowing that I was riding by myself, Faulkner hurried to my father, saying Indians were chasing stock on top of the canyon, and maybe they had captured me. At once the order was given to saddle up, and the troop started up the steep side of the canyon, fully armed, and prepared to rescue me from the Apaches. I managed just then to make the cow start down, calling to my father not to help, or he could not have the cow.

So the soldiers and my father watched my struggles until the cow actually was in front of the house, then they took charge of her. Later I learned that old Mr. Riggs had "put up a job" on me, as he knew I was a tenderfoot. The cow had a calf. That calf was kept at the ranch, and the hardest thing any cowhand faces is to drive a solitary cow away from her calf. No one at the ranch had supposed I could succeed, but I turned the joke on them.

A STARTER OF YEAST

Yeast was another problem. Jenny's bread would not rise. The yeast cakes in the commissary at Fort Bowie were evidently stale. I spoke of the lovely bread Mrs. Prue made, and my mother instructed me to get a "starter of yeast" from Mrs. Prue.

Private Michael Finnegan, colored, had been assigned by my father to act as my bodyguard when I was riding. Finnegan bubbled with the joy of living and felt highly honored at the new duty. Twenty feet behind me and

Don, he rode. Cartridges filled the belt about his waist; the pistol and his gun were ready for service. The last cartridge, if we were surprised, Finnegan would use on me, rather than let the Apaches capture me. So one day we started for the Prue Ranch. Finnegan was carrying a small tin lard pail, with flat cover, intending to bring back the "starter of yeast."

Mrs. Prue gave it cheerfully and said something to Finnegan which I did not understand, for Don already was dashing toward the canyon and his stable. Finnegan rode after me. Don decided to race. My guard tried to keep his distance of twenty feet, which made Don go faster. Then I heard a loud report. I knew it must be Apaches shooting at us, so I kicked and whipped Don to greater speed. I dared not turn back or slacken Don's gait, though I wondered why Finnegan did not shoot. Then Finnegan's horse reached me, passed, and raced madly toward the camp.

As he passed, I had seen Finnegan bending over his saddle, brushing his hand across his eyes. Something grayish was on his face. I knew he had been shot, and felt that his brains were oozing from the wound. I beat Don with my riding whip, kicked him with my heels, and he dashed madly into the canyon.

We rushed past the stables, past the lines of tents where soldiers were running out, but I still could not see Finnegan. I expected to find his body on the ground as I rode. Turning into the open space in front of our cabin I saw Finnegan. He had dismounted and was standing in front of my parents and old Jenny, saying something.

Don reached the group, and I called out, "Oh, Finnegan, did they shoot you?" He turned with a broad grin, remnants of the gray brains still splotched his face, but he was wiping it off with his red cotton handkerchief.

"Dat yeast got lively, Miss Birdie, and it done shot off the lid of the can, and I thought you was ahead of me, so I had to catch up with you if I could."

By that time we were all hysterical, but Jenny was mad when she took the tin can that was absolutely devoid of any yeast. Neither Finnegan nor I was sent for more yeast, but Prue himself, hearing of the incident, drove down with his wife and a bucket of fresh yeast for our bread.

The Prue Ranch stood on the flat just at the bottom of the mountains where the road twisted into Apache Pass toward Fort Bowie. Mrs. Prue one day told me an incident that I have never forgotten. It was when Geronimo had just "jumped the reservation" at Fort Apache in 1885, and the news had not yet permeated Arizona where isolated ranches were numerous. Prue was absent from the ranch, leaving Mrs. Prue and a nine-year-old adopted child, Rosa, alone.

Prue had been a soldier, and another soldier, dying, had left his motherless child to Prue's care. Prue and his wife adopted the child, who was a dark-eyed, curly haired youngster, bright, pretty, and well mannered. Mrs. Prue showed me where she had seen the entire Geronimo band riding down the mountainside, and told how she had hidden Rosa in a trunk, leaving a slight space for air and a blanket tossed over the lid.

Bidding the child to remain perfectly quiet, the desperate woman stood by that window, pistol in hand, ready to fight to the last bullets, then kill the child and herself. But Geronimo did not even turn aside. He was hurrying down to the mountains in Mexico where the United States soldiers could not cross. National law prohibits it, as the Apaches were well aware.

Mrs. Prue could not believe her eyes when she saw the Apaches scurry past the ranch, then disappear toward the south. She told me that she was so weak her knees doubled up, and she fell on the floor. Finally she controlled her muscles, and called to Rosa. But the child was too frightened to lift the cover of the trunk until Mrs. Prue was able to assist.

Rosa stood beside Mrs. Prue as I heard this story. I looked out the window and pictured Geronimo's one hundred twenty-five savages riding down the trail toward the little ranch. The part that women played during those frontier Indian days has never been recorded in history, nor awarded by medals.

MY INDIAN BEAU

Camp Bonita, twelve miles as the crow flies from Fort Bowie, was the headquarters courier camp. Couriers rode with mail, official or personal, much as the old pony express riders, but soldiers of the regular army were used instead of civilians. The first stop from Fort Bowie was at our camp. Here all mail for our little settlement was left in a locked mail sack. My father had the key. The first courier took this sack back to Fort Bowie with any mail to go to General Crook, officers at any other point, or to be sent to the Southern Pacific station, Bowie, sixteen miles north of Fort Bowie.

From Camp Bonita a soldier of "H" or "E" Troop of the Tenth Cavalry rode on toward the Mexican border to the next "courier camp." So personal and official mail went on to the Mexican border, and often was carried by an Indian runner over mountains that no horses could climb and only an Indian could locate. These Apache runners were remarkable.

Sometimes they have been known to go without water for seventy-two hours in the rare atmosphere, and while moving at a rate of one hundred twenty miles during twenty-four hours. Their keen sight and training from childhood to endure hardships, and at the same time miss nothing in the way of a trail sign, made them almost invaluable.

Yet, blood is thicker than water, and officers could not place implicit confidence in their loyalty. The Chiricahuas were of the same tribe as Geronimo's band of hostiles. The White Mountain Indians were foes, but for years had been intimidated by the Chiricahuas, and knew that if Geronimo again "surrendered," as he had already done three times, the White Mountain Apaches, being on the same reservation at Fort Apache, would certainly pay dearly for aiding the soldiers.

Many times on the trail, officers felt that the scouts left "signs" for the hostiles, and in our own camp, each cartridge issued to an Indian was tallied by my father. The scouts would ask permission to go deer hunting for a day. An Indian never wastes ammunition. He will stalk his objective until so near that his shot will be fatal. The scouts did bring in deer meat, but too much ammunition was used to attain the result. So my father refused to issue any ammunition to the scouts, except when on a hot trail. Even then he tallied the cartridges each night, to prevent the Indians from burying it where the hostiles could recognize the cache from some sign that only they would understand.

Yet there were many faithful scouts. In our camp, H Troop had five San Carlos Apache scouts, while Captain Kelley's E Troop had the same number. Among them was a young Indian, about eighteen or nineteen, but all the other scouts were much older. I had not noticed this Indian until one day, as I sat on a low doorstep in front of our cabin, he seemed to actually jump out of the ground in front of me.

It did not startle me, and I saw he was smiling. In his hands he held something. Before I realized what he was doing, he laid a young rabbit in my lap and placed my hands over it, then disappeared. I called to my mother, who was inside the two-room house, and then Jenny and I fixed a box for the frightened creature. I wanted to free it, but knew the Indian might be on the watch, so we kept it until Jenny, almost at midnight, tore off the mosquito netting, and thus permitted the rabbit to escape naturally. Later this scout brought other gifts to me.

The top of a tin baking powder can, with the rim removed, had been notched evenly and a red string thrust through a perforation so I could wear the gift as a chain and pendant. Another time it was a beautifully braided chain like a man's watch chain, with slides made of black and white horsehair jerked from the tails of horses. Had my admirer been caught by the soldiers who adored their horses, he would have gotten a severe lesson.

Then one morning my mother called to me from the front room to come in and locate a bug that was making an unfamiliar sound. I hunted every possible place in the vicinity of the funny, squeaky noise, which was loudest underneath her bed in the very farthest corner. No visible insect was there. I went into my own room and examined the corner, heard the noise, but found nothing.

Poisonous insects were common acquaintances, but none of us wished one on any of us during the night. I crawled again under her bed, while she poked from my room. The little sliding window was above her head, and she investigated the cracks around it. Pushing aside the sash, she thrust out her head. I heard her call to me, and rushed to the room. She was laughing.

"It's your Indian beau," she whispered. "He's outside your window serenading you. Look out at him."

There he stood, unconscious that we had seen him. He had a queer instrument, evidently constructed by himself, and with a funny little bow made of a green twig and horsehair, he was sawing back and forth and producing the squeak that we had mistaken for a new sort of bug. As he heard us move, he looked up quickly, and saw us both laughing at him, I am sorry to say. Everything was a joke to me in those days. With sober eyes he stared at me, then at my mother, and drawing himself up with real dignity, he walked away. I have always been ashamed of that incident.

Not long afterward the soldiers of our troop, who had a baseball team and often played against Captain Kelley's troop, decided to try baseball with the Indian scouts of H Troop. Four of the Indians of our troop and some of E Troop took a real interest, and had watched the colored soldiers when the two troops played against one another.

Just above our house, toward the end of the canyon which ended in a slit so narrow that no horse could pass through, a clear space had been found where the baseball games were played. When the players had taken their places, my parents and I walked out to watch the game, for the scouts were mingled evenly with the colored soldiers.

Before the game actually began, my mother called attention to a group of scouts who were beneath a spreading oak tree. They were very hilarious over something, and kept looking back of the tree, then toward us. Suddenly two of them darted back of the tree and pushed another scout into plain view. It was my Indian beau. The other scouts were convulsed with mirth and pointed to us. Then we understood.

My beau had discarded the usual scout's apparel, and was arrayed in the uniform of a soldier. He had a brand new suit of the regulation army blue worn by an enlisted man, a white shirt and collar, four-in-hand red necktie with black polka dots, and was wearing the same kind of shoes that were issued to the soldiers.

He stood there the picture of misery, while Indians and soldiers shouted together. But, at last, he drew himself up, and ignoring the soldiers and the other Indians, he looked steadily at my parents and me. There was no smile this time. With a little tug at the blouse, exactly like the young officers who almost invariably jerked the wrinkles from their coats when they stood up, the Indian turned and walked past us, with an absolutely perfect imitation of a West Point graduate.

This episode, and fearing the ridicule of the soldiers as well as the other nine Indians might cause resentment, caused my father to "swap" my Indian beau for another scout shortly after the baseball game that day. He had never made any attempt to approach me except when I was very close to our cabin, and then only to give me a present.

WE WAIT FOR NEWS

Officers coming and going to other camps or commands from Bowie or down below the border to Mexico always stopped at Camp Bonita, and usually had time for a talk with my father, or a simple lunch in our tent dining room. So I heard the Apache campaign discussed freely from the angle of the officers who were actively engaged. Couriers carrying the mailbags retailed unofficial information to the enlisted soldiers, and this was told to Jenny, or Sergeant Miller, her husband. Consequently, Jenny retold it to us while she was cleaning up and my father was down at the stables, or some other daily duty in the soldiers' part of camp.

Thick brushwood gave privacy to our own location, but often at night we would hear the men singing; then my father and I would sneak through the brush and get close enough to see the colored soldiers sitting around a huge campfire, talking, laughing, and singing. H Troop had a fine quartet, as one of the men, Jenny's husband, had a magnificent bass voice, and had sung with professional colored singers before he enlisted.

The effect of those voices, often in full chorus, the uniformed figures grouped around the campfire, above them towering the rocky sides of the narrow canyon, and higher the brilliant Arizona stars, or moonlight so intense that one could actually read ordinary print, formed a picture that has never faded in my memory.

The jokes, laughable conversations, and the music would have been instantly silenced had the men suspected that the "Captain and Miss Birdie" were hiding in the brush, listening. Yet at any moment those carefree soldiers of the Tenth would change to grim fighters at the sound of a bugle call, "Boots and Saddles." Their fighting qualities had made a record for the entire regiment, and the Fighting Tenth never failed their officers.

Into our camp came news that Captain Wirt Davis with his troop of the Fourth Cavalry and one hundred Indian scouts had surprised the Apaches in their camp near Nácori, Sonora. Soon after that we heard of another fight between the Indians and the Fourth Cavalry, aided by seventy-eight Indian scouts. Then followed a meager account regarding an encounter between the scouts under Captain Crawford and the subchief Chihuahua in which Chihuahua and fifteen squaws had been captured.

Back and forth, like threads of a great shuttle, the campaign was waged in Arizona, New Mexico, and Mexico. Soldiers, horses, Indian scouts, troops of Mexicans in Mexico, each making strenuous efforts in a common cause—the capture and subjugation of the Chiricahua Apaches, who for generations harassed and dominated even the other Indians of that section.

Forty-three companies of United States Infantry and forty troops of cavalry, in addition to the Indian scouts who had been enlisted for six months' term, endured hardships and privations, exposure to intense heat and extreme cold, with such slight advantages that the result was practically negligible. The ranchers and citizens, as well as the newspapers of Arizona, were vitriolic in their abuse of the soldiers and officers.

Insinuations grew to statements that the army was not trying to catch the Apaches, and were permitting them to kill, steal, and plunder in Arizona. Officers were infuriated at the injustice of the public opinion, for well they knew the herculean work that was being done to end the campaign and punish the Apaches.

Stories of raids, murders, and plundering of ranches below the Mexican border kept "the pot boiling," as the officers expressed it. Captain Crawford was down in the Bavispe Valley of Mexico in the middle of December, constantly on the alert to avoid complications between the Mexicans in small primitive, isolated settlements, and the Indian scouts to whom they willingly sold mescal. Most of these Mexicans had been terrorized by the Apaches for years, and had heard stories from former generations regarding Apache atrocities, so they were more than ready to exterminate any Indian if conditions were favorable.

This in addition to the tremendous physical strain on Crawford in his already exhausted condition, and the fact that it would be due to his personal influence if the Chiricahuas surrendered if found, added to the anxiety and responsibility of an officer who already was hardly able to keep on his feet. The other officers, Lieutenants Maus and Shipp, tried to lighten Crawford's duties, but the march had to be maintained over unbroken country, through tortuous canyons, and up mountains that were almost perpendicular. Water, too, was often hard to find. But Crawford was a true soldier. As long as he could drag himself along, he made no complaint.

How do I know? We knew the man himself. Lieutenant Shipp was second lieutenant of my father's troop on detached service. And finally, Lieutenant Marion P. Maus was personally known to us, and had been stationed at Fort Grant before Crawford took his last dinner there in our home.

Back and forth rode the couriers between the troops and Indian scouts in Mexico, through Camp Bonita and the bloodstained Apache Pass into Fort Bowie, field head-quarters of General George Crook, commander of the Department of Arizona. At times my father's troop, and the troop of Captain Kelley, mounted hurriedly and rode in response to news that the hostiles had been seen in a certain vicinity. Then my mother, Jenny, and I were left alone in Camp Bonita until the troops returned.

Christmas of 1885 came and went. New Year's was uneventful. Winter rain storms pounded our tents and the little two-room cabin, and then we thought of the fine men whom we knew were exposed to the cold, wind, and rain. Their beds were the rough soaking earth, saddles became pillows, and often with a minimum supply of rations, foot sore, and with no certainty of how long they must go on. Yet at daybreak, they were up and ready to press forward.

That was the stamina of those officers and men when the regular United States Army of the frontier Indian days gave heart and soul and every ounce of strength in their bodies for the "Good of the service, and the honor of the regiment."

READING NEWSPAPERS

During the evening at Camp Bonita, when all our maga-zines and newspapers had been read and reread, my father and I had two unfailing sources of amusement while my mother knitted or did fancy work. One was a series of games of bezique, the old French variety which required four decks of cards and a score of two thousand points. So only one game could be played before bedtime. We kept a careful record, and our excitement at times was so noisy that my mother would have to suppress us.

Another entertainment was derived from the walls of the room which were covered with newspapers from the top of the wall to the floor. My father and I tried to outvie one another with tidbits of news. Often I would climb onto a chair to read some fresh item located near the ceiling, and after I had read it aloud, would turn to see my father's six-foot, two-inch frame flattened on the floor as he answered my challenge by saying, "That's not new. I read that long ago, but here's something you have missed." Then he would triumphantly read an item located at the junction of the wall and floor.

We were constantly playing pranks on one another, and always swapping jokes. One pleasant December day, my mother and I decided to take a short walk while my father was superintending the men at stables. A fine box of candies had arrived for me at camp, but as I already had a partially eaten box, I refused to start eating the new one, though my father eyed it hungrily. I had hidden the new box in my "dresser" under a shelf for towels and covered by cretonne curtains.

The walk was extended, but when we returned, my father was not in the room, and we supposed he was down at the troop. I went into my little room to put away wrap and hood, when I saw Midget, our tiny black dog, half under the flounce of cretonne that hid the supports of my crude bed. Midget's tail protruded and that tail was wagging hysterically.

I stooped, lifted the flounce, and understood the situation at once, calling to my mother, "There's a man hiding under my bed!" She cried out in alarm, but I grabbed a broom and began poling viciously, as I said, "Get out of there, you scoundrel. Get out at once." My mother hovered in the door opening, while I poked at the man.

"Hold on, Buck," my father pleaded. "I'll come out. I only took one little piece from the box."

Midget came out, too, licking his chops, as my father meekly handed me my new box of candy, and was sentenced to eat the candy in the old box while Mama and I would eat every piece in the new box. And that sentence was fully carried out.

⚛15⚛

WORD COMES OF CAPTAIN
CRAWFORD IN MEXICO

It was the last week in January 1886. My parents and I were seated in our front room of our little cabin where a huge log in the fireplace gave warmth and cheer. A frightful storm of wind and rain that was mixed with sleet had been raging all day and the previous night and still continued. Aided by the striker, Jenny had served our meals in the cabin so that we would not have to go outside, even for a few paces to the dining tent. Any ordinary rain storm we considered a joke, as we scurried under umbrellas between the cabin and our canvas dining room.

The clock struck nine, and my father, according to his invariable custom, rose to wind it, saying as usual, "When I wind the clock it is time to go to bed." But he turned and looked toward the closed door. My mother and I had also heard above the din of the storm the hoof beats of a galloping horse. We knew that no troop horses were permitted out of the stables without a written order from my father to the stable guard, stating the exact time the man and horse must return, and if not back at the specified hour, the stable guard was obliged to immediately report to my father.

No order had been issued that day for any man or horse to leave camp. In fact, no soldier wanted to get away from his comfortable tent and face the elements. Our first thought was that a messenger was bringing word of Indians somewhere, and that the soldiers would have to saddle and pick up the trail at once. The horse stopped at the door. We waited for a knock or a voice, but heard nothing except the storm beating on the window and door. Lighting a glassed lantern, which he used when he went to the soldiers' camp after dark on inspection, father opened the door slightly, for the rain and sleet dashed into the room.

Nothing was visible at first, then in a flash of lightning he saw a riderless horse cowering in the storm. At once he handed me the lantern. "Stand back of the door and hold the lantern so I can see what man has been taking his horse out in this storm without my permission."

He flung his rubber coat over his shoulders and went out. I watched him. It was not a troop horse with a McClellan saddle, but a small cow pony with a high-horned Visalia common to Arizona and California. My father walked around the horse, then shouted, and immediately voices replied from the soldiers' tents.

Men came running. I held the lantern as the colored soldiers lifted an unconscious white man from the ground and carried him into the room where he was placed in a large reclining chair. The pony was led to the stables, and Jenny, aroused, came into the door. My mother was at the emergency medicine chest, pouring a little French brandy into a glass. Jenny hurried to make coffee.

The man was exhausted. The brandy, forced between his lips, stimulated him and the heat from the open fire reached his body, for his clothing was saturated, and he was numb from the cold. As we stood about him, wondering what had brought him to our door, his eyes were opened slowly, and as he saw us, he turned to my father. "Captain Crawford is dead." For a few seconds no one spoke. The news was a shock.

"Did his scouts turn on him, or was it Geronimo's band?" my father said.

"Neither. He was talking to Mexican soldiers and under a flag of truce, when one of the Mexicans shot him in the head."

So came the news of our dear friend, my father's comrade in youth, and the dear "Guard of Honor" who had carried me in his arms when I was a baby at Ship Island, and who had guided my first steps and heard my first attempt to speak. Killed while talking under a flag of truce. Each of us remembered his words that night in our home at Fort Grant: "If I go down there, I have a feeling that I will never come back."

The courier drank the hot coffee and ate the warm food Jenny brought and arranged on our center table. After the man had eaten, he gave a few details, saying, "I was not with them, but I am carrying the news from Lieutenant Maus to General Crook at Fort Bowie, and I must go on at once if you will give me a fresh horse. I have ridden day and night, and got relay horses at ranches as I came along."

My father remonstrated, and said he would at once send two soldiers with the reports, but the courier had better rest a few hours. The man refused. "I promised I would go through myself," he said.

So old Jake, the easiest riding horse of H Troop, was led up, and two soldiers ordered to accompany the man. He got up to his feet with an effort, but when he tried to mount, he could not get into the saddle. I held the lantern once more, as my father and the two soldiers lifted the man to Jake's back. "I can ride if I can only get on the horse," he said.

They rode away in the storm. The courier was bent over and swaying, but the soldiers rode closely at either side of old Jake, and their outstretched arms were supporting the courier. We three watched from the doorway in spite of the storm, and for a short distance the light from the lantern silhouetted their figures against the night. Then the shadows closed down on them, as the darker shadow had closed down on Captain Crawford in the wild, isolated mountains of Mexico.

TRAGEDY IN MEXICO

Details of the tragedy came to us later. Crawford's command had crossed the Aros River and dragged toward the *Espinosa del Diablo*—the Devil's Spine—where the sharp peaks had the appearance of jagged spines. It was frightfully cold in the high altitude, making it hard to sleep at night, for each man had but one blanket. The trail was easy to follow, for the hostiles were so sure no white man could find them in that section that they took no pains to cover their own trails.

On the ninth of January, a hard day's march ended at sunset, but Noche, who was sergeant major of the Indian scouts, hurried back with news to be cautious. Noche and Dutchy were excited and announced that Geronimo was encamped twelve miles ahead of Crawford's command, but on a high and almost inaccessible ridge. Though all the men were tired and cold, Crawford dared not permit a campfire, even to make hot coffee or cook food. The smoke would betray their presence to Geronimo's band. Hard bread and raw bacon, twenty minutes' rest, then they pressed on in spite of exhaustion, cold, and the darkness of an impending storm.

In narrating this incident, both Lieutenant Maus and Lieutenant Shipp told how Crawford, worn with exhaustion and almost too weak to crawl along, doggedly kept behind the Indian scout, Noche, over trails that led up and down jagged mountainsides, with rocks that cut through the moccasins that the officers were wearing, so that their feet might make no noise and betray their presence. At dawn they reached Geronimo's camp. But in order to cover the twelve miles, it had been necessary to actually travel eighteen, and everyone in that command was on foot.

As they completed their arrangements to take the camp entirely by surprise, a burro brayed, and warned the sleeping Chiricahuas. At once the hostile Apaches fired. Crawford's command sent volleys into the camp, but the fog was heavy, the rocks afforded hiding spots, and the hostiles slipped out of sight and sound. Thousands of huge boulders aided the Indians under Geronimo and Natchez to effect their escape, but the camp, with its pony herd, ammunition, and food supplies, were in Crawford's possession, while the fleeing Apaches were without the actual necessities of life, and no ponies to help them evade the Indians with Crawford.

The officers understood Apache tactics, and felt no surprise when they saw a squaw making signs. She brought a message from the two leaders of the hostiles that they wanted to talk, and she asked for food. That was a usual procedure under such circumstances. Food was sent by her and arrangements were made for a talk the next day. While the worn-out party rested by the campfire, one Indian scout kept on guard. He distrusted Geronimo and was listening for the least sound that might mean an attack on the camp by the hostiles.

When he heard a suspicious sound of approaching feet, he gave the alarm and the scouts began their shrill war cries. Crawford and Maus could not distinctly see the figures, but as Captain Wirt Davis was operating below the border, they concluded his command had found the same and was approaching. The officers reached a high point and were looking down at the advancing command when a volley of shots was fired and dropped three scouts. At once, Crawford's scouts hid in the rocks and opened fire on the men below them.

Crawford and Maus were confident the newcomers were the command of Captain Wirt Davis, so shouted the order to "Cease firing!" The scouts obeyed. Then about thirteen Mexican soldiers left the main force and approached. Crawford did not speak Spanish, but Maus and Tom Horn, chief of scouts, spoke it, and to them fell the obligation of talking with Major Mauricio Corredor, who commanded the Mexicans. The American officers stood in front of Major Corredor and his companion, a young lieutenant named Juan de la Cruz. Near them was the group of thirteen Mexicans, and some distance away the rest of the Mexicans awaited developments.

Maus explained the situation, and the danger of a clash seemed to be passed, but the scouts, hidden in the rocks, were not satisfied. Their keen eyes had seen another party of Mexicans crawling toward the place where Crawford was standing with Maus and the two Mexican officers. Crawford, noticing the situation, called to his scouts, "Don't shoot!" Maus and Horn echoed the command in Spanish, so did the two Mexican officers facing their own men.

One shot sounded. Then volleys fired. Major Corredor fell, Lieutenant de la Cruz started to run, but went down with thirteen bullets in his body. A group of Mexicans tried to find shelter back of a sapling, but bullets from Crawford's loyal scouts perforated the tree and killed every Mexican back of it. When order had been enforced, many men were dead, Tom Horn was wounded in the left arm, and Crawford was nowhere in sight.

Maus found him lying back of a boulder with a red handkerchief over his face. That handkerchief belonged to Dutchy and had been worn as a band about the Indian's head. It meant that Dutchy was a scout and loyal to his pledge. Dutchy had placed the handkerchief over the face of his fallen commander, and was standing on guard with arms folded across his breast.

When Maus lifted the handkerchief, he saw that Crawford was not yet dead, though part of his brains oozed down and spattered the rock. More shots sounded, and Lieutenant Maus, now in command, hastened to prevent more bloodshed. The Mexicans were double his own forces and were better armed. Maus's ammunition had been heavily depleted in the fight with Geronimo and then with the Mexicans. For two hours the engagement continued sporadically.

Owing to someone's blunder, Crawford's command had left Fort Bowie with Lieutenant Samuel Faison, of the First Infantry, in command of the pack train. Later it was discovered that Faison's men, who carried .50-caliber guns, were supplied with only .45-caliber ammunition in the heart of a country that was antagonistic to Americans, and especially American soldiers who were in that country.

Dr. Tom Davis had been ill and lagged behind, so it was not until late that afternoon that he joined Maus. Crawford was still breathing, though unconscious, and death was possible at any moment. The next morning he still lingered and it was decided by the officers to attempt to get Crawford to the Mexican border, if it could be accomplished with that terrible wound in his head.

A litter, or travois, made of willows bound with canvas was being made when some Mexicans approached and told Maus they wanted to talk with him. A furious storm had begun, and Maus was invited to step under the shelter of an overhanging ledge. There he was confronted by fifty armed Mexicans who demanded his papers, used insulting terms, and called him a marauder.

The Mexicans had no authoritative leader and were of the common grade of illiterate peons or worse. The situation was acute, but Maus had instructed Lieutenant Shipp to fire on the Mexicans regardless of himself if the Mexicans held him prisoner.

At this time old Geronimo, realizing that Crawford was dead or badly wounded, signaled to Crawford's scouts that they would help them thrash the Mexicans. The war cries of the scouts, added to those of Geronimo's followers, caused the Mexicans to change their plans and release Lieutenant Maus. Crawford was shot on January 11, and the first day's march covered only two or three miles. Over narrow, rocky defiles, across streams that were swollen from the recent rains, up and down steep mountains, they carried Crawford in the travois.

The first night of this march an Apache woman came into camp and said that Geronimo wanted to talk. Maus met him early the next day about two miles on the trail, and taking a white man, Tom Horn, who could interpret the Indian language, went without arms as Geronimo had stipulated. Geronimo and Natchez failed to materialize, but another warrior was there. Once more Maus was told to come without arms the following day.

Geronimo, Natchez, Nana, and Chihuahua, all of the chiefs, appeared fully armed. With them were fourteen warriors each fully armed and wearing belts of cartridges. They had agreed to come unarmed, as Maus had agreed to do, but only he was now unarmed. The Indians squatted in a circle, with Geronimo in front. His gun was held upright, but eventually Geronimo agreed to meet General Crook near San Bernardino on the border in two moons.

Hampered by high streams and by hamlets populated with unfriendly Mexicans suspicious of the command, Maus went on until January 17, but Crawford had shown no sign of consciousness during that interval. On that date while Maus was sitting beside Crawford, the wounded officer suddenly opened his eyes and looked straight at Maus, and pressed the hand Maus was holding. He could not speak, though Maus tried to obtain a word, and assured him that he would take care of him and his affairs.

Crawford shook his head, reached out his arm, and drew Maus to him, then became unconscious. The next day he died. There was no struggle. In fact, no one knew when he slipped away. He had said to us at Fort Grant that he was so tired and wanted to rest, that he felt if he went into Mexico he would not return.

But he did come back. Maus and the others carried his body as they marched on that awful trail. Wrapped in canvas, they placed him on a pack mule to the Sátachi River, but it was too high to cross over. A day went by, but the body of Crawford had begun to decompose, so when they crossed the river a day later and reached Nácori, it was necessary to bury him there.

So wrapped in canvas, and placed in a crude coffin constructed by the officers from four rough slabs of wood, Captain Emmet Crawford, our dear friend, was left to rest until his body could be claimed and removed to an honored grave in the country he had served so loyally from 1861, until he gave his life for it in the lonely mountains of Mexico. Today he sleeps in Arlington National Cemetery. Near him lie officers who shared his hardships in the Civil War and the regular army of the frontier days.

After the death of Captain Crawford and his temporary burial at Nácori, Mexico, Lieutenant Maus reached Lang's Ranch in the Los Animas Valley near the Mexican border on February 1. The command had covered a thousand miles on foot to that date. The scouts were dissatisfied and eager to get to their own camps, but four days later orders were received for them all to return to Mexico, and remain on alert for signals from Geronimo's band as had been agreed upon. It was March 15 when the signal was seen from a high peak.

GERONIMO MEETS GENERAL CROOK

Maus went out with several scouts and twenty miles from the rest of the command encountered messengers sent by Geronimo and Natchez. The balance of the hostiles were still forty miles distant, but it was agreed they would all come to Maus's camp. Accordingly on March 19, the entire band of hostile Indians under Geronimo and Natchez camped a half-mile from Maus and his command, but refused to go into Fort Bowie and surrender to General Crook. However, they agreed to proceed with Maus to a point twelve miles below the border at Cañon de los Embudos.

General Crook had been notified and reached Maus's camp on March 25 to talk with Geronimo, who had daily inquired when the general would be there. Crook had a talk with the Apaches, who agreed to surrender. Afterwards, Crook ordered Maus to bring the Apaches into Fort Bowie. Probably all would have gone as planned had not the Apaches obtained mescal from a rancher and bootlegger nearby, and started to fight among themselves as they were still in possession of all their arms and ammunition.

Lieutenant Shipp was ordered to destroy all the mescal at the ranch where the Apaches had been buying the liquor, and the trouble ceased. But the next morning, March 30, it was found that Geronimo and Natchez, with nineteen warriors, thirteen women, and six children, had vanished. At once Maus and Shipp picked up the trail, while Faison, commanding a detail, took the remaining seventy-seven

Apache prisoners—including Chihuahua, Nana, and Jolsanny—to Fort Bowie. It was found impossible to follow the trail of the hostiles, as it scattered and was lost when the Apaches avoided stepping on the dirt, but moved from rock to rock.

So the command under Maus had no alternative but to return to Fort Bowie which they reached on April 3. Then followed an official situation that was bitter. General Sheridan in one official telegram (I have the exact copies of all the telegrams passing between Sheridan and Crook during this crucial time) said, "Your dispatch of yesterday received. It has occasioned great disappointment. It seems strange that Geronimo and party could have escaped without the knowledge of the scouts."

Later Sheridan telegraphed, "You have in your department forty-three companies of infantry and forty troops of cavalry, and ought to be able to do a good deal with such a force. Please send me a statement of what you contemplate for the future."

On April 1 Crook wired Sheridan, "As I have spent nearly eight years of the hardest work of my life in this department, I respectfully request that I may now be relieved from its command."

From Washington on April 2 came the telegram to Crook. "General Miles has been ordered to relieve you in command of the Department of Arizona and orders issued today. Advise General Miles where you will be."

From Fort Bowie on April 3, Crook wired Miles at Fort Leavenworth: "Adjutant General of the Army telegraphs that you have been directed to relieve me in command of Department of Arizona. Shall remain at Fort Bowie. When can I expect you here?"

Through whispered rumors, officers and soldiers realized the official upheaval before General Miles arrived at

Fort Bowie on April 12, 1886, to relieve General Crook from command of the Department. Out in camp we were vitally interested, and my father cogitated as to what steps would be taken by General Miles to carry on the campaign against Geronimo and Natchez, who remained quiescent somewhere after they had slipped away from Maus's command, breaking their promises to surrender to Crook at Fort Bowie.

Miles arrived on April 12 and on the 20th my father received a copy of orders similar to that sent to every other officer in the Department of Arizona. Briefly, it meant that troops were to guard all waterholes, while other troops were to take up the trail of the hostiles and keep on that trail until relieved by another troop, or until men and horses were completely exhausted.

We were still in Camp Bonita with my father, and as the campaign under General Miles developed force, officers passing through our camp would talk enthusiastically of the new vigor in the work. Miles waited for Geronimo to make the first move, thereby betraying the location of the renegade Apaches. At last it came.

⚜ 16 ⚜

THE GERONIMO CAMPAIGN,
LIEUTENANT CLARKE,
AND GENERAL MILES

In the middle of April 1886, depredations were reported in Mexico near the border of Arizona. Then the Apaches drove across and on April 27 they reached the A. L. Peck Ranch in the Santa Cruz Valley near Nogales, Arizona. The ranch was attacked. Mrs. Peck and her youngest child were tortured to death, while Peck was bound to a fence post and forced to watch his wife and child slowly die.

Peck became temporarily insane and was freed by the Apaches, who have a superstitious awe of the insane, believing they have been touched by the Great Spirit, who will avenge any injury to that person. Cowboys employed on the ranch were also killed, and then the Apaches went on their way carrying Peck's niece, age twelve, their prisoner. Troops were ordered in immediate pursuit.

Before the attack on the Peck Ranch, my father, with his troop and Captain Kelley's E Troop, were ordered over to the Mowry Mine, which had been attacked. After they reached there and buried the men killed by the Apaches, they continued scouting after the renegade Indians. Thus my mother, Jenny, and I were left alone in Camp Bonita with one colored soldier. Sergeant Charles Faulkner was very old. He had almost finished twenty years' service. A mule was sick and Faulkner was doctoring it, as well as in charge of the property in the camp, which could not be left without protection.

We had no thought of danger, and when Faulkner suggested that he would bring his blankets to the kitchen tent for the night, it rather amused my mother, Jenny, and me. That night Jenny brought her bedding into the house and slept in my back room, while I shared my mother's room in the front of mine. We slept serenely and were eating breakfast in our tent dining room, when Faulkner scratched at the tent flap, which was closed together.

His white head and wrinkled black face appeared between the parted canvas, but his face was ashy gray, his eyes popping wide.

"Fo' Gawd," he exclaimed. "I wuz afeered to come up dis mawnin'. I thought you all was daid."

It was our turn to stare. We believed the old man had become suddenly demented. Then he told us that a trail of unshod ponies had been made during the night, right between our cabin and the empty tents of the two troops. We saw that trail. It was a big one. Evidently the Apaches had made a short cut through the canyon, which had been their usual trail for years, and had been surprised at seeing the tents of two troops. They did not investigate the tents, but sneaked out of the place as quietly as they possibly could.

It certainly would have resulted in a horrible tragedy had the Indians learned that those lines of tents were vacant, and only old Sergeant Faulkner was there to protect the wife and daughter of an officer of the Tenth Cavalry, and old Jenny Miller, wife of Sergeant Miller. But the news of the Peck massacre went like wild fire over the country, and the soldiers followed it like hounds on a trail. My father decided it would be better for my mother and me to return to Fort Grant, as at any hour the soldiers might be ordered out from Camp Bonita, and we would be left alone again.

A LOST LETTER

I must now go back to an incident that was not a part of the official records of the Geronimo campaign, and yet that outbreak of Geronimo was pivotal in the outcome. After Lieutenant Clarke had said good-bye, or rather *au revoir* at the sycamore tree on Grant Creek, he had been on duty patrolling the Mexican border. It was shortly after he had left Fort Grant that the wife of an officer of our own regiment informed me that I had mistaken his attitude, and that consequently he had volunteered for field service.

I was very much a child and also very proud, but still could hardly credit what she said. However, I did not keep my promise to write to him, determined that he must be the one to write first. Later when we met, both of us were able to grasp the situation properly, but that was three years after I had been married.

While at Camp Bonita, Dr. Peter Egan came to inspect the camp at intervals, and one day he told me that Lieutenant Clarke had sent a message to me by himself. That he had been dangerously ill at Fort Bowie, and as soon as he was off "sick report," he would come to the camp. Dr. Egan asked if I had any message, and all my wounded pride flared up, so I replied politely, "Tell him I am glad he is recovering. That is all."

Dr. Egan eyed me sharply, but I looked steadily at him, and he drove away from the camp in the buckboard drawn by two very fast mules. After he had gone, I wrote a hasty note, addressing it to Powhatan and sealing the envelope, then I had Don saddled and rode after the doctor. But I had wasted time, writing and getting ready. He was too far for me to catch.

Outside the canyon about a mile away was the Prue Ranch. When I realized that I could not overtake Dr. Egan, I rode to the ranch. Prue, who had formerly been a soldier, was up working on the windmill, and climbed down. I told him I had missed Dr. Egan, and asked if Prue were going into Fort Bowie soon. He said he was going the next day to see about his hay contract, and would take my message then.

I had enclosed my note in an addressed envelope, but the larger outer envelope had no address. So Prue handed me a pencil from his vest pocket, and on it I wrote the name of Dr. Egan. I thought that if Prue did not see Egan personally, he could leave the note at the hospital for Dr. Egan, who I was sure would deliver the sealed envelope and the message it contained.

For several weeks I daily expected a reply, or that Lieutenant Clarke would ride into our camp. Then I decided that my information had been correct. In my note I had referred to the talk at the sycamore tree, and told what had been said to me as to his reason for volunteering for field duty. That if I did not hear from him, or he did not come to the camp, I would take the silence as confirmation of what had been told me as to his attitude.

No word came in reply. We went back to Fort Grant, and on May 4, 1886, I was married to another man. The day before my wedding, down in the Pinito Mountains of Sonora, Mexico, Captain Lebo's Troop K, of which Powhatan Clarke was second lieutenant, had a fight in a rocky canyon while following the Indians who had captured the little Peck girl.

During the fight, Corporal Edward Scott was badly wounded and unable to escape as the Apaches, behind boulders, made him a target for their bullets as he lay help-less on the ground. Then Lieutenant Clarke dashed to the side of the Negro soldier without thought of his own dan-ger, and carried the man to a place of safety. Later a Medal of Honor was awarded him for that daring deed. The res-cue took place on May 3, the day before I was married.

We did not meet again until December 24, 1889, when I was visiting the Hooker Ranch where my father-in-law and his wife resided. My little girl was then almost three, my boy a year and a half old. The Tenth Cavalry had a reunion at Fort Grant, and four young officers—Charles Grierson, James Watson, Alexander Dade, and Clarke—all of the Tenth Cavalry, learning I was at the ranch ten miles from the garrison, rode over with invitations for Mrs. Henry Hooker, Mrs. Ida Stewart (my sister-in-law), and myself, to attend the dance and stay overnight as the guests of Miss Bessie Dwyer, who had charge of the two Nordstrom girls while Captain and Mrs. Charles Nordstrom were absent in the East.

Powhatan elected himself my escort that night, and between dances we tried to puzzle out what had happened to my note, which he had never received, and his note that had never reached me, asking me to write. The statement as to his reason for applying for field duty had been with-out any foundation, and he said that he was sure I under-stood, "and would wait for him to come back." It was a frank talk on both sides, and we understood each other perfectly. The next morning I went back to the ranch, and then to Los Angeles. He returned to his station at Fort Thomas, and we never saw one another again, but I heard from him by letters at intervals.

On July 21, 1893, in the Little Big Horn River near Fort Custer, Montana, the soldiers had been practicing swimming their horses, and a number of officers of the Tenth Cavalry were supervising the drill, among them Lieutenant Clarke and his friend and classmate, Lieutenant Jim Hughes. Powhatan passed him as he was lying on the ground, rather the worse for a kick his horse had given him while in the water. Powhatan asked if he were sick, and then went on, saying: "I'm going in once more, then I'll go on."

A few seconds later a soldier cried out in alarm. Lieutenant Hughes and the other officers, who had sent the troops back to the garrison, sprang to their feet. Though there were a number of officers swimming around under water, the swift current carried the half-conscious Clarke away. Hughes caught his wrist, but it was wrenched from his grasp. Two hours later the body was recovered. Cuts on the head, and examination of the place where he had taken his dive, showed that he had struck in shallow water on jagged rocks in the riverbed at that point.

The loss of his dearest friend and classmate was not only a shock, but a lasting sorrow to Lieutenant Hughes. I can say the same thing for myself, but I was glad that conversation had taken place at Fort Grant on Christmas Eve, 1889, during the reunion dance of the old regiment, and that we had understood one another, but "played the game squarely," to the end.

When my daughter was nine years old we were living at Willcox. Louis Prue, the rancher, was thrown from his horse near Bonita Canyon where our camp had been located. His wife sold the ranch and one day came to see me. She handed me a yellow envelope, with pencil address that was almost illegible. It had been opened. In it was another opened envelope, and the note I had expected Dr. Egan would deliver to Lieutenant Clarke.

It had been thrust into a pigeon hole of Prue's desk, and there it had remained until his death when his widow discovered it. Not knowing what it contained, and unable to decipher the penciled name, she opened the letter. Fort Bowie had long since been abandoned, and only ruins of the garrison remained. She did not know where to send the letter, because she was aware that Lieutenant Clarke was dead, and as she had known me when I had lived at Camp Bonita, she drove almost forty miles to place that note in my hands.

And Dr. Egan, who was stationed at Fort Custer when Powhatan was drowned, never knew of the note I had expected him to give to the young officer for me. So the story ended. But I have never forgotten, and I know that he, too, always remembered the old sycamore tree up Grant Creek, and the monogram he had carved the day I promised to "come back to our tree."

That was forty-three years ago. I was just past eighteen and he was twenty-three. The fast-trotting mules, and Mr. Prue's forgetfulness that day, changed the course of both our lives, as well as influencing others.

GENERAL MILES TAKES CONTROL

A plan conceived by General Miles to establish heliograph stations in New Mexico and Arizona was carried out. Fourteen stations in Arizona and thirteen in New Mexico were set up to flash messages over distant mountains and inaccessible canyons, and thus enable troops in the field to cooperate intelligently, though far apart. Heliographs had never before been used in America.

They originated in India, and General Miles had become interested when he had seen the instrument in Washington. He considered the conditions of Arizona, New Mexico, and Mexico almost identical with that of India in climate, clarity of air, temperature, dryness, as well as sandy stretches and mountains that were practically unscalable.

During the expeditions against the Sioux, he had made the Indians grasp the fact that the telegraph, telephones, and railroads were allies of the soldiers against the Indians. A demonstration with telephones caused the Indians to call it the "whispering spirit," and realize that there was something they could not comprehend or kill. Their superstitious awe of things beyond their knowledge invested it with supernatural power. He was right in his supposition about the value of the heliograph.

My mother and I had returned to Fort Grant from Camp Bonita, but my father and his troop remained there on duty. General Miles was planning details of his intensive campaign and no one could tell when or where the first blow would be struck at the hostiles. My wedding had been set for May 4, 1886, at Fort Grant, with only the immediate families present, as my father did not expect to be able to leave his command to come to Fort Grant.

Then the unexpected happened. One of the officers stationed at Fort Bowie, which Miles used as field headquarters after General Crook had been relieved, told General Miles of my approaching wedding, and of my mother and myself having been at Camp Bonita for the past several months. Thus General Miles learned that my father had not even asked permission to go to Grant and be present at the wedding. The result was that my father received an order from General Miles to turn his troop over to another officer and proceed to Fort Grant to reach there May 2.

This was the first of many kindly acts of General Miles, and at once won my loyal friendship. When my father arrived, he told us that H Troop was to move to Fort Apache, so would follow him to Grant under Lieutenant Matthias Day of the Ninth Cavalry. My mother and I were sitting alone on the porch of the Folly that evening, both of us rather unhappy because my father would not be with us, and as my brother and sister were in the East at school, my mother and I would have no blood connection at the ceremony, and afterward she would be left alone.

An ambulance was driven to our door, and to our surprise and joy, my father hurried up the steps and told of the kindness of General Miles, for my father had not even thought of asking to be granted leave for two days because of the critical condition of the Indian situation at that time.

GOOD-BYE TO MY TROOP

A very informal ceremony followed at noon of May 4, and Mr. Edwin Russell Hooker and I started to Willcox, twenty-seven miles southwest to catch the eastbound Southern Pacific train which was due around five in the afternoon. The Hooker trotters were famous, the day clear, and road excellent. At a distance halfway to Willcox, I saw a troop of cavalry coming toward us, and finally realized that it was my father's troop.

I did not know the officer in command, but the soldiers recognized me. Just then I noticed Prince, my spotted black and white cur, and Hector, the pointer, so I called to them. Instantly the two dogs bolted toward the buggy, yelping hysterically. Prince scrambled between the wheels and up across my lap, crying with delight, and licking my face wherever he was able to touch it with his tongue.

Hector, unable to reach me over Prince's big sprawling body, managed to climb halfway across the dash, back of the legs of the nervous team. It was a ticklish situation, but I pushed Prince to the ground and got out of the buggy, then Hector ran to me.

While I was almost mangled by the two affectionate animals, the troop had halted, and the soldiers, dismounted, crowded about me. Sergeant Finnegan led my horse, Don, so that I could see that he was all right, and Don poked at my hand, but I had not the usual lump of sugar that day. Each soldier of the troop shook hands with me, and I know that some of them had tears in their eyes.

At that moment the officer, who had stopped his horse at a short distance, rode back, and lifting his campaign hat, said, "I am sure you must be Miss Cooper. I am Lieutenant Day of the Ninth Cavalry. I served with the Tenth Cavalry for almost a year after graduating from the Academy."

The men stepped back, but he left my side and turned to speak to Mr. Hooker, so that the soldiers would feel no restraint in saying good-bye to me. Then the men mounted their horses, calling "Good-bye and good luck, Miss Birdie." The night before we had left Bonita Canyon, the entire troop had come up to the outside of our cabin and serenaded me. I had gone out then to speak to them and thank them, and Jenny had made coffee and lemonade, and luckily had cake for them.

I had not then, or at any time after, appreciated that I really was leaving the old regiment, until I stood watching the troop ride on its way toward Fort Grant. Hector and Prince did not show any inclination to follow the soldiers, though Finnegan was whistling to them. Finally I made the dogs understand they must go on. Though they hesitated, at last they obeyed.

I stood alone in the road, looking after the troop, until the tears in my eyes shut it away. I wanted to go back with them, back to the old troop, with its familiar black faces, back to the garrison, to my father who had always been my pal, and back to the regiment in which I had spent my life from babyhood.

There was a lump in my throat. My eyes were blinded by tears, and there was an ache in my heart that nobody ever knew, except myself. When I had been very small, my father had said, "Don't be a deserter. Head up, eyes front. Face the bullets. It's no disgrace to die with a bullet in the breast, but a bullet in the back is a disgrace to the whole regiment." I went back to the buggy.

CAPTAIN LAWTON CHASES GERONIMO

General Miles selected Captain Henry Ware Lawton, of the Fourth Cavalry, and a young doctor named Leonard Wood, twenty-five years old, who was then an assistant contract surgeon in the army and stationed at Fort Huachuca, Arizona, in organizing a pursuing force to hammer the Apaches, while other commands guarded every known waterhole. Lawton's command consisted of Indian scouts, cavalry, and infantry.

Though various officers were assigned to duty under Lawton, only Lawton himself and Dr. Wood remained for the entire period with the pursuit. The seventy-seven Apaches who refused to leave when Geronimo and Natchez had slipped away from Lieutenant Maus had been shipped to Florida as prisoners of war. But a number of Chiricahuas were still on the reservation at Fort Apache.

My father and mother moved to Fort Apache in May, while I remained at the Hooker Ranch ten miles from Fort Grant. The people of Arizona were demanding that all of the Apaches should be removed permanently from the territory. As I heard the viewpoint of the citizens, and also that of the army people, it gave me a general idea of the Indian problem of Arizona in 1885 and 1886.

I knew that General Miles had been at Fort Apache in the middle of August, but letters from my parents gave interesting sidelights. Later I learned further details from General Miles, as well as my own parents. Official letters and telegrams passing between President Cleveland and

General Sheridan at Washington and General Miles at Fort Bowie had resulted in full authorization of Miles to round up all the Chiricahua Apaches in Arizona and ship them to Florida. It explicitly commanded that when such steps were taken, not one Chiricahua Apache was to be left in Arizona Territory. Even the presence of one or two would constitute a menace to safety.

On the Apache Reservation a number of this band had made no attempt to join Geronimo's forces, but their motives could not be relied upon, nor guarantee their future actions. Consequently, these apparently peaceful Chiricahuas had to be surrounded, disarmed, and held prisoners without any suspicion of the plans for their transportation.

Sunday morning, after the usual inspection of barracks and soldiers, the Apaches were instructed to gather in the parade ground so that they might be counted. This was a usual proceeding, so awoke no suspicion on the part of the Chiricahuas. Colonel James F. Wade, lieutenant colonel of the Tenth, commanded Fort Apache.

When leaving our quarters that morning, my father told my mother of the plan to round up the Chiricahuas. He added that she must not divulge this information to anyone, as the plan had to be kept absolutely secret for fear of its discovery by the Indians. That would have caused them to leave the reservation at once. "Keep inside the house, whatever you do," he cautioned her. "Even if you hear shooting, do not come outside."

Fort Apache was a hundred ten miles from Holbrook, the nearest settlement on the north. Fort Thomas lay sixty miles south. The balance of the surrounding country consisted of the wildest mountain country. While my mother watched from her windows, she saw the Indians gather on the parade ground; the soldiers apparently were drilling, but gradually worked to positions surrounding the Apaches, who were seated on the ground.

Suddenly they realized the situation, as the soldiers closed about them, armed, and ready in case of resistance. Some of the Indians leaped to their feet, but the businesslike guns halted any hostile demonstrations, and those who were armed gave up their guns. Not one shot was fired. The entire band of Chiricahuas offered no further resistance. At this moment a terrific mountain thunderstorm broke over the garrison, saturating both prisoners and their captors, thus making the scene even more dramatic.

Then an old Indian, his white hair hanging about his face, stepped between the soldiers and his own people. Lifting his face and thin arms to the sky while the rain beat down upon him, he called out in a shrill, mournful voice, "The Great Father is weeping because his children are prisoners." Other voices uttered a mournful wail, like their cry of grief when a warrior dies. Even the officers and soldiers felt pity for the forlorn little group who were destined to be exiled for life.

In the meantime Captain Lawton had surprised the Apaches under Geronimo on July 13, and captured their supplies, but the Apaches escaped, and were followed by the command. Lawton, Dr. Wood, and Lieutenant Leighton Finley, the latter of our own regiment, encountered a troop of Mexicans who had been in a fight with the Apaches and had rescued the little twelve-year-old Peck girl. The Mexicans turned the child over to the American officers.

The next news that we heard was when Lieutenant Charles Gatewood of the Sixth Cavalry, who had joined Lawton, went alone and unarmed into the camp of Geronimo. The Indian had sent word to Lawton that he wanted Gatewood to come alone and unarmed to talk with him. Without hesitation, Lieutenant Gatewood accepted the terms, though everyone in Lawton's command realized the danger. He returned, but as Geronimo had been very defiant and unfriendly, Gatewood was sure his trip had been wasted, and the situation unchanged.

However, the next day Geronimo suddenly appeared in the camp, and greeted Lawton effusively, throwing his arms about that officer's neck. With Geronimo came Natchez and a dozen more warriors. Then followed the balance of the hostile band, agreeing to surrender, but insisting their surrender must be personally to General Miles. Lawton had full authority to accept their surrender, but the Indians insisted that they would surrender to no one but Miles himself.

So they marched parallel, about half a mile away from Lawton's command, until they reached a place called Skeleton Canyon in far southeastern Arizona, a historic place a dozen miles north of the Mexican border that opens out on the Valley of the San Simon.

The only promise the Chiricahuas had received from Lawton was that the hostiles would not be killed after surrendering to Miles. That assurance, of course, was given. Previous to this acceptance, the Indians had tried to make the same terms as in years past. That meant merely giving up arms and returning to their reservation. General Miles was adamant. Guarantee of their lives was the only condition offered them.

On September 4, 1886, Geronimo and General Miles met at Skeleton Canyon in the camp of Captain Lawton, and there he made his final surrender. Miles told him the lives of the band would be spared, but that they would all be taken away from Arizona. Geronimo and Natchez realized they were powerless and accepted the ultimatum. The heliostat had pursued and puzzled them, for they had detected the flashes of light and considered it came from a supernatural power. Miles demonstrated the power of the heliostat, and that practically was the last straw of the Indians' resistance.

On September 8 the Apaches, now numbering twenty-four men and fourteen women and children, were placed aboard a special train at Bowie Station on the Southern Pacific Railroad which would take them first to San Antonio, where they arrived two days later. Geronimo and his followers remained at Fort Sam Houston until October 22, when they departed for Fort Pickens, Florida, arriving three days later.

THE
CAPTURE OF
CHIEF MANGUS

General Miles proceeded to Washington to make a personal report, but received a frigid reception. General Sheridan and also President Cleveland considered that Miles had disobeyed their orders that all of the Chiricahuas should be captured and taken away, and not one of them left behind in Arizona. General Sheridan called General Miles' attention to the fact that Chief Mangus, "the Big One," was still at large with his band, thus leaving a formidable enemy in Arizona Territory. Though General Miles insisted that troops formed such a close network in the section where Mangus was known to be hiding that his capture was expected momentarily, General Sheridan held his opinion that Miles should not have shipped one Chiricahua until the entire tribe had been captured.

Miles left General Sheridan's presence and went to the home of Mrs. Donald Cameron, sister of Mrs. Miles. As he was hanging his hat on a hall rack, the doorbell rang, and General Miles opened the door. A telegram was handed him. He read it, seized his hat, and hurried back to General Sheridan.

"There is my answer." He lay the message on Sheridan's desk. It read:

Fort Apache
October 19, 1886

Chief Mangus captured by Captain Charles L. Cooper, Tenth Cavalry, after five days' hard chase. Unconditional surrender. Arrangements being made to transport entire band to Florida, probably October 30th.

J. F. Wade
Lieut. Colonel, Commanding

General Miles, himself, related the above incident to my father, and later to me. He also told it to my father's father, James G. Cooper, who was on the staff of the *New York Tribune* with Horace Greeley and later Whitelaw Reid. I have the letter from my grandfather to my father giving intimate conversation with General Miles in the *New York Tribune* office.

UNCONDITIONAL SURRENDER

The capture of Chief Mangus was the only absolutely unconditional surrender of any Indian during the Apache campaign of 1885–86. My father, with twenty men of H Troop, left Fort Apache on October 14, and after scouting the country along the Bonito Fork of the Black River, found a trail of unshod stock, mostly mules, on the evening of the 17th. The next morning they took up the trail and followed it over forty-five miles of almost impassable mountains.

The Indians under Mangus were just going over the peak of a mountain that towered two thousand feet almost perpendicularly, when my father, at the foot of the mountain, discovered them. At the same time, the Indians saw his command. Chief Mangus was holding a fine pair of LeMaire field glasses, looking down, while my father looking upward with his own field glasses, realized that the man at the top of the mountain was actually Chief Mangus himself.

For two hours the chase continued, covering five mountains as high and difficult as the first one, until men and horses were almost exhausted, not only by their hard riding, but aggravated by the high rare atmosphere. Fifteen miles of this work terminated by the Indians abandoning their mules and ponies in order to slip unobserved among rocks and thick brush. The command was so close that the Indians could be observed individually. Each soldier was ordered to select an Indian and keep after him until captured. No shooting was to be done except in absolute necessity. It was "capture" them, not "kill" them.

One by one they were caught. An old squaw, glancing backward, fell into a small pool of water, and was hauled out dripping from head to foot. A second squaw actually burrowed into a hole made by an animal, but one foot protruded, and was noted. So she was dragged out in spite of kicks and squeals. These two women after a few words together became almost hysterical with laughter over being caught, and even the soldiers who had captured them enjoyed the joke with them.

Two of the entire band escaped the soldiers. One of the two was Mangus. My father knew that Mangus had no food, no mule or horse, and just one squaw remained at large with the chief. So ordering the soldiers to camp with the prisoners, a good supper was prepared. The Apaches enjoyed the meal, sitting socially with the Negro soldiers who had captured them. Spanish was a common language among the Apaches, and many of the soldiers had a fairly good knowledge of it. So the supper was quite a celebration for prisoners and captors.

My father was sure that Mangus watched from a hiding place in the large rocks. The spot where the Indian was hiding could not be taken in open attack; neither could Mangus escape without being detected by the alert eyes of the soldiers. It was not a surprise when the squaw came from Mangus with a message. He was hungry. Food was furnished the woman, who carried it to the Apache. Again she returned. Mangus wanted to smoke.

My father gave her tobacco and she vanished. The third time she came to say that Mangus would talk to the captain the next morning, but all the soldiers must be sent away, and the officer carry no arms. He agreed. The soldiers protested, but were ordered to take their prisoners to a distant point. The final words spoken to the soldiers bade them not to allow an Indian to escape, and above all, to pay no attention to the captain, but if Mangus proved treacherous, "Don't let him get away. Get him dead or alive, no matter what happens to me."

The soldiers and captured Apaches rode away, leaving my father alone by the campfire. Not a soul was in sight and he could not hear a step. His pipe was in his mouth, and he stooped down to light it with an ember from the fire. As he rose to his feet, Mangus stood in front of him, a few feet distant. The chief was the same height and build as my father, over six feet two inches tall. He was wrapped in a blanket, but the barrel of a rifle protruded.

The two of them stood looking at one another without a word. Then Mangus tossed back his blanket and laid the loaded gun at my father's feet, saying in excellent Spanish: "You are great *nantan* (commander). I am not ashamed to surrender to you. You are a better soldier than I am."

PRISONER

My father shook the Indian's hand, then they sat down by the campfire together and talked. Mangus told my father that he had had a quarrel with Geronimo and Natchez just after the fight in Guadalupe Canyon with Captain Charles Hatfield of the Fourth Cavalry at the beginning of the campaign. He had not seen Geronimo or Natchez since then. Further, he said he had committed no depredations in the United States after separating from Geronimo and Natchez. These statements were later confirmed as being true. General Miles told me there was no evidence of raids or attacks by Mangus, except below the Mexican border.

An old feud existed between the Chiricahuas and the Mexicans after an act of treachery when Apaches, invited to a "love feast" at a Mexican mine, were seated enjoying the food. Near them was a pile of harnesses, saddles, and such camp equipment, over which a canvas had been drawn. A white man stood beside this heap. His hand moved. A small cannon poured out broken nails, shot, and glass among the Indians, wounding men, women, and children.

A few escaped, though armed Mexicans shot those writhing on the ground and most of those who attempted to escape. From that date, vengeance on Mexicans had been the code of the Chiricahuas.

Mangus did not deny that he had killed, stolen, and burned wherever he could do so in Mexico. It was now unconditional surrender. Then as the soldiers started to ride with their thirteen prisoners, twenty-nine mules, and five ponies toward Fort Apache, Mangus turned to my father and said, "Will you grant me one thing? Let me ride beside you into Fort Apache, not following as a prisoner among the others." My father understood and granted the request. So they rode side by side into Fort Apache.

Not until Mangus noticed there were no tents where the Chiricahuas had lived did he have any idea what had happened to the balance of the tribe. My father explained. Mangus said nothing. The last of the Chiricahuas were held prisoners while preparations were made for shipping them to Florida. The squaws and children were almost totally unclothed. They were gaunt from hunger and privation of their long struggle to avoid capture since they had broken away from Geronimo and Natchez a year and a half earlier.

Ladies at Fort Apache sent clothing for them. Mangus refused it, but said he would accept what my mother might send. So she assembled what she could, and it was accepted gratefully. Mangus sent a message to my mother, saying he would like a suit of my father's uniform. It was taken out of a field chest and a soldier carried it to the chief. After that, a shirt, stockings, and shoes reached the Indian, who dressed himself in the clothes and felt it no dishonor to wear the uniform of a cavalry officer who had captured him and his band.

My father admired Mangus as a chief, a soldier, and a man of honor. During the time Mangus was prisoner, my father frequently visited and talked with him. When the Indians were to start for Holbrook, the railroad point, on October 30, my father went to say farewell to Mangus. The Indian chief rose to meet him and held out his two hands. On either wrist was an iron band, and between these bands hung a heavy chain.

"If you were going with us," said Mangus bitterly, "I would not be wearing these." My father felt the indignity as deeply as did Chief Mangus.

"No," he replied. "You would not wear them if I could help it, or if you went with me. Your word is enough for me, Mangus."

The Indian looked his gratitude, and took my father's hands in his own two hands. "If you went with me, I would not try to escape, but go like a child. I would give you my word. Mangus does not lie. But now they have put on these." He held out his hands again. "I will try to escape if I can." My father stood beside Mangus talking with him until, at last, the wagon with the prisoners started toward the railroad on the long journey to Florida exile.

ATTEMPT TO ESCAPE

The desperate courage of Mangus may be better understood by the facts regarding his journey toward Fort Pickens, Florida. On the night of November 3, when three miles east of Pueblo, Colorado, while the train was running at forty miles an hour, Mangus asked Sergeant John Casey for permission to go to the retiring room. Once inside, the Indian locked the door, smashed the glass, and jumped from the window.

In spite of the immediate alarm, the train went almost a mile before it could be stopped, and backed up to the place in search of him. The colored soldiers held the other Indians at pistol point to prevent a general attempt to escape through glass windows. Mangus was lying beside the track, unconscious, bleeding, and with three broken ribs.

When he recovered consciousness on board the train, he put up a desperate fight. The hands of Apaches are very small and flexible, with well-developed wrists. Consequently, Mangus was able to slip one hand free from his handcuffs, and grasping it as a weapon, he suddenly struck Sergeant Casey across the face, partially stunning the soldier, who fell to the floor.

Mangus scrambled under a seat grappling with six Negro soldiers and uttering weird howls or war cries. The other prisoners joined in the cries and attempted to aid their chief, but the men of H Troop, with cocked rifles, held them at bay until other soldiers had overpowered Mangus. Then he was stretched across two seats while the bell cord of the car was used to wrap about his ankles, legs, and body, as a fly is wrapped by a spider. New manacles were adjusted and also leg-irons which frustrated any possibility of other attempts to escape.

And so the Negro soldiers of my father's troop escorted to Fort Pickens, Florida, the Apache chief, Mangus, whom my father alone and unarmed had met in the mountains of Arizona, when Mangus lay down his gun at Captain Cooper's feet in unconditional surrender. This was the only unconditional surrender during the entire campaign.

THE END OF THE GERONIMO CAMPAIGN

I have a letter lying on my desk at this moment that may be of interest. It is from my grandfather, James G. Cooper, of the *New York Tribune*, to my father.

December 24, 1886

Dear Charlie,
General Miles was in to see our W. R. [Whitelaw Reid] today. Perhaps this fact may not be published or dwelt upon (between you and me) but they were together about an hour.

When he came out I had a very interesting conversation with him. To give you an idea how he values your work, I'll give you (privately) about what was said in one sentence: "When we had captured Geronimo, all the efforts of those parties were brought to bear to belittle the result. They kept saying, 'Geronimo! Geronimo is a small man to capture. He's not the one to get in, especially by questionable methods. Why don't you get the Big One, Mangus?' and, confound them, before their growls and sneers had hardly got cold in the papers, your son, Captain Cooper, had captured this same 'Big One' as they called him, in open field. Yes, sir. In the open field, captured their 'Big One' and brought him and his men in as prisoners, Sir."

But in view of the state of feelings in Washington and as a matter of business wisdom, you'd better burn this after having read it. Don't make any mistake about this part.

Love to all and a Merry Christmas and Happy New Year.

Aff'y, Father

P.S. While General M. and your dad were talking, Phil Fitzpatrick came in, soon after Louis Abry, our Mr. Clarke's clerk also came in.

Curiously enough (as I found out afterwards) they each mistook the Gen. for you, come on to visit during the holidays.

Mr. Clarke himself then said, "I had a good look at him, with his stovepipe hat off, as he sat talking with Mr. Reid. He looks astonishingly like your son, Captain Cooper."

Later, various leading participants in the campaign were singled out for "specially meritorious acts or conduct in service." Among them were Captain Emmet Crawford, Lieutenant Charles B. Gatewood, Captain Thomas C. Lebo, Captain Charles A. P. Hatfield, Captain Henry W. Lawton, Lieutenant Matthias W. Day, and Captain Charles L. Cooper.

Lieutenants Powhatan H. Clarke, Marion P. Maus, and Dr. Leonard Wood all received the Medal of Honor. Both Lieutenants Charles B. Gatewood and William E. Shipp were recommended for one.

That was the last chapter of the Geronimo campaign. The last blow had been struck and the big Indian outbreaks in Arizona were over.

~18~

FRIENDS AND MEMORIES
OF FORT APACHE

In the early fall of 1888, I went for a visit to Fort Apache where my father and mother were then living. The garrison was about a hundred ten miles south of Holbrook on the Atlantic and Pacific Railroad, and the three days' drive led through a beautiful mountainous country with many streams. This section was entirely different from the southern parts of Arizona Territory.

We stopped at the small Mormon village of Snowflake, and found every comfort of an old-fashioned home the first night at Mrs. Minnerally's. The Mormon town was laid out like a toy village, with snow white houses, green blinds, gardens, and trees. I learned that all the men gave portions of their services in cooperating with the others for the general upkeep of neatness, as well as in farming work.

About the middle of October, the families learned that General Miles had invited Mr. Welsh, organizer and corresponding secretary of the Indian Rights Association, to meet him at San Carlos while my father was the commanding officer at that garrison. Newspapers and individuals had been criticizing methods employed by the army officers toward the Indians, and General Miles by this method allowed full contact with the Indians themselves and those of the distant eastern cities, who were thus enabled to judge matters firsthand on the reservation of San Carlos.

Fort Apache, like most frontier garrisons in those days, was over a hundred miles from the railroad, and visitors to the garrisons, whether private individuals or officials, had to be cared for by the families of the officers stationed there. It was customary to inquire of each household as to the housing of such guests.

MOTHER'S BATHTUB BED

When my mother was asked by Captain Charles Nordstrom whether we could help out, and she heard that a Mr. Welsh of Philadelphia was to be one of the party, she at once declared she would arrange to make him comfortable in our house. Then she explained that Mr. Welsh had been a friend of Captain John Green's, so she would be delighted. I wondered at the time how so old a man as Mr. John Welsh was able to take such a strenuous trip, not only from Holbrook by carriage to Fort Apache, but later to continue sixty-five miles over the rough road down to San Carlos.

When Mr. Welsh, agile, dapper, and apparently about thirty-five or -six years old, alighted from the army conveyance at our door one Sunday evening, my mother's face was a study of surprise. She had expected John Welsh, the father, and had drawn as her house guest, Herbert Welsh, the son. I enjoyed the joke hugely. However, I was still unable to agree with her plans of hospitality. We had a large living room adjoining the dining room and kitchen on one side of a wide hallway. Across that hall was one fairly good-sized front bedroom which my parents used. A door led into a small room which we called the bathroom.

It was not a modern bathroom in any sense of the word, but just a long narrow room in which had been installed a large zinc tub encased in a half-wooden frame, like a box.

No washstand or any other bathroom conveniences were in any of the army quarters at Apache. But those who possessed a coffinlike tub felt quite luxurious.

Back of this bathroom was another bedroom. I occupied that room with my nursemaid, Mary Kilroy, who had accompanied me to Fort Apache. With us were my two children, Forrestine, "Tots," nineteen months old, and my baby boy, Harry, two and a half months old when Mr. Welsh arrived at Fort Apache. I had suggested that my mother use the double bed with Tots, so that Mary and I could each use a cot. The baby had his crib. But my mother, with an air of mystery, announced she had everything arranged, and we would not be upset.

That evening after dinner when Mr. Welsh, unaware of the limited quarters in our home, had gone to bed, my mother explained that Johnson, the soldier striker, and Dual, the old Creole cook, would bring a set of single springs into the bathroom, and that she intended to have it placed above the tub. In spite of the urgings of Mary and myself that one of us use the springs in the back room, my mother carried out her plan.

The weather was quite cool up in the White Mountains in the middle of October, and as she feared a frost might nip her window plants when our wood fires died down during the night hours, we had aided her to set her pet geraniums, planted in painted tomato cans, down inside the bathtub for the night. The springs formed a roof above these flowerpots. Everyone quieted down for the night, hoping our guest would rest peacefully.

About two hours later, Mary and I sat bolt upright in our beds, awakened by a frightful crash. Without a word, we darted into the bathroom. There by the flickering light of a candle, we sized up the situation. My mother was nowhere in evidence, but muffled tones came from the bathtub. The wire mattress was cocked at an angle from the tub, while the mattress and bedding made a canopy over my mother's jerking head. We tried to lift the wire springs, but could not do so.

Then we both tugged at the mattress, while asking if she was hurt. Her reply was unintelligible. After strenuous efforts, we removed the mattress, then lifted the bedding. My mother was sitting in the wreckage of her plants, her face distorted with suppressed laughter, as she tried to make us keep quiet. It was useless. Mary and I were hysterical, and my mother spluttered. We tried to help her from the tub, but our laughter and her inability to lift herself made matters worse.

"Don't wake Mr. Welsh," she kept whispering between her gasps. Finally she was extricated. Mary and I wanted her to take my bed, but she was adamant. The wire springs were laid flat on the bathroom floor, as she commanded, then with the bedding arranged, she managed to get down to the level of the springs.

Early the next morning, in fact before dawn, she limped into our room, asking us to get the springs and bedding out of the bathroom so that Mr. Welsh could use the room whenever he was ready. Mary and I lugged the springs, mattress, and bedding into our room, and my mother began to dress. But the combination of the tumble into the tub among the geraniums, and later on the floor, where the springs had flattened beneath her, had bruised her flesh and stiffened every muscle of her body.

However, like an early Christian martyr dying with a smile, she fulfilled the duties of a hostess at the breakfast table. Her usual dignity, which combined with her silver hair, had won her the nickname of "The Duchess" that October morning, and throughout the day was more impressive than ever, but Mary and I knew the reason.

Before the day was over, everyone else in the garrison was aware of what had happened during the night in our quarters. Mr. Welsh was not enlightened then or at any subsequent time, but only a few years ago in Washington, I told General Miles all about it, and he enjoyed the story immensely.

Mr. Welsh was to remain at our home until General Miles, traveling by the Southern Pacific Railroad from Los Angeles, had reached Willcox, and from that point traveled by ambulance to San Carlos. Upon his arrival there, a telegram was to be sent to Mr. Welsh at Fort Apache, and an ambulance with escort furnished by the post commander, Lieutenant Colonel George Huntt.

Several days elapsed before the telegram was received. The second night my mother insisted that Mary and I must not give up our beds to her, and with the still stiff muscles as reminders, she discarded her former plans and had the servants bring in four wooden-seated dining chairs on which the springs were laid. Even this was a precarious arrangement, so in the morning, Mary and I held the chairs in place while my mother got out of bed.

OUR KITCHEN FORAY

That evening another catastrophe occurred, and Mr. Welsh was witness to part of it. He had been entertained at dinner formally by Colonel Huntt, and was wearing his dinner suit. On his return to our house, he sat talking with us a little while, then as he was saying good night, my mother asked if there was anything he needed in his room. His reply was that he was accustomed to eating a small piece of bread before retiring. My mother at once offered to arrange a luncheon for him, but he declined, insisting that "just a little piece of bread" was all that he could eat.

The kitchen was closed for the night, and the servants had gone. A small butler's pantry between the dining room and kitchen held our fancy groceries. While I took a candle into the pantry, followed by Mr. Welsh, my mother, without a light, invaded the kitchen. Duel, the cook, was a crank. He kept his kitchen immaculate. A crumb was his mortal enemy. Servants were impossible to obtain at Holbrook, and, as Duel was a real chef, he was a despot in our home.

The bread box was always on the kitchen table. My mother reached out for it in the dark, and hauled it toward herself, intending to bring the bread into the pantry and thus avoid any telltale crumbs. Then came a crash, a horrified exclamation, and Mr. Welsh followed me into the kitchen. I held the candle above my head.

There stood my mother, dripping wet from waist to hem of her skirt. The kitchen floor was a veritable milky way. Duel had set a pan of milk on the table so that the cream would "rise," and be ready for him to skim for our morning meal. She had jerked the bread box and sent the pan of milk in a regular Niagara over herself and the floor.

Mr. Welsh exclaimed, "Oh, Mrs. Cooper! What will your servant say?"

My mother, looking every inch a duchess, replied loftily, "Nothing at all."

Mr. Welsh gallantly offered to mop it up for her, evidently intending to help shield her from an irate cook, but the offer was declined. I made an offer, but was told that it must be left for Duel to clean in the morning. We all left the kitchen as was.

Mr. Welsh was given a slice of bread, and went to his room. Mary wanted to mop up the floor, but my mother insisted that it must be left for Duel. The wool challis dress she had been wearing for the first time had been made by a rather expensive dressmaker in Philadelphia. It was practically ruined, as we all knew. At last we settled down for the night.

I was awakened by Mary whispering, "There's someone tiptoeing in the kitchen." We listened, then I picked up the pistol, which we kept during my father's absence, and followed by Mary, I sneaked across the hall and flung open the kitchen door. My mother, arrayed in *robe de nuit*, was busy mopping up that ocean of milk.

She looked at us in a guilty manner, and then as Mary took the mop, I could not resist mimicking the entire episode, including Mr. Welsh when he made his chivalrous offer to mop the kitchen floor of his hostess, and my mother's lofty assertion, "I will leave it for Duel to clean in the morning." The floor was spotless when we three went giggling across the hall and once more into our beds.

I PLAY FOR GENERAL MILES

The telegram from San Carlos brought Mr. Welsh's farewells, and my mother that night slept in her own room. About a week later my father wired us from San Carlos, "General Miles and his party will be your guests at dinner tonight." Duel was still with us (thanks to the kitchen mop) so dinner was not a problem. The visitors were to remain one night only at Fort Apache, then proceed to Holbrook and their destinations. At once Duel got busy.

Dinner had to be promptly at six, as Colonel Huntt was to give a formal reception at his own home that evening in honor of General Miles and his party. Everyone in the garrison was expected to attend the reception.

At the dinner, besides General Miles, was Mr. Welsh (again our house guest, while once more the faithful wire springs on the four chairs supported my mother's form), Mr. Booth of Santa Barbara, a friend of General Miles, and Colonel Huntt, commander of Fort Apache. My mother and I completed the list among those present, and the dinner went off smoothly.

After dinner Colonel Huntt excused himself, as did Mr. Booth and Mr. Welsh, but General Miles remained seated in a big, comfortable lounging chair, enjoying a cigar. I had been given a very thorough music education in the East, and General Miles was an ardent lover of music. As he sat smoking, he had a pile of my music on a low stool beside his chair, and while I played one number, he would select another. Time passed. I forgot the reception, so did General Miles, and my mother felt diffident about reminding him he ought to go.

Then a knocking at our front door, which I opened, brought Lieutenant Charles Gatewood, the aide-de-camp of General Miles. The same Gatewood, who alone, had gone unarmed into the camp of the hostile Apaches headed by Geronimo.

"Good gracious, General. I've been looking all over the garrison for you."

General Miles was surprised. "What is the matter?"

"Have you forgotten? Colonel Huntt is having a formal reception in your honor. Everyone else is there, waiting for you."

General Miles smiled, "I'll come right away, but I'm sorry you found me. I was enjoying the music."

Late that night Lieutenant Gatewood knocked on our door, and when my mother opened it, he handed her a handwritten telegram, a copy of one to be sent to my father the next morning.

Fort Apache, A.T.
October 21, 1888
To Captain Cooper
San Carlos, A.T.

General Miles says you may exercise the usual pre-
rogative of a commanding officer in visiting surrounding country by which you can visit your
family remaining with them a reasonable time.

(Signed) Gatewood
ADC

HOMESICK FOR FATHER

For the third time General Miles had placed me under a
debt of gratitude, first, when he had ordered my father to
Fort Grant in time to be present at my wedding on May 4,
1886. A second time in Los Angeles in March of 1887 just
after the birth of my daughter, the General and Mrs. Miles,
accompanied by Captain and Mrs. Wesson, called on my
mother and me.

My mother had come on a visit to me, but I was very
homesick for my father, who was then at Fort Apache and
unable to obtain a leave of absence. As General Miles was
talking during his call, he suddenly turned to me, asking
how long since I had seen my father.

That was the last straw. I began to cry and hurried from
the room. General Miles was quick to grasp the situation,
when my mother told him I had not seen my father since
my marriage. That evening Lieutenant Gatewood brought
a copy of an official telegram to the bungalow where we
were living. It was an order to my father to report immediately to Los Angeles as a member of an examining board.
He was in Los Angeles with us for three weeks.

During that time General Miles requested my father to attend a banquet given by the Los Angeles Chamber of Commerce in honor of the general. Captain Henry Lawton (who later as a major general of volunteers was killed on the battlefield in the Philippines) was also in full-dress cavalry uniform, and as the two officers, both well over six feet tall, were walking together on the way to the banquet, several newsboys spied them. Impressed by the brilliant yellow and blue uniforms and helmets with flowing yellow horsehair plumes, the newsboys asked, "Say, where is your band going to play tonight?"

At the banquet, when General Miles had been introduced as the soldier who had ended the Apache troubles in Arizona, he in turn introduced my father as the officer who actually had ended that problem by the capture of Chief Mangus, and added, "The only real and unconditional surrender effected during the Geronimo campaign."

An incident not on official records occurred at San Carlos during the visit of Mr. Welsh and General Miles. My father, being instructed to assemble the Indians to meet Mr. Welsh and General Miles, sent Indian runners to all the camps, bidding the Apaches to come for a pow-wow in the garrison. There were many Indians noted for recurring atrocities, and to these he sent especially urgent commands. So when the Apaches assembled to meet Mr. Welsh, he saw the worst renegades on the San Carlos Reservation.

One villainous-looking Apache came up to Mr. Welsh, and laid his arms on that gentleman's shoulders as a token of esteem and comradeship. But when the Indian announced proudly, "Me heap good Indian. Me bring in my cousin's head for reward. Heap good Indian, me," the officers afterward told that the expression of horror on the face of Mr. Welsh amused them all. The Indian actually had trailed, killed, and decapitated his relative in order to get a reward, as the cousin was an outlaw.

That same Indian, after killing his cousin and bringing in the head as proof of the death, had later accosted an officer and said, "Me get another cousin's head for you, for nice horse." No doubt the renegade would have been delighted to have received a commission for another Apache's head, had Mr. Welsh desired it.

General Miles, Mr. Welsh, and the others in the party left Fort Apache on October 22, 1888, and I did not again meet General Miles until 1922 in Washington. There I was privileged to rank him as one of my most valued and loyal friends until his death. In November 1923 I wrote General Miles that *Star: The Story of an Indian Pony,* for which he had written the foreword on July 21, had been accepted for publication in Germany after having been published in the United States by Doubleday, Page and Company. I am glad that he lived to write that foreword for my third book, *Star.*

Six months later at the old Shoreham Hotel in Washington, now a lost landmark, General Miles sat beside me, while officers who were distinguished generals, but who had as young lieutenants served under him during the Geronimo campaign, surrounded him and heard a review of my book, *When Geronimo Rode,* broadcast over WRC in the National Capital. The autographed copy which I presented him that day was inscribed as follows: "The West is his monument. He needs no other."

The days of Indian fighting are over forever, and soldiers like Miles, Wood, Crawford, Mills, the Custers, Sherman, Crook, Clarke, Gatewood, Lawton, and Shipp, with my father, have answered the last roll call. The Indian trails of my western yesterdays ended in 1889 with my visit to Fort Apache. After that I faced the cattle trails of the open range in Arizona.

CHRONOLOGY

1862   At seventeen, Charles Lawrence Cooper, of New York City, enlists as a private in Company B of the Seventy-first New York State Militia, taking part in the defense of Washington, D.C., and the Gettysburg campaign

1864   Sergeant Cooper is commissioned a second lieutenant, serving in Companies A, K, and B of the 127th U.S. Colored Infantry

1865   The Civil War ends. Twenty-year-old Charles Cooper and nineteen-year-old Flora Green are married in Philadelphia

1867   Forrestine Cooper is born in Philadelphia

Second Lieutenant Cooper is promoted to first lieutenant in the Thirty-ninth Infantry at Ship Island, Mississippi

1871   Lieutenant Cooper is reassigned to Company A of the Tenth U.S. Cavalry, black troops with white officers, later to become known as the Buffalo Soldiers

Company A is ordered to Fort Sill in the Kiowa and Comanche country, where it arrives after a march of 225 miles from Camp Supply

1872   Lieutenant Cooper performs special duty as post treasurer, acting signal officer, and post librarian. Company A performs usual garrison duty and numerous details for completion of the new post

1873   Company A is ordered to Fort Concho, Texas, 290 miles southwestward

1874   Company A is ordered on a scout of the North Fork of the Red River in Indian Territory and marches through the Wichita Mountains, forcing the Indians to take shelter on the Fort Sill reservation

1875   Quanah, chief of the Comanches, leads his tribe of 100 warriors, 300 women and children, and 1,400 ponies into Fort Sill in a peaceful surrender of the Quohada tribe

1876   Lieutenant Cooper conducts convicts to San Antonio, commands troop in absence of Captain Nicholas Nolan, leads scout after hostile Indians, and goes on detached service conducting new recruits to Fort Concho

1877   Captain Nolan and Lieutenant Cooper leave Fort Concho with Company A to search for hostile Indians on the Staked Plains. Soon they become lost and go without water for 86 hours

1878   Company A leaves Fort Concho for assignment at Fort Sill, Indian Territory. Second Lieutenant Henry O. Flipper, first black graduate of the United States Military Academy at West Point, joins Company A

1879   Cattleman Charles Goodnight of the Palo Duro Ranch, Texas, gives 14 head of beef to starving Kiowas from Fort Sill

Lieutenant Colonel John W. Davidson and Company A transfer to Fort Elliott in the Texas Panhandle, arriving after a march of 170 miles northwest of Fort Sill

1880   Captain Nicholas Nolan, Lieutenant Henry Flipper, and Company A ride to the Rio Grande in southwest Texas to join Colonel Benjamin Grierson in the Victorio campaign.

Lieutenant Cooper joins Captain Stevens T. Norvell's Company M at Fort Concho

1881   Lieutenant Cooper, commanding Company M, is ordered to Fort Reno, Indian Territory, to assist in controlling the Northern Cheyenne Indians

1882   Captain Stevens Norvell, Lieutenant Cooper, and Troop M leave Fort Concho for Fort Davis, Texas, 240 miles westward

1883   Lieutenant Cooper is promoted to captain at Fort Davis, serving special duty as post adjutant, acting ordnance officer, and acting signal officer. He assumes command of Troop H, Tenth Cavalry

1884   Forrestine Cooper graduates finishing school at Mount Saint Joseph Academy at Chestnut Hill in Philadelphia and joins her family at Fort Davis

1885   Eleven troops of the Tenth Cavalry come together at Fort Davis and join the remaining 12th at Camp Rice on the Rio Grande while en route to posts in Arizona, where they would participate in the Geronimo campaign

1886   Nineteen-year-old Forrestine Cooper marries twenty-five-year-old Edwin Russell Hooker, son of cattle baron Henry Clay Hooker, at Fort Grant.

Geronimo surrenders to U.S. Army in Arizona, formally ending the Apache wars

1887   Hooker's daughter, also named Forrestine, or "Tots," is born in Los Angeles

1888   Hooker's son, Harry Edwin Hooker, is born

1889   Captain Charles Cooper and Troop H return from duty at San Carlos Reservation to Fort Apache

1892   The Tenth Cavalry exchanges posts in Arizona with the First Cavalry in Montana

PLACES TO VISIT

Chiricahua National Monument
13063 East Bonita Canyon Road
Willcox, AZ 85643
(520) 824-3560
www.nps.gov/chir
> Thirty-eight miles southeast of Willcox, this 12,000-acre attraction for hikers and birders includes Bonita Canyon and Faraway Ranch, site of the nearby Tenth Cavalry camp and Birdie Cooper's home in 1885–86.

Fort Apache Historic Park
P.O. Box 628, Fort Apache, AZ 85926
(928) 338-1392
www.wmonline.com/attract/ftapache.htm
> Owned by the White Mountain Apache tribe. Today, visitors to the 288-acre site are able to view more than 20 buildings at the frontier fort, which dates from the 1870s through the 1930s.

Fort Bowie National Historic Site
3203 South Old Fort Bowie Road, Bowie, AZ 85805
(520) 847-2500
www.nps.gov/fobo
> Thirteen miles south of Bowie, adobe ruins and the site of Butterfield Overland Stage Station greet visitors in the fabled Apache Pass.

Fort Concho National Historic Landmark
630 South Oakes, San Angelo, TX 76903
(325) 481-2646
www.fortconcho.com/index.htm
> Most of the stone buildings of the frontier post have been preserved. The site offers exhibits and educational programming.

Fort Davis National Historic Site
P.O. Box 1379, Lieutenant Henry Flipper Drive
Fort Davis, TX 79734
(432) 426-3224, Ext. 20
www.nps.gov/foda
> One of the best preserved and restored posts in the Southwest. The fort protected travelers on the San Antonio–El Paso Road from 1854 to 1891. Outstanding exhibits and educational programs are available on the 474-acre site.

Fort Hays State Historic Site
1472 Highway 183 Alt, Hays, KS 67601
(785) 625-6812
www.kshs.org/places/forthays/index.htm
> Famous figures once stationed at Fort Hays include General Nelson Miles, General Philip Sheridan, and Lieutenant Colonel George Armstrong Custer.

Fort Huachuca Historical Museum
Building 41401, Fort Huachuca, AZ 85613
(520) 533-5736
huachuca-www.army.mil/HISTORY/museum.htm
> Much of this 1880s post, once prominent in the Apache wars of Arizona, survives. The museum interprets the U.S. Army in the Southwest.

Fort McKavett State Historic Site

P.O. Box 867, Fort McKavett, TX 76841

(325) 396-2358

www.tpwd.state.tx.us/park/fortmcka

Founded in 1852 and abandoned in 1883, the partially restored post on eighty acres offers exhibits and living history program.

Fort Sill National Historic Landmark and Museum

437 Quanah Road, Fort Sill, OK 73505

(580) 442-5123

sill-www.army.mil/Museum

North of Lawton, the historic site includes much of original stone post and offers a special children's exhibit commemorating Birdie Cooper, called "Cricket's Corner." Quanah Parker, Geronimo, and other Indian notables are buried at post cemeteries.

Fort Supply Historic Site

P. O. Box 247, Fort Supply, OK 73841

(580) 766-3767

www.ok-history.mus.ok.us/mus-sites

Located one mile east of the town of Fort Supply on State Highway 3, the site preserves historic structures and replica stockade of 1868–1894 frontier post.

Wichita Mountains Wildlife Refuge

Route 1, Box 448, Indiahoma, OK 73552

(580) 429-3222

southwest.fws.gov/refuges/oklahoma/Wichita/index.html

Twenty miles northwest of Lawton, the rugged, 59,000-acre mountain preserve is home to Texas longhorns, bison, and other big game. An automobile road leads to the top of Mount Scott. The visitor center lies midway through refuge.

FURTHER READING

NATIVE AMERICANS

Debo, Angie. *Geronimo: The Man, His Time, His Place*. Norman: University of Oklahoma Press, 1976.

Fehrenbach, T. R. *Comanches: The Destruction of a People*. 1974. Reprint, New York: Da Capo, 1994.

Hagan, William T. *Quanah Parker, Comanche Chief*. Norman: University of Oklahoma Press, 1993.

Nye, Wilbur Sturtevant. *Plains Indian Raiders: The Final Phases of Warfare from the Arkansas to the Red River*. Norman: University of Oklahoma Press, 1968.

Reedstrom, E. Lisle. *Apache Wars: An Illustrated Battle History*. New York: Sterling, 1990.

Roberts, David. *Once They Moved Like the Wind: Cochise, Geronimo, and the Apache Wars*. New York: Simon & Schuster, 1993.

BUFFALO SOLDIERS

Burton, Art T. *Black, Buckskin, and Blue: African American Scouts and Soldiers on the Western Frontier*. Austin, Tex.: Eakin, 1999.

Carroll, John M., ed. *The Black Military Experience in the American West*. New York: Liveright, 1971.

Cox, Clinton. *The Forgotten Heroes: The Story of the Buffalo Soldiers*. New York: Scholastic, 1993.

Haskins, Jim. *Black Stars: African-American Military Heroes*. New York: John Wiley & Sons, 1998.

Leckie, William H. *The Buffalo Soldiers: A Narrative of the Negro Cavalry in the West.* Norman: University of Oklahoma Press, 1967.

Schubert, Frank N. *Black Valor: Buffalo Soldiers and the Medal of Honor, 1870–1898.* Wilmington, Del.: Scholarly Resources, 1997.

FRONTIER WOMEN

Eales, Anne Bruner. *Army Wives on the American Frontier: Living by the Bugles.* Boulder, Colo.: Johnson, 1996.

Laurence, Mary Leefe. *Daughter of the Regiment: Memoirs of a Childhood in the Frontier Army, 1878–1898.* Edited by Thomas T. Smith. Lincoln: University of Nebraska Press, 1996.

Leckie, Shirley Anne, ed. *The Colonel's Lady on the Western Frontier: The Correspondence of Alice Kirk Grierson.* Norman: University of Oklahoma Press, 1989.

Palmer-Ramsey, Paige. *Young Troopers: Stories of Army Children on the Frontier.* Tucson, Ariz.: Southwest Parks & Monuments Associa-tion, 1997.

Roe, Frances M. A. *Army Letters from an Officer's Wife, 1871–1888.* 1909. Reprint, Lincoln: University of Nebraska Press, 1981.

Stallard, Patricia Y. *Glittering Misery: Dependents of the Indian Fighting Army.* 1978. Reprint, Norman: University of Oklahoma Press, 1992.

THE FRONTIER ARMY

Aleshire, Peter. *Reaping the Whirlwind: The Apache Wars.* New York: Facts on File, 1998.

Haley, James L. *The Buffalo War: The History of the Red River Indian Uprising of 1874.* Garden City, N.Y.: Doubleday, 1976.

McDermott, John D. *A Guide to the Indian Wars of the West.* Lincoln: University of Nebraska Press, 1998.

Nye, W. S. *Carbine & Lance: The Story of Old Fort Sill.* 1937. Reprint, Norman: University of Oklahoma Press, 1969.

Pate, J'Nell L. *Ranald Slidell Mackenzie: Brave Cavalry Colonel.* Austin, Tex.: Eakin, 1994.

Wooster, Robert. *Soldiers, Sutlers, and Settlers: Garrison Life on the Texas Frontier.* College Station: Texas A&M University Press, 1987.

ACKNOWLEDGMENTS

My wife, Linda, introduced me to Forrestine C. Hooker through her own copy of Hooker's *Cricket: A Little Girl of the Old West,* published in 1925. The late Gillett Griswold, Fort Sill Museum director, provided still more background, as we discussed at length what surely must have been the actual experiences of a child who lived the story she so aptly chronicled. Barbara Fisher found Hooker's manuscript four decades ago, and used a small portion of it for her 1963 thesis.

Finally, I met Hooker's granddaughter, Mrs. Jacqueline Hooker Hughes, known affectionately as "Rinki," at the Sierra Bonita Ranch north of Willcox, Arizona. Her interest in her grandmother's forgotten manuscript, and my own research into the Tenth Cavalry, made possible the editing of those memoirs. When I followed Captain Henry Lawton's trail in his pursuit of Geronimo in the wilds of Mexico—a century after Lawton—I ended that trail at the Sierra Bonita Ranch. Rinki helped celebrate with cooking the best steak I had eaten in what seemed like months. She has generously provided family material and photographs, making this book possible.

My pursuit in Mexico led me to Bill Hoy, then superintendent of the Fort Bowie National Historic Site, who invited me to participate in the centennial commemoration of the end of the Apache wars in the Southwest, and the festivities held at the ruins of Fort Bowie. I have returned to Fort Bowie, or Apache Pass, or the Chiricahua Mountains countless times over the years. Always Bill Hoy was there, providing cheer, lodging, fellowship, and helping me research my latest quest.

Only three years ago we stood in the stone breastwork atop the mountain peak overlooking Faraway Ranch in Bonita Canyon of the Chiricahua National Monument. Buffalo Soldiers had watched from that vantage when Forrestine Cooper lived in the cabin at that location with her parents. Many of them carved their names on monument stones that were later used to build the ranch house fireplace.

Others also helped greatly. Hooker's great-granddaughters, Ginna Froelich James and her sister, Judy Cocke, and Judy's husband, J J, were helpful with both research material and photographs and allowed me to photograph the 1873 Winchester that Mangus surrendered to Captain Cooper. Ginna and Judy's father, the late Forrest Hooker Froelich, also was helpful. Mary Williams, park ranger historian, of the Fort Davis National Historic Site, has been a gracious host for many years, never failing to try to answer questions or seek answers. She also was kind enough to read the manuscript and offer suggestions.

The late Dr. Waldo and Mildred Mott Wedel, archaeologist emeritus and research associate, respectively, of the Smithsonian Institution, generously allowed me to "house sit" while researching in the archives. The late Sara D. Jackson, who guided many a graduate student through the military records at the National Archives, provided both guidance and goodwill. My daughter, Kimberly, and son Chris, and his wife, Kathryn, all living in Washington, D.C., now make it possible for me to spend long sojourns at those treasured institutions.

Todd Mills, who studied Hooker Hot Springs, graciously supplied material. Thomas D. Phillips, independent historian of the black regulars, has shared much research, good conversation, and enthusiasm. Bruce Dinges, of the Arizona Historical Society, has done likewise. Evelyn Lemons, archivist at Fort Concho National Historic Landmark; James Finley, director of the Fort Huachuca Museum; William Secrest, Jr., of the California History and Genealogy Room, Fresno County Library; Larry Ludwig, superintendent of the Fort Bowie National Historic Site, all assisted with special requests.

Historian Lynda Sánchez and her husband, James, provided lodging and warm meals at their Lincoln County ranch on many a westward trip through New Mexico, as did former Fort Bliss Museum director, Sam Hoyle, and his wife, Helen. Transplanted Oklahoman James Johnston of Tucson provided lodging and good cheer for extended trips to southern Arizona.

Sister Patricia Annas, archivist of Mount St. Joseph Convent, kindly copied the program of the Twenty-fifth Annual Commencement of the Mount St. Joseph's Academy at Chestnut Hill, Philadelphia, showing Forrestine Cooper's graduation in 1884. Dale Durham, director of the U.S. Army Chemical Corps Museum at Fort Leonard Wood, assisted in many ways. Max Gartenberg of New York was also helpful.

Staffs of the National Archives, Library of Congress, Smithsonian Institution, New York Public Library, Special Collections of the United States Military Academy Library, United States Military History Institute, Arizona Historical Society, Special Collections of the University of Arizona Library, Chiricahua National Monument, Western History Collections of the University of Oklahoma Library, Museum of New Mexico, and Montana Historical Society, were equally helpful.

My wife, Linda, who introduced me to Hooker, also provided long hours of standing at copying machines, as I tabbed documents and reports. She might have hidden *Cricket*, had she known what it would lead to. I must also thank Nancy Toff, vice president and editorial director at Oxford University Press, who believed in the book; Karen S. Fein, development editor, who helped guide it to conclusion; and Brigit Dermott, managing editor, and Janielle Keith, assistant editor, who with a careful eye, guided it through production.

INDEX

Picture Credits: Arizona Historical Society: cover; courtesy Judy Froelich Cocke: fig. 5; courtesy Jacqueline Hooker Hughes: fig. 14; courtesy Ginna James and Judy Cocke: cover inset; Fort Concho National Historic Landmark: frontispiece; Library of Congress: figs. 3, 8, 9; Montana Historical Society: fig. 13; Museum of New Mexico: fig. 11; National Archives: fig. 7; Smithsonian Institution, National Anthropological Archives: fig. 4; University of Arizona Library, Special Collections: fig. 10; University of Oklahoma Libraries, Western History Collections: figs. 1, 2, 6, 12.